experience design 1

Nathan Shedroff

New Riders

201 West 103rd Street, Indianapolis, Indiana 46290.

While everything, technically, is an experience of some sort, there is something important and special to many experiences that make them worth discussing. In particular,

the elements that contribute to superior experiences are knowable and reproducible, which make them designable.

These elements aren't always obvious and, surely, they aren't always foolproof. So it's important to realize that great experiences can be deliberate, and they are based upon principles that have been proven. This book explores the most important of these principles.

The design of experiences isn't any newer than the recognition of experiences. As a discipline, though, Experience Design is still somewhat in its infancy. Simultaneously having no history (since it is a discipline only recently defined), and the longest history (since it is the culmination of many, ancient disciplines), Experience Design has become newly recognized and named. However, it is really the combination of many previous disciplines; but never before have these disciplines been so interrelated, nor have the possibilities for integrating them into whole solutions been so great.

Experience Design as a discipline is also so new that its very definition is in flux. Many see it only as a field for digital media, while others view it in broad-brush terms that encompass traditional, established, and other such diverse disciplines as theater, graphic design, storytelling, exhibit design, theme-park design, online design, game design, interior design, architecture, and so forth. The list is long enough that the space it describes has not been formally defined.

The most important concept to grasp is that *all* experiences are importan

experience design nathan shedroff

experience desig

...d that we can learn from them whether they ...e traditional, physical, or offline experiences; ...whether they are digital, online, or other ...chnological experiences. In fact, we know a great deal about ...eriences and their creation through these other established disciplines that can— ...must—be used to develop new solutions. Most technological experiences— ...uding digital and, especially, online experiences—have paled in comparison to

real-world experiences and have been relatively unsuccessful as a result. What these solutions require first and foremost is an understanding by their developers of what makes a good experience; then to translate these principles, as well as possible, into the desired media without the technology dictating the form of the experience.

This book contains real-world, "offline" examples to counterbalance the online examples so that we can learn from them how to create more successful experiences in new media.

Experiences are the foundation for all life events and form the core of what interactive media have to offer.

One of the most important ways to define an experience is to search its boundaries. While many experiences are ongoing, sometimes even indefinitely, most have edges that define their start, middle, and end. Much like a story (a special and important type of experience), these boundaries help us differentiate meaning, pacing, and completion. Whether it is due to attention span, energy, or emotion, most people cannot continue an experience indefinitely, or they will grow tired, confused, or distracted if an experience—however consistent—doesn't conclude.

At the very least, think of an experience as requiring an **attraction**, an engagement, and a conclusion.

The attraction is necessary to initiate the experience. It can be cognitive, visual, auditory, or a signal to any of our senses. The attraction can be intentional on the part of the experience, not just the experience creator. For example, the attraction for filling-out your taxes is based on a need, and not a flashy introduction. However, there still needs to be cues as to where and how to begin the experience.

The engagement is the experience itself. It needs to be
sufficiently different than the surrounding environment of the experience to hold the attention of the experience, as well as cognitively important (or relevant) enough for someone to continue the experience.

The **conclusion** can come in many ways, but it must provide some sort of resolution, whether through meaning—story or context—or activity to make an otherwise enjoyable experience satisfactory. Often, an experience that is engaging has no real end. This leaves participants dissatisfied or even confused about the experience, the ideas, or the emotions they just felt. An experience creator that does not spend enough (or any) attention on the conclusion—whether through inattention to detail, boredom, or speed—has just wasted his or her effort and the audience's time.

It is possible, and appropriate, for an experience to have an **extension**, which can merely prolong the experience, revive it, or form a bridge to another experience. In this sense, a larger conclusion with greater meaning can be alluded to so that experiences can be elicited. Each experience still needs a satisfactory conclusion on its own level in order to justify more time for further experiences. Hanging your audience completely out to dry will more likely disappoint them than keep their attention for more experiences. Just like serial narratives (such as episodes of television or comic books), all experiences must reward attention at their end.

Experiences are crucial to our lives and our understanding of the world, as well as to our ability to function within it. Indeed, to be creative at all requires a wealth of experience from which to draw. As turn-of-the Century educator John Dewey described in his book *Experience and Education*, there are three natural mental resources: "a store of experiences and facts from which suggestions proceed; promptness, flexibility, and fertility of suggestions; and orderliness, consecutiveness, and appropriateness of what is suggested."

Finally, it is critical to remember that **while all experiences aren't created equally, all must compete for the attention of the audience and participants**.

This means that websites don't just compete with websites, or parties with parties or environments with environments. People searching for experiences—especially if those experiences inform—will choose from various media to meet their needs. One misconception in the digital world has been that CD-ROMs and websites in particular somehow don't need to be as interesting, compelling, or useful as traditional experiences in the same genre—that novelty alone was enough to be successful. What most developers have found is that successful digital media are those that offer experiences unique to their medium and compete with traditional media in usefulness and satisfaction.

experience design nathan shedroff

"It is not enough to insist upon the necessity of experience, nor even of activity in experience. Everything depends on the *quality* of the experience which is had….

Just as no man lives or dies to himself, so no experience lives or dies to itself. Wholly independent of desire or intent, every experience lives on in further experiences. Hence the central problem of an education based upon experience is to select the kind of present experiences that live fruitfully and creatively in subsequent experiences."
—John Dewey, *Experience and Education*

One aspect of an experience that can make it surprising and amazing is that of confronting one's beliefs. When we are challenged to rethink possibilities (when our beliefs and expectations are confronted by the evidence in front of our eyes), we can have a profound reaction.

This was my experience at the Institut de Monde Arabe in Paris. On approaching the entrance, the South-facing glass wall of the building, which is also part of the entrance courtyard, appears to be backed by Arabic latticework. This isn't so surprising or puzzling, and seems like a rational interior design motif for a building representing traditions that go back over 1,000 years.

Upon entering the building, one is immediately surprised by the technological modernity of the building's interior. In fact, this building is one of the most technologically sophisticated in the world. Its mediatique is buzzing with robot arms switching video tapes into a bank of players, and then images are displayed on a wall of monitors, each representing a different Arabic world.

However, it is when one climbs a floor or two and approaches the South wall— this time from the inside—that one is confronted with a contradiction of reality. The latticework that easily could have been assumed from the outside is, in fact, an array of working metal apertures, some tiny, others large, in each pane of glass. The sheer number of apertures multiplied from pane to pane over the entire length and height of the building is staggering and unbelievable. Like the pyramids themselves, the amount of work involved in their creation is difficult—almost impossible—to process, or to believe.

There are nearly 20,000 working apertures that open and close automatically to regulate light into the building. The prospect of such a detailed undertaking is so difficult to calculate that I was left staring in awe, silence, and disbelief that someone, anyone, would actually attempt it. Part of my brain told me it could not exist—no one in their right mind would try; yet my eyes were informing another part of my brain. Yes, indeed, it did exist, right in front of my face.

I have rarely encountered such an experience—not just the surprise or the reversal of expectations, but the vision and determination of those who created it. When you create your next experience, consider how it might exceed not only your assumptions and expectations but those of your audience as well.

institut de monde arabe   1 rue des Fossés St-Bernard (5è), Paris, France
www.imarabe.org

experience design nathan shedroff

ENTRÉE PRINCIPALE

INSTITUT DU MONDE ARABE

العالم العربي معهد

institut du monde ara

Seduction? in the interface?

Seduction is not an adjective most people would associate with a computer interface or media, but whether they realize it or not, **most people have been either seduced or the target of seduction** by almost all forms of media. Successful seduction, however, is a careful art that is not easily mastered nor invoked.

Seduction, in fact, **has always been a part of design**, whether graphic, industrial, environmental, electronic. For many, seduction immediately connotes sex appeal or sexual enticement. In fact, the sexual aspect is n the essence of its meaning as much as **enticement** and **appeal**.

Seduction is a portion of a field of study into the persuasive aspects of computing and other media, called **CAPTology.**

I believe that it's important to view the interface as **an opportunity to seduce people**--not for nefarious reasons, for in order to **enhance their experiences and lives.**

While the Dialectizer may not be the quintessential experience, it is an unexpectedly funny one. Simply, the Dialectizer will rewrite a site on-the-fly, so the site takes on a different manner of style or personality when read. It's hard to come up with a real-world use for this application, but this website presents the ability to create a different perspective, albeit a stereotypical one, that changes the experience of every other website.

Combining choice, and a type of adaptiveness, it allows users to control their experience and spin the browsing experience into something different.

www.rinkworks.com/dialect/

experience design nathan shedroff

Seducshun? in de interface?

Seducshun be not an adjective most sucka's would associate wid some clunker interface o' media, but wheda' dey realize it o' not, most sucka's gots been eida' seduced o' de target uh seducshun by mos' all fo'ms uh media. WORD! Successful seducshun, however, be a careful art dat be not easily mastered no' invoked.

Seducshun, in fact, has always been some part uh design, wheder graphic, industrial, environmental, o' electronic. Co' got d' beat! Fo' many, seducshun immediately connotes sex appeal o' sexual enticement. Man! In fact, de sexual aspect be not da damn essence uh its meanin' as much as enticement and appeal.

Seducshun be a po'shun uh a field uh study into de puh'suasive aspects uh computin' and oda' media, called CAPTology.

I recon' dat it's impo'tant to view de interface as an oppo'tunity t'seduce sucka's--not fo' nefarious reasons, fo' in o'da' to enhance deir 'espuh'iences and lives.

nathan shedroff **experience design**

How many different types of experiences are there? Most likely, the diversity isn't infinite. Functionally, however, the diversity is large enough to define an incredible amount of variety. This variety forms a palette for us to both define and discover what experiences have to offer—that is, what we can learn from them as well as how we can build new variations.

One way to understand what makes experiences successful is to build taxonomies of some the experiences that we can identify (ultimately, an endless list). This allows us to explore what makes various experiences distinct and what makes them special. The chart on this page offers only a few of the possible attributes of experiences and matches them against just a sliver of all the possible experiences. However, they were chosen because they have presented some of the best results and have revealed some of the most important insights.

The best way to explore your own opinions and insights about experiences is to expand this chart yourself.

One of the most apparent values of a chart like this is that it makes it clear how related experiences compare in different ways. In particular, it becomes apparent that many experiences, though different in medium (such as print versus live versus digital) are similar in activity, meaning, and success. This leads to one of the most important understandings about experiences, especially digital ones—that is, all experiences compete with each other on many levels and in different media. Historically, this has been poorly understood by developers of "new media," because these developers assumed that their competition was other similar media and not all possible experiences around that topic or purpose.

For example, developers during the CD-ROM explosion rushed to create CD-ROMs on every conceivable topic—most often with dubious and misguided understandings of interactivity and of its strengths and weaknesses. What they created were mostly exotic experiences that, in the end, weren't successful for their audiences once their curiosity was satisfied. Any of the criteria on an experience taxonomy could have helped them discover what was potentially important about their products next to other experiences on similar topics in other media. For example, a CD-ROM about, say, tropical fish would clearly need to compete against other tropical fish experiences, such as television specials, scuba diving, visiting an aquarium, and so forth on *some* important level to capture an audience's attention, and in order to be successful.

The same phenomenon has occurred in the online world of websites. So many websites that have been created cannot compete with traditional experiences in the same milieu and are failing (often for a variety of reasons, though this is an important contributing one).

Producing/Processing
Experience
Brainstorming
Planning/Arranging/Organizing/Reorg
Processing/Transforming
Making/Building/Preparing/Cooking
Reflecting/Contemplating
Classifying
Learning
Asking
Storing
Indexing
Issues
Orga
Med
Storage
Transmitting
Transmitting/Sending/Receiving
Awareness
Answering
Advising
Facilitating
Analyzing
Teaching
Helping
Performing
Simulations/Re-enactments/F
Speaking/Telling/Showing/E
Performing/Acting/Demons
Testing/Quizzes/Exams
Playing/Sports/Games...
Practicing?
Listening/Watching
Consuming
Conversations
Indulging/Eating/Dri
Waiting
Traveling
Governing (Responsibilities)
Judging
Feeling

www.nathan.com/projects/experience.html

Others?

Scope

Medium

Abilities, Available Data
/Skills, Available Data

Desirable
Not Neccessary
Not Neccessary

Personal
Personal
Personal

Role   Action   Inspiration   Few Resources   Internal Res.   Staging Materials Performance Skills Setting the Stage Interact

Producer   Inter/Active
Producer   Inter/Active
Producer   Inter/Active
Producer   Inter/Active

Compression, Quality, Longevity

Not Neccessary

Personal

Archiver   Active

dium, Quality, Bandwidth

Not Neccessary

Personal

Transmitter   Active

Quantity
Quality

One to Few?
One to Few?
One to Few?

Broad/Narrow/Personal
Broad/Narrow/Personal
Broad/Narrow/Personal

Helper   Inter/Active
Helper   Inter/Active
Helper   Inter/Active
Helper   Inter/Active

Suspension of Disbelief
Ability, Fear, Anxiety, Quality (see Performing)
Ability, Audience (FYI 9 categories)
Ability, Time, Quality, Depth, Fear, Anxiety
Ability, Interest, Equipment

Possibly
Few to many
Few to Many
Not Neccessary
Not Neccessary
Not Neccessary
Two Minimum
Few
Not Neccessary

Personal
Broad/Narrow
Broad/Narrow
Personal
Personal
Personal
Broad/Narrow
Personal
Personal

Lectures/Seminars/Conversations
Theater/Opera/Recitals/Concerts...

Lectures/Movies/Performances/TV...

Producer   Interactive
Transmitter   Active
Transmitter   Inter/Active
Producer   Interactive
Producer   Interactive
Producer   Active
Consumer   Passive
Producer   Interactive
Consumer   Active

Time, Context, Level of Complexity
Interest, Ability
Nutrition? Texture? Quantity?

Possibly
Not Neccessary
Power, Authority, Leadership/Capabilities

Personal
Personal

Few to Many

Passive
Consumer   Passive?
Broad/Narrow
Leader   Inter/Active   Leader   Active

Time, Space, Available activities
Speed, Timeliness, Space

Some of the happiest memories from our youth include the fun and excitement of amusement parks. Whether it was the rides themselves or just the environment, the excitement was always a result of exploring an unusual environment with often fantastical features. Most amusement rides offer us the ability to experience things we could not otherwise, or play on our senses in ways that would be difficult outside the parks. Rides that twirl us at high speed or lift us off the ground are usually novel and stimulate our adrenaline and emotions. Even walking around the park is often a visual, sonic, and olfactory treat, as we smell, see, and hear novel things created especially to grab our attention and enhance the experience.

experience design nathan shedroff

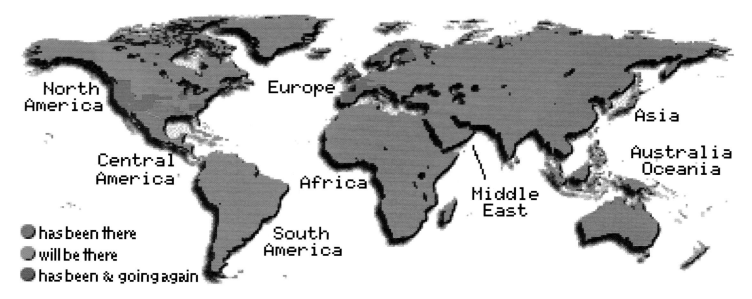

has been there
will be there
has been & going again

Travel is a universal experience.

Whether you travel across the world, or to a part of a city you never have visited before, there's something important and magical about finding new situations and seeing new sights. While travel is often an observational experience, many travelers specifically travel to participate in the action—whether it's an extreme or action sport, or whether it is to immerse themselves in another culture directly, such as working in another country or teaching a language to locals.

There's definitely a difference between traveling and touring. The former requires an authentic interest in new things and an openness and willingness to experience them. The latter is usually limited to "seeing" the sights—often through the lens of a photo or video camera. Tourists tend to gravitate to the familiar for meals and companionship while travelers abhor both, instead going out of their way to meet new people.

VirtualTourist.com is a fantastic site for both traveler and tourist, though the emphasis is on travelers, and often on adventure travel. The site excels in knowledge since it allows everyone to post their experiences, photos, stories, and travel histories for others to share. The site makes it easy to meet and communicate with others as well as to search for people who have been to the places you've visited or are planning to visit.

One of the nicest features is a visual map of each member's travels that is compiled automatically when members enter their travel histories. This map shows where travelers have been, as well as where they intend to go next.

experience design nathan shedroff

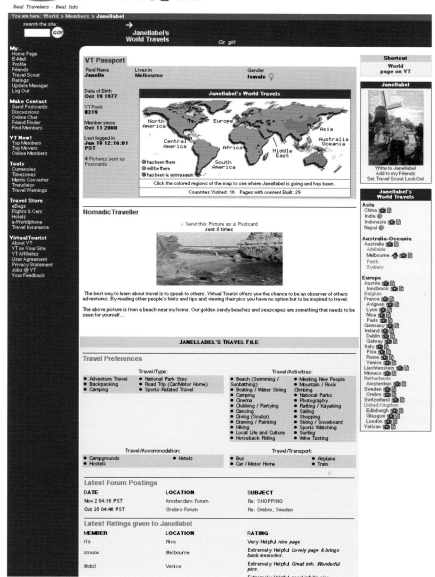

Another way to understand experiences is to identify the different media within which they occur. It's easiest, then, to identify the prominent attributes that differentiate products and media. There are no "right" answers here, and the differences in opinion and perception among people vary wildly. You might try discussing these in a group of people to gain an understanding about how media are viewed by others. This is an exercise I often use in classes and presentations, and the conclusions people make are some of the most valuable insights they will ever have.

experience design nathan shedroff

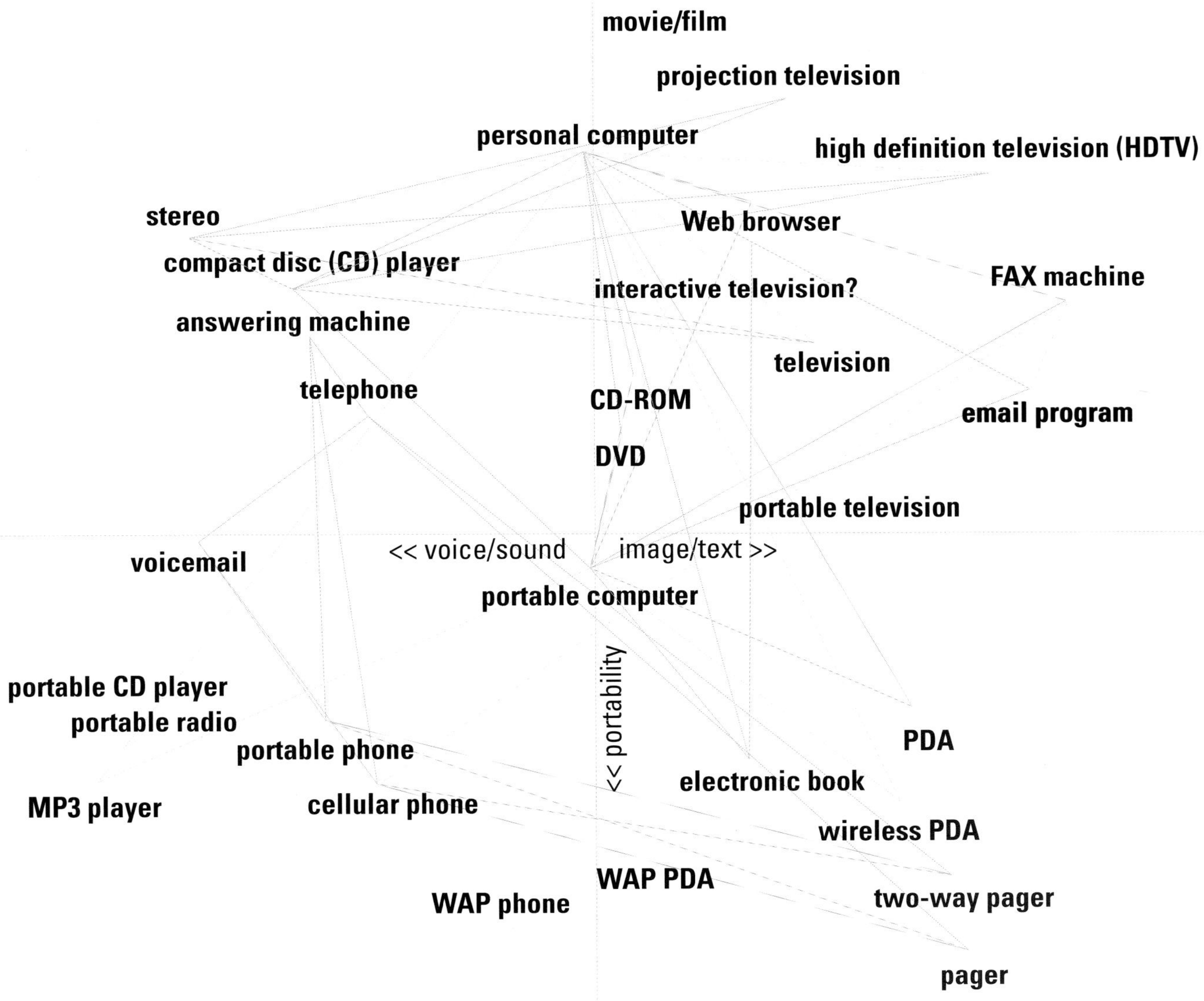

movie/film

projection television

personal computer

high definition television (HDTV)

stereo

Web browser

compact disc (CD) player

FAX machine

interactive television?

answering machine

television

telephone

CD-ROM

email program

DVD

portable television

<< voice/sound   image/text >>

voicemail

portable computer

<< portability

portable CD player

portable radio

PDA

portable phone

MP3 player

electronic book

cellular phone

wireless PDA

WAP PDA

WAP phone

two-way pager

pager

For a product that has been around for 20 years and has become such an important part of our daily life, automatic teller machines (ATMs) have evolved very little. The interfaces are still difficult for many people to use, though they do offer more options and, often, multiple languages now. Advertising within the screens have heightened our annoyance with them, while at the same time new functions have expanded our interactions (in Hong Kong, for example, some allow people to trade stocks).

ATMs have become so ubiquitous that when they aren't accessible, either through malfunction or availability (Tonga and Samoa, for example, still have no ATMs), we are unprepared for alternatives. In fact, travelers to other countries use them as an easy way to get money without having to interact with bank tellers in a foreign language. Compared to the experience they replace (waiting in line and then interacting with a bank teller), these devices give us an enormous amount of new freedom. ATMs pop-up in places that are

too small to have a bank branch, or where they can extend a bank's hours of operation, or where they can help us to purchase movie tickets or train fares. Where suspicion, fear, and unease were often associated with ATMs when they were first introduced (Would they dispense the correct amount of money? Would deposits actually get to our accounts? Would we be able to correctly use the machine?), we now associate convenience with them.

The Black Berry is the current wireless device-of-choice for wired (or unwired as this case may be) Internet enthusiasts and business people. The Black Berry is bigger than a pager but acts as a two-way communications device for text. It includes a small keyboard so people can enter text messages using two-thumbed typing, and it is always connected to a wireless paging service. The Black Berry is a pager, email system, personal organizer with schedule and address book, and notepad; and, it is compatible with sophisticated email servers already installed in many companies, including security protocols. This makes it an easily integrated solution for people on-the-move who mostly need email services and paging, and not a full computer.

Users of the Black Berry swear by its features and rave about its intuitive interface. For sure, it is easily learnable. Though not ubiquitous—mostly due to its relatively high cost—the Black Berry is growing in popularity because it does well exactly what it set out to do and never attempts to offer features that neither perform well for such small devices, or aren't essential for the needs of most users.

RIM 957 Wireless Handheld
www.blackberry.net

date launched: April 2000

In 100 years, there will be no computers.
In 100 years, MPEG and QuickTime will be forgotten.
In 100 years, CD-ROMs will not exist (whether quad-speed or even faster).
In 100 years, there will be no Basic, C++, Perl, or HTML.
In 100 years, Mighty Morphin Power Rangers will (thankfully) be only a memory.
In 100 years, RISC chips will be extinct.
In 100 years, there will be no PowerBooks.
In 100 years, Windows® will not exist (Bob® should be gone in less than 5).
In 100 years, DOS will still be around somewhere.
In 100 years, there will be no Mosaic, Netscape, CompuServe, Prodigy, or America Online.
In 100 years, Barney will be extinct.
In 100 years, set-top boxes, ITV, and HDTV will be forgotten.

It is not that these things aren't important to somebody, but they should not be important to you. These should not be foremost in your thoughts. However...

In 100 years, Dr. Seuss will still excite both kids and adults.
In 100 years, people will still buy, sell, and trade things that are important to them.
In 100 years, spirituality will still help people guide their lives.
In 100 years, sex will still have its allure, excitement, suspicion, and danger.
In 100 years, there will still be intolerance, hatred, bigotry, and greed.
In 100 years, conversations will still illuminate, enrage, engage, and inspire.
In 100 years, creativity will be even more important.
In 100 years, art will still be revered.
In 100 years, AT&T will still be here.
In 100 years, people will still throw dinner parties,
In 100 years, travelers will still explore the world.
In 100 years, there will still be holes in the ozone layer.
In 100 years, people will still wait in lines.

In 100 years, life will seem just as complex and difficult to organize.
In 100 years, people will still fall in love.

Nathan Shedroff
from a presentation at Intermedia, 1995

One way of measuring experiences is to qualify them against personal value. This is intentionally vague because there is such a wide variety of meanings that people can associate with things. One way to do this is to research which experiences people will spend the most time with and for which they would pay the most money. Since we can't look ahead in time for a comparison to current experiences, we need to look back. And we need to look back over a time period that's long enough to give us some perspective, **like 100 years.**

This looking back over our shoulder is critical because most technological industries have almost nonexistent attention spans and proclaim it worthless to look ahead more than six months. This short-sightedness is one of the reasons the industry is so hit-and-miss, having soaring successes as well as spectacular failures—and many more failures than successes. Looking back and understanding people in a longer, broader context allows us to find more universal aspects of **human values** that we can tap into for designing more

100 years ago.... Only 14 percent of the homes in the United States had a bathtub. There were only 8,000 cars in the US and only 144 miles of paved roads. Alabama, Mississippi, Iowa, and Tennessee were each more heavily populated than California. With a mere 1.4 million residents, California was only the twenty-first most populous state in the Union. The tallest structure in the world was the Eiffel Tower.

The average wage in the US was twenty-two cents an hour. The average US worker made between $200 and $400 per year. Sugar cost four cents a pound. Eggs were fourteen cents a dozen. Coffee was fifteen cents a pound. Most women only washed their hair once a month and used borax or egg yolks for shampoo.

Professor Marcello Truzzi

Drive-by-shootings—in which teenage boys galloped down the street on horses and started randomly shooting at houses, carriages, or anything else that caught their fancy—were an ongoing problem in Denver and other cities in the West. Plutonium, insulin, and antibiotics hadn't been discovered yet.

Scotch tape, crossword puzzles, canned beer, and iced tea hadn't been invented. Some medical authorities warned that professional seamstresses were apt to become sexually aroused by the steady rhythm of the sewing machine's foot pedals. They recommended slipping bromide, which was thought to diminish sexual desire, into the woman's drinking water. Marijuana, heroin, and morphine were all available over the counter at corner drugstores.

successful experiences. This is an approach that doesn't always work for fads but is valuable for products and experiences that hope to have more longevity and a greater impact.

According to one pharmacist, "Heroin clears the complexion, gives buoyancy to the mind, regulates the stomach and the bowels and is, in fact, a perfect guardian of health." Coca-Cola contained cocaine instead of caffeine. There are about 230 reported murders in the U.S. annually.

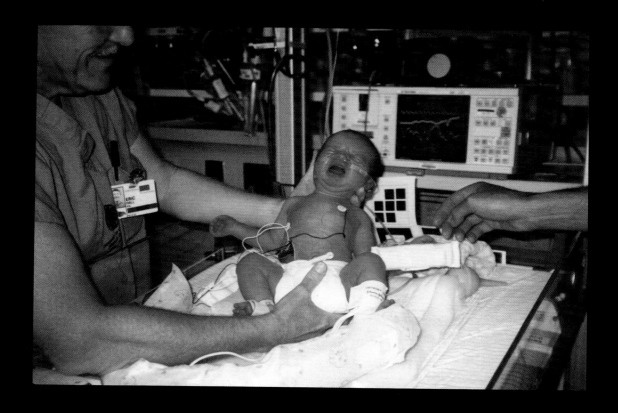

The two quintessential and ubiquitous experiences of one's life are birth and death. Their constancy make them experiences worth studying—all the more so since they're so emotionally charged. Our feelings about each experience vary greatly from culture to culture and change substantially as we age. While some people are perpetually trying to avoid death, others embrace it as a natural and necessary part of life. Psychologists attribute many of our emotional problems to our inabilities to deal with birth and death issues, our own mortality, and the deaths and births of those around us.

Both birth and death are experiences that have much to teach us: about design, about life, about our psyches, and about ourselves. Mostly, our views haven't changed substantially over the years and centuries, at least within our faiths and cultures, and they provide a set of values upon which to base new experiences.

experience design nathan shedroff

Matchmaking is an activity as old as history itself. In fact, the history of finding a partner or spouse tells a great deal about a culture. In some mainly older cultures, matches were made by a third-party or by parents. In Western culture, and increasingly elsewhere in the world, people now make their own decisions about whom to marry or, at least, spend their lives with.

There are many online services for matchmaking and these have been active and popular for the Web's entire history. Match.com was one of the first and is still one of the best, due to its clear and easy design and its wealth of descriptive information. Several people have even found their present spouses over its five-year history.

Welcome

free search | create profile | register now | home

join now   log in   tour   matchscene   help   contact us

Welcome

Welcome to Match.com!
You've found the smart way to date,
relate and find your
soul mate.

Register for Free
It's quick, simple and gives you
Full Search, our expanded search
tool. Plus email deliveries of your
ideal profiles.

Post a Free Profile
Create your profile in minutes and
our exclusive Match technology
will find the members that match
you! Venus will deliver profiles
direct to your email. Add a photo
for 8 times greater response.

Take the Site Tour
Here's your chance to learn all
about Match.com, the web's most
exciting online matchmaking site.

Join the MatchClub
Take advantage of all the
benefits of being a Match
member!

The Buzz
from MatchScene, Match.com's relationship webzine

when harry met sally sweepstakes

Can a man and a woman just be friends? **Take our poll**
and find out. Enter to win a New York City romantic
getaway.

 Love Letters
Could This Be You?
Read about our Match of the Week and other Tales of
Success!

Meet Our Spotlight Members!

She's an actress in Sherman Oaks,
California

He's a PR executive in
Washington, DC

 Feature Story:
Before you decide to ask out
the cutie in Accounting, check out:
**Seven Deadly Sins
of an Office Romance**

Out & About
Two college
professors meet.
Are they
sexually
compatible?

Conv. Starters
Learn how to
move from day
to night in
style.

Tools For Guys
Whistle While
You Work: The
Office Fling
Survival Guide.

Horoscopes
What do the
stars say about
your love life?

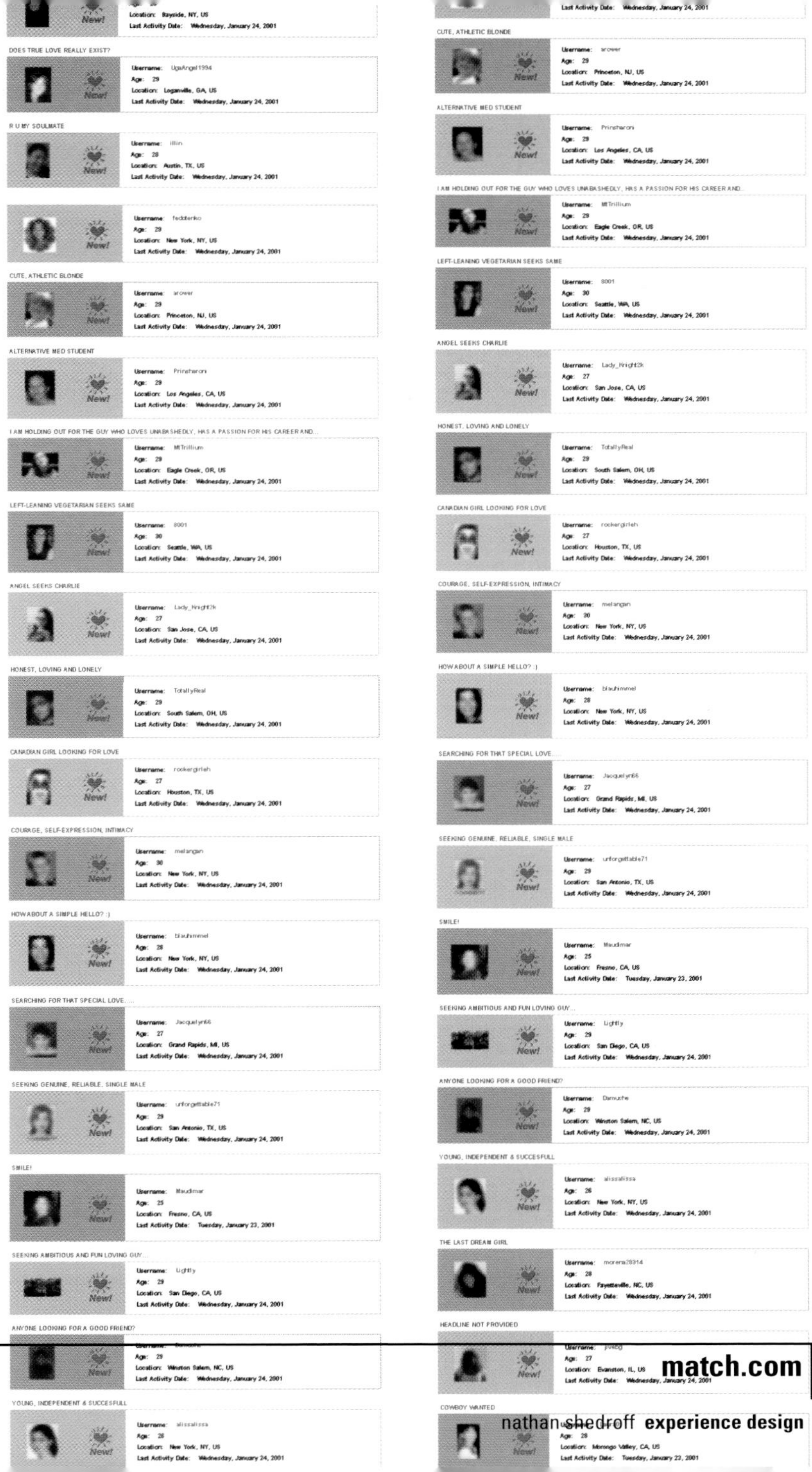

Member listings (left column):

DOES TRUE LOVE REALLY EXIST?
Username: UgaAngel1994
Age: 29
Location: Loganville, GA, US
Last Activity Date: Wednesday, January 24, 2001

R U MY SOULMATE

Username: itlin
Age: 29
Location: Austin, TX, US
Last Activity Date: Wednesday, January 24, 2001

CUTE, ATHLETIC BLONDE

Username: arower
Age: 29
Location: Princeton, NJ, US
Last Activity Date: Wednesday, January 24, 2001

ALTERNATIVE MED STUDENT

Username: Princeheron
Age: 29
Location: Los Angeles, CA, US
Last Activity Date: Wednesday, January 24, 2001

I AM HOLDING OUT FOR THE GUY WHO LOVES UNABASHEDLY, HAS A PASSION FOR HIS CAREER AND...
Username: MTrillium
Age: 29
Location: Eagle Creek, OR, US
Last Activity Date: Wednesday, January 24, 2001

LEFT-LEANING VEGETARIAN SEEKS SAME
Username: 0001
Age: 30
Location: Seattle, WA, US
Last Activity Date: Wednesday, January 24, 2001

ANGEL SEEKS CHARLIE

Username: Lady_hright3k
Age: 27
Location: San Jose, CA, US
Last Activity Date: Wednesday, January 24, 2001

HONEST, LOVING AND LONELY

Username: TotallyReal
Age: 29
Location: South Salem, OH, US
Last Activity Date: Wednesday, January 24, 2001

CANADIAN GIRL LOOKING FOR LOVE

Username: rockergirlah
Age: 27
Location: Houston, TX, US
Last Activity Date: Wednesday, January 24, 2001

COURAGE, SELF-EXPRESSION, INTIMACY
Username: melangan
Age: 30
Location: New York, NY, US
Last Activity Date: Wednesday, January 24, 2001

HOW ABOUT A SIMPLE HELLO? :)
Username: blushmemel
Age: 28
Location: New York, NY, US
Last Activity Date: Wednesday, January 24, 2001

SEARCHING FOR THAT SPECIAL LOVE...

Username: Jacquelyn66
Age: 27
Location: Grand Rapids, MI, US
Last Activity Date: Wednesday, January 24, 2001

SEEKING GENUINE, RELIABLE, SINGLE MALE
Username: unforgettable71
Age: 29
Location: San Antonio, TX, US
Last Activity Date: Wednesday, January 24, 2001

SMILE!

Username: Maudimar
Age: 25
Location: Fresno, CA, US
Last Activity Date: Tuesday, January 23, 2001

SEEKING AMBITIOUS AND FUN LOVING GUY...
Username: Lightfly
Age: 29
Location: San Diego, CA, US
Last Activity Date: Wednesday, January 24, 2001

ANYONE LOOKING FOR A GOOD FRIEND?
Username: Danushe
Age: 29
Location: Winston Salem, NC, US
Last Activity Date: Wednesday, January 24, 2001

YOUNG, INDEPENDENT & SUCCESSFULL
Username: alexcafossa
Age: 26
Location: New York, NY, US
Last Activity Date: Wednesday, January 24, 2001

Member listings (right column):

Username: [unreadable]
Location: Bayside, NY, US
Last Activity Date: Wednesday, January 24, 2001

CUTE, ATHLETIC BLONDE

Username: arower
Age: 29
Location: Princeton, NJ, US
Last Activity Date: Wednesday, January 24, 2001

ALTERNATIVE MED STUDENT

Username: Princeheron
Age: 29
Location: Los Angeles, CA, US
Last Activity Date: Wednesday, January 24, 2001

I AM HOLDING OUT FOR THE GUY WHO LOVES UNABASHEDLY, HAS A PASSION FOR HIS CAREER AND...

Username: MTrillium
Age: 29
Location: Eagle Creek, OR, US
Last Activity Date: Wednesday, January 24, 2001

LEFT-LEANING VEGETARIAN SEEKS SAME

Username: 0001
Age: 30
Location: Seattle, WA, US
Last Activity Date: Wednesday, January 24, 2001

ANGEL SEEKS CHARLIE

Username: Lady_hright3k
Age: 27
Location: San Jose, CA, US
Last Activity Date: Wednesday, January 24, 2001

HONEST, LOVING AND LONELY

Username: TotallyReal
Age: 29
Location: South Salem, OH, US
Last Activity Date: Wednesday, January 24, 2001

CANADIAN GIRL LOOKING FOR LOVE

Username: rockergirlah
Age: 27
Location: Houston, TX, US
Last Activity Date: Wednesday, January 24, 2001

COURAGE, SELF-EXPRESSION, INTIMACY

Username: melangan
Age: 30
Location: New York, NY, US
Last Activity Date: Wednesday, January 24, 2001

HOW ABOUT A SIMPLE HELLO? :)
Username: blushmemel
Age: 28
Location: New York, NY, US
Last Activity Date: Wednesday, January 24, 2001

SEARCHING FOR THAT SPECIAL LOVE...

Username: Jacquelyn66
Age: 27
Location: Grand Rapids, MI, US
Last Activity Date: Wednesday, January 24, 2001

SEEKING GENUINE, RELIABLE, SINGLE MALE

Username: unforgettable71
Age: 29
Location: San Antonio, TX, US
Last Activity Date: Wednesday, January 24, 2001

SMILE!
Username: Maudimar
Age: 25
Location: Fresno, CA, US
Last Activity Date: Tuesday, January 23, 2001

SEEKING AMBITIOUS AND FUN LOVING GUY...
Username: Lightfly
Age: 29
Location: San Diego, CA, US
Last Activity Date: Wednesday, January 24, 2001

ANYONE LOOKING FOR A GOOD FRIEND?
Username: Danushe
Age: 29
Location: Winston Salem, NC, US
Last Activity Date: Wednesday, January 24, 2001

YOUNG, INDEPENDENT & SUCCESSFULL
Username: alexcafossa
Age: 26
Location: New York, NY, US
Last Activity Date: Wednesday, January 24, 2001

THE LAST DREAM GIRL
Username: morena28314
Age: 28
Location: Fayetteville, NC, US
Last Activity Date: Wednesday, January 24, 2001

HEADLINE NOT PROVIDED

Username: jvileg
Age: 27
Location: Evanston, IL, US
Last Activity Date: Wednesday, January 24, 2001

COWBOY WANTED
Username: [unreadable]
Age: 28
Location: Morongo Valley, CA, US
Last Activity Date: Tuesday, January 22, 2001

nathan shedroff experience design

In his novel, *Generation X: Tales for an Accelerated Culture*, author Douglas Coupland describes a "takeaway" as "that one memory of Earth that you'll take away with you when you die that proves that you were alive."

Takeaways are another exercise that helps us derive meaning from the things we experience. Ponder for a moment what memories you have that might qualify as a takeaway. Perhaps you don't have one yet, but you probably have an idea as to what it might be. Think about what is important to you in your life. What will you remember? What makes your life worth living?

It's likely that your takeaway doesn't involve technology—few people's do; most likely, it doesn't involve media like TV or radio either. It just may be that technological experiences are sufficiently mediated so that they become less direct and, therefore, more difficult to become important. Perhaps it's because technological and media experiences are so often reproduced, their rarity or specialness is lessened.

In any case, it's useful to deconstruct the meaning of these important experiences in order to understand why they are so important to us. In fact, these attributes are some of the most important we can discover and, hopefully, reproduce in the experiences we create for others. Transformative experiences, those that help people change in some way that is important to them, are typically good for measuring value.

Some of the attributes we have uncovered appear on the following pages—especially those in the Interaction Design section. However, these are only the tip of the experiential iceberg. It is up to you to discover and explore more.

The setting is a ... ... large apartment complex where a few twenty-something friends sit and tell stories to each other.

"Let me see your eyes."

Tobias leans over to allow Elvissa to put a hand around his jaw and extract information from his eyes, the blue color of Dutch souvenir plates. She takes an awfully long time. "We're okay. Maybe you're not all that bad. I might even tell you a special story in a few minutes. Remind me. But it depends. I want you to tell me something first: after you're dead and buried and floating around whatever place we go to, what's going to be your best memory of earth?"

"What do you mean? I don't get it."

"What one moment for you defines what it's like to be alive on this planet. What's your takeaway?"

There is silence. Tobias doesn't get her point, and frankly, neither do I. She continues. "Like yuppie experiences that you had to spend money on, like white water rafting or elephant rides in Thailand don't count. I want to hear some small moment from your life that proves you're really alive."

Tobias does not readily volunteer any info. I think he needs an example first."

"I've got one," says Claire. All eyes turn to her.

"Snow," she says to us. At the very momenta hailstorm of doves erupts upward from the brown silk soil of the MacArthurs' yard next door.

..."I'll always remember the first time I saw snow. I was twelve and it was just after the first and biggest divorce. I was in New York visiting my mother and was standing beside a traffic island in the middle of Park Avenue. I'd never been out of L.A. before. I was entranced by the big city. I was looking up at the Pan Am Building and contemplating the essential problem of Manhattan.

"Which is--?" I ask.

"Which is that there's too much weight improperly distributed towers and elevators, steel, stone, and cement. So much mass up so high that gravity itself could end up being warped some dreadful inversion--an exchange program with the sky." (I love it when Claire gets weird.) "I was shuddering at the thought of this. But right then my brother Allan yanked my sleeve because the walk signal light was green. And ...

experience design nathan shedroff

Generation X: Tales for an Accelerated Culture
isbn: 031205436X
www.coupland.com

ven know what it was at first, but then I saw millions of
akes--all white and smelling like ozone, floating downward
ke the shed skin of angels. Even Allan stopped. Traffic was
onking at us, but time stood still. And so, yes--if I take one
emory of earth away with me, that moment will be the one.
o this day I consider my right eye charmed."

'erfect," says Elvissa. She turns to Tobias. "Get the drift?"

...econd."

ve got one," says Dag with some enthusiasm, partially the
spirit, I suspect, of wanting to score brownie points with
vissa. "It happened in 1974. In

ngston, Ontario." He lights a cigarette and we wait. "My
ad and I were at a gas station and I was given the task of
lling up the gas tank--a Galaxy 500, snazzy car. And filling
up was a big responsibility for me. I was one of those
oofy kids who always got colds and never got the hang of
ings like filling up gas tanks or unraveling tangled fishing
ds. I'd always screw things up somehow; break something;
ave it...

Anyway, Dad was in the station shop buying a map, and I
...feeling so manly and just so proud of how I
...d anything up yet--set fire to the gas station or
...you--and the tank was almost full. Well, Dad
me out just as I was topping the tank off, at which point
e nozzle simply went nuts. It started spraying all over. I
on't know why--it just did--all over my jeans, my running
noes, the license plate, the cement--like purple alcohol.

...saw everything and I thought I was going to catch total
it. I felt so small. But instead he smiled and said to me,
...Isn't the smell of gasoline great? Close your eyes
...ale. So clean. It smells like the future.'

Well, I did that--I closed my eyes just as he asked, and
eathed in deeply. And at that point I saw the bright orange
ght of the sun coming through my eyelids, smelled the
asoline and my knees buckled. But it was the most perfect
oment of my life, and so if you ask me (and I have a lot of
opes pinned on this), heaven just has to be an awful lot
ke those few seconds. That's my memory of earth."

Was it leaded or unleaded?" asks Tobias.

eaded," replies Dag.

...Tobias can barely contain himself. His body is poised forward, like a child in a shopping cart waiting to lunge for the presweetened breakast cereals: "I know what my memory is! I know what it is now!"

"Well just tell us then," says Elvissa.

"It's like this--" (God only knows what it will be) "Every summer back in Tacoma Park" (Washington, DC. I knew it was an eastern city) "my dad and I would rig up a shortwave radio that he had leftover from 1950s. We'd string a wire across the yard at sunset and tether it up to the linden tree to act as an antenna.

We'd try all of the bands, and if the radiation in the Van Allen belt was low, then we'd pick up just about everywhere: Johannesburg, Radio Moscow, Japan, Punjabi stuff. But more than anything we'd get signals from South America, these weird haunted-sounding bolero-samba transmissions from dinner theaters in Ecador and Caracas and Rio. The music would come in faintly--fainely but clearly.

"One night Mom came out onto the patio in a sundress and carrying a glass pitcher of lemonade. Dad swept her into his arms and they danced to the samba music with Mom still holding the pitcher. She was squealing but loving it. I think she was enjoying that little bit of danger the threat of broken glass added to the dancing. And there were crickets cricking and the transformer humming on the power lines behind the garage and I had my suddenly young parents all to myself--them and this faint music that sounded like heaven--faraway, clear, and impossible to contact--coming from this faceless place that was always summer and where beautiful people were always dancing and where it was impossible to call by telephone, even if you wanted to. Now that's earth to me."

Well, who'd have thought Tobias was capable of such thoughts? We're going to have to do a reevaluation of this lad.

"Andy?" Elvissa looks to me. "You?"

"I know my earth memory. It's a smell--the smell of bacon. It was a Sunday morning at home and we were all having breakfast, an unprecedented occurence since me and all six of my brothers and sisters inherited my mother's tendency to detest the sight of food in the morning. We'd sleep in instead.

"Anyhow, there wasn't even a special reason for the meal. All nine of us simply ended up in the kitchen by accident

Unfortunately, I only have a handful of candidates for "takeaways." The memories most important and wondrous to me are few, but I will share one…

Driving back to our rooms in a calm, pitch-black night in Costa Rica, my friends and I pulled-off to the side of the road to talk. We were in the middle of trees and fields on the edge of a jungle. At first, no one even paid attention to the absolute darkness and still silence that surrounded our truck, but slowly we lost our will to continue speaking as our eyes adjusted to the dark and the jungle came alive with the light of thousands of fireflies.

We were speechless as we watched their visual mating signals from a hundred yards a way to right in front of us on our windshield. The twinkling lights from the fireflies were as much like a field of stars, as a field of fireflies were like a field of fairies. It was a magical, unexpected moment and a reminder of how stunning nature can be when you take the time to look. It was also a timeless moment—not that I wasn't aware of time passing, but because it felt like it could go on forever, without end.

nathan shedroff experience design

today my house fell into the water.
the pacific ocean.

the last month has been saturated with persistent
rains and insistent waves and northern california
seems to be prepping for the apocalypse. the rains
had been degrading our cliff and we would watch daily
as different elements of the thing would deteriorate
and drop, school busses in size, sub-audio plops
onto the beach some 70 feet below our back porch.

                --

i went to karate at 8. i got back at 9:30. it was
warm and i opened the door to let some of the rare
sunlight- in the garage my cats interpreting as i
moved boxes around and i heard a noise on the side
of the house like someone kicking something and i
thought it impossible that there was someone there
and i opened the door to look at the ocean.. the
cliff was breaking away so fast, deep, and moving
toward me like a huge anti-matter snake and the
dirt was falling away like there was someone under-
neath pulling at it like a carpet. the ground was
falling out from under the house.

stood there as the cliff slid toward me 6 feet in
half that many seconds, like an invisible predator,
enough to convince me it was time to move more than
my eyebrows. grabbed cats. jumped out garage door.
lisa was in the living room. talking on the phone...
i told her to get out of the house. she did. and
we waited in the front yard and listened and waited
and wondered and the wind blew a bit and we heard the
ocean and the world seemed very still and blue.

we heard a thud, or so it seemed.

the razorbladeopportunity to really part with

designer/writer/photographer:
Mark Meadows

> 24 1998, opinion on the collapse.

2479 Feb 23 23:29 house_collapse.html

> 24 1998, some pictures   some'i took.

12180 Feb 26 08:48 cnn_snap.jpg
32035 Feb 24 20:44 lisa01.jpg
69025 Feb 24 21:53 pix02.jpg
62276 Feb 24 21:55 pix03.jpg
90512 Feb 24 21:56 pix04.jpg
50197 Feb 24 21:52 pix05.jpg
41335 Feb 24 21:53 pix06.jpg
47433 Feb 24 20:46 duo.jpg

> 25 1998, newspaper clips.

245267 Feb 24 20:53 chronicle_cover.jpg
105873 Feb 24 20:54 examiner_cover.jpg
192905 Feb 24 20:53 chronicle_cover_detail.jpg

> 25 1998, phone call from a friend.

707186 Feb 24 20:25 marko.wav

Sometimes an event can leave a lasting impression—especially a personal catastrophe. When Mark Meadow's house slid into the sea, it changed his thinking about what a home is. He chronicles here what he and his girlfriend went through in the days prior to losing his home.

images: copyright 1999 Mark Meadows

nathan shedroff **experience design**

Information design only recently has been identified as a discipline; it is one in which we all participate and, in some way, we always have. Information is really data transformed into something more valuable by building context around it so that it becomes understandable.

One of the first things we can learn about understanding is that it is a continuum from Data, a somewhat raw ingredient, to Wisdom, an ultimate achievement. Along this spectrum is an ever-increasing value chain of understanding, which is derived from an increasing level of context and meaning that becomes more personal and more sophisticated—not to mention more valuable—as it approaches Wisdom.

There are many ways to describe this spectrum. In *The Experience Economy,* H. Joseph Pine II and James H. Gilmore equate this spectrum with the following parts:

Noise	=	Commodities:	Value is for raw materials.
Data	=	Products:	Value is for tangible things.
Information	=	Services:	Value is for activities.
Knowledge	=	Experiences:	Value is the time customers spend with you.
Wisdom	=	Transformations:	Value is the demonstrated outcome the customer achieves.

We have learned from information design that structure, itself, has meanin

and it can affect not only the effectiveness but the meaning of a message. This axiom has been proven time and time again in the presentation of "statistics" and in their "interpretation." People readily agree and believe that statistics can "lie." For years, Richard Saul Wurman has shown us that simply reorganizing the same pieces in different ways changes our understanding of them, as well as the whole. A quick survey in any medium shows a notable lack of innovation in most products of communication in terms of their structure and form. This is mostly due to a lack of initiative and imagination rather than a lack of ability or opportunity. To build more effective communications, we must experiment much more with the form these might take.

The term **information overload** has been used for several decades now but I don't think that this is really the problem. Instead, consider Richard Saul Wurman's definition of **information anxiety**. In his latest book, *Information Anxiety 2,* he and I define this malady in terms of its social effect: a lack of context and meaning in our world. It isn't so much that there's more to read (although this is certainly the case), but that there is such a paucity of valuable insights and meaning; no one has shown that there is, in fact, any greater number of meanings to understand than ever before.

The way to lessen this condition is to create more insight, perhaps the most valuable product of all

Insight is what is created as we add context and give care to both the presentation and organization of data as well as the particular needs of our audience. And as insight is increased by building with more care and context, communication is pushed higher up or deeper into the understanding chain.

In the following pages, you'll see examples of all of these concepts, including multiple ways of organizing data and the emotional impact it can have on the message. Information presentations often can be seductive, sometimes in the content, often in visual presentation, but most important is their form and ability to communicate clearly.

experience design nathan shedroff

The Experience Economy, Joseph Pine II and James H. Gilmore, isbn: 0875848192
Information Anxiety 2, Richard Saul Wurman, isbn: 0789724103

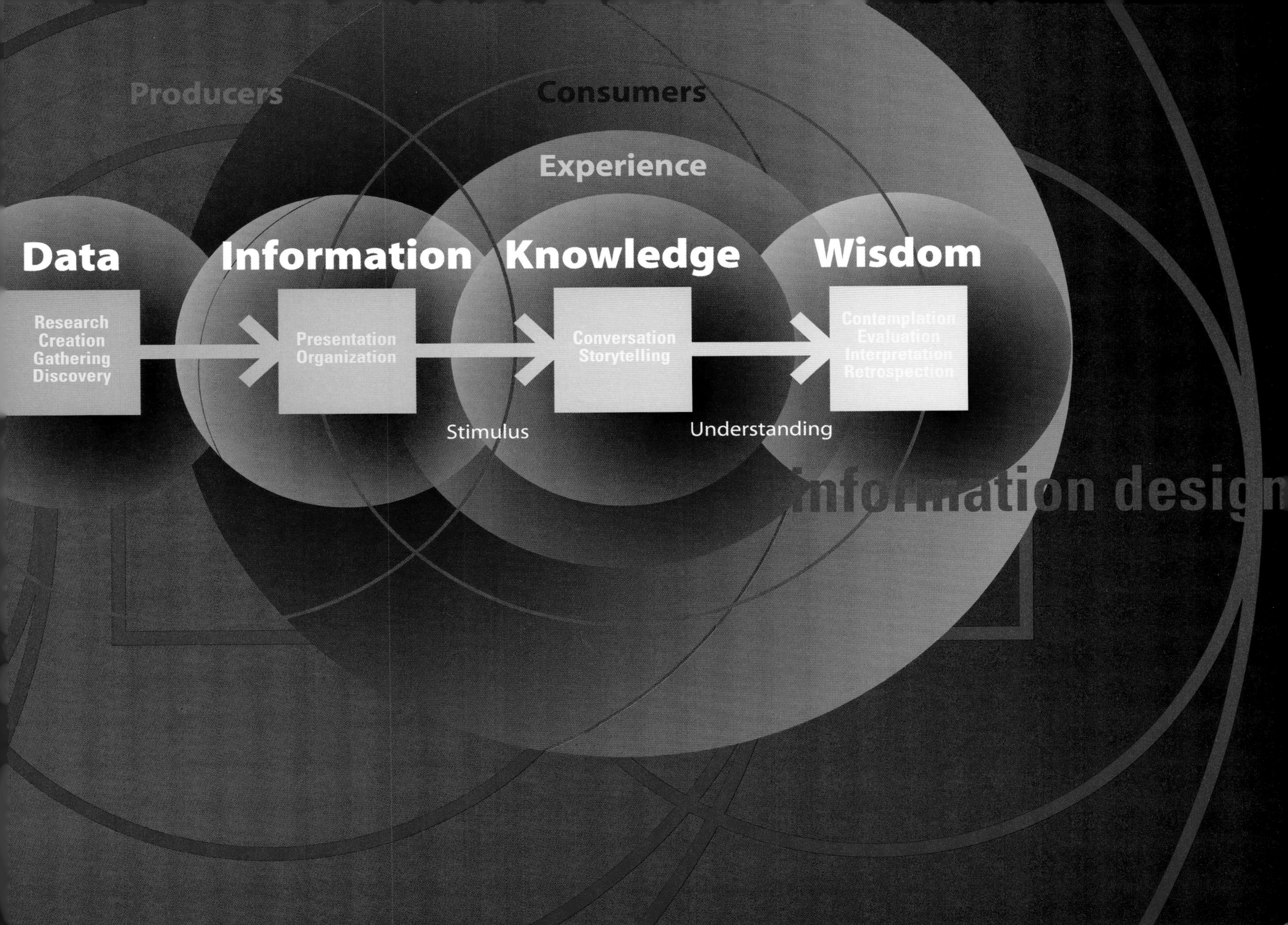

Producers

Consumers

Experience

Data

Research
Creation
Gathering
Discovery

Information

Presentation
Organization

Knowledge

Conversation
Storytelling

Wisdom

Contemplation
Evaluation
Interpretation
Retrospection

Stimulus

Understanding

information design

nathan shedroff experience design

| data

Data is not information.

This is paramount to realize. Though we use the two terms interchangeably in our culture—mostly to glorify data that has no right to be ennobled—they mean distinctly different things.

Data is raw and often overabundant. While it may have meaning to experts, it is, for the most part, only the building blocks on which relevance is built. It also should never be produced for delivery in raw form to an audience—especially a consumer audience. This isn't so that it can be kept secret but because it has no inherent value. Until it is transformed into information (with context), its meaning is of little value and only contributes to the anxiety we feel dealing with so much information in our lives.

An unfortunate fallacy we live under is that this is an "Age of Information."

Never before has so much data been produced. Yet our lives are not enhanced by any of it. Worse, this situation will only become more pervasive.

Data is often passed off as information, while the bulk of it doesn't even qualify. For example, CNN often fills the space between advertising and news on its television channels with "factoids"—probably the best word yet to ensure that there isn't any meaning, information, or value attached to it. These serve not to inform, but to create the perception of information. Each is a wasted opportunity for actually enlightening us with insightful observations about the news around us. Instead, they serve only as worthless trivia that mostly divert our attention from more important things, while giving the illusion that accuracy and obscurity are replacements for understanding.

Likewise, titles like Chief Information Officer (CIO) and even Information Technology (IT) further mask the problem. In most cases, neither has anything to do with information, communication, or any systems for generating these. Rather they are merely steeped in data, data systems, data technologies, and data processes. The famed "productivity paradox" (the lack of proof that any gains in increased productivity stem from computers and related technologies) is mostly a crisis arising from this misunderstanding of data and information. What we tend to measure is only data and while this has increased in our society, it has not—and cannot—improve productivity or anything else because it lacks the value to do so, or the value to make meaningful change. Once we re-educate ourselves as to what information really is, then we may be able to find the opportunities for increased understanding and productivity.

Data is so uninforming that we can liken it to heavy-winter clothing, enshrouding us as we interact with each other. It doesn't completely stop us from communicating, but it makes it much more difficult, and it surely makes any complex interactions more laborious.

nathan shedroff **experience design**

CCL 30   CCMPR 23 3/16   CPG 37   CPJ 29 13/16   CPK 18 1

5 1/2   CPY 10 3/16   CPY 19 15/16   CPZPRA 24 3/4   CQPRA

10   DAJ 0   DAL 52 3/4   DAP 6 1/4   DBD 33 1/8   DCA 2

PRB 71 1/4   DDF 12 1/2   DDR 13 3/8   DDRPRA 22 3/4   DDF

DJM 12 7/16   DJT 2   DK 8 7/8   DL 11 15/16   DLJPRA

DMH 16 3/4   DMN 5 3/16   DNA 66 5/8   DNB 24 1/8   DN

Raw data is easy to find in our world—but useful raw data is more rare. Stock tickers have been one of the few commonly accepted forms of data in our lives that have garnered respect. This is beginning to change with new technologies that offer easier tracking tools (filtering only the stocks that interest us), and richer presentations of market information (such as the *Map of the Market* on page 94).

experience design nathan shedroff

```
CPMPRA 25 1/16      CPN 35 1/16      CPO 26 5/8      CPQ 16.67

/16    CQB 2 1/16    CQBPRA 6    CQBPRB 7 1/8    CR 27 15/16


  DCI 28    DCN 17 5/8    DCO 11 15/16    DCP 57 5/8    DCS

22 13/16    DDRPRC 21 1/16    DDRPRD 21 1/4    DDS 13 1/2


DLJPRB 0    DLJPRT 25 1/16    DLM 8 5/16    DLP 21 9/16    D

  DNR 9 9/16    DNT 24 7/8    DNY 26    DO 37 9/16    DOL 15
```

The data streaming off the archetypal ticker is about as raw as can be imagined, yet it still holds a lot of respect in both the professional investment world and among amateur investors. Without knowing a great deal about the market (common measures such as volumes, volatility, average prices, political climate, etc.), trying to interpret any great meaning in a particular stock's performance is difficult, if not impossible, without context—yet we still publish this data everyday in newspapers.

nathan shedroff **experience design**

This is one of those online experiences that never could have existed before the Web. J-track enables anyone to view the tracking data for all the satellites in orbit around the Earth—at least the ones that NASA tracks. There is no meaning or evaluation provided, nor synopsis or knowledge, but the novel nature of the data itself—certainly for those of us outside the aerospace industry—is a rare glimpse into a phenomenon that we can barely perceive otherwise.

http://liftoff.msfc.nasa.gov/realtime/JTrack/   principal designers: Patrick Meyer, Tim Hervath, and Becky Bray

experience design nathan shedroff

STATION

INTELSAT 603

2

nathan shedroff **experience design**

Information is the beginning of meaning.

Information is data put into context with thought given to its organization and presentation. And even at that, it is only the lowest form of meaning as the context involved in creating and presenting data is usually basically generalized. However, at least there *is* context, unlike data.

Because information is so basic, it tends to be formal and rather impersonal. Also, most of us have such poor information skills—that is, the skills necessary for reorganizing, analyzing, synthesizing, and presenting data—information tends to be even less sophisticated when it finally comes into being.

We all create information on some level, though most of us aren't consciously aware of doing so. However, we do make note of those people or sources that we tend to trust and understand better than others. We do feel a difference when we feel we're being understood, and a frustration when we aren't. Because information is part of our lives, we all are both producers and consumers. This is why it is so critical for us to have basic information skills. Without these skills we relinquish the responsibility and the ability to create information for ourselves and those around us—to add value, if for no other purpose than to relate our own personal stories and experiences.

Like data, information can be captured and frozen in time. It can be printed in books or inherent in natural phenomena (like tides). However, it is only of value if we know how to decode it, if we can speak the language with which it has been encoded, and if the information hasn't been obscured by other phenomena.

Unfortunately, there are very few products that help us create information. Software manufacturers, in particular, have been adept at creating tools that allow us to manipulate data, color and animate it, but not help us create meaning from it. Usually, these tools only make things worse as their effects only mask meaning further.

Organizing Things

The organization and presentation of data can profoundly change its understanding. Presentation can affect the knowledge people build and the experience people have. This is where information design can have its greatest impact. It is the discipline concerned with transforming data into information by creating context and structure. Information design is the method through which graphic design and other visual disciplines are expressed.

Though data organization is a profoundly important process, it isn't necessarily a foreboding one. As Richard Saul Wurman has so often shown, there are only a few ways to organize data in order to create information. In fact, it is often a fun exercise that yields surprising and satisfying results. Meaning is formed by the arrangement of data and transformed as we restructure it.

Consider the basic ways we can organize data, being mindful that organization and presentation are different concepts. Data can only be organized within a few principles: **Magnitude, Time, Numbers, Alphabet, Category, Location**, and **Randomness.**

 **Magnitude**, Time, Number, and Alphabet are all sequences of some type, which we can use to organize things based on a similar characteristic shared by all the data. The last three of these attributes (**Time, Number,** and **Alphabet**) are special, simple sequences that we've come to understand through training but which often have no inherent meaning for the data. These organizational structures are merely easy for us to use, even though their use can seem somewhat artificial.

 Category and **Location** are organizations that also use some inherently meaningful aspect of the data around which the data can be oriented. Because these organizations are more qualitative than quantitative, they often seem more "natural" and less artificial. These two organizations can be thought of as two-dimensional (and sometimes even three-dimensional) in that they each orient data, necessarily in at least two directions (whereas sequences like those above are fundamentally one-dimensional). There is no greater value necessarily in data arranged two- or three-dimensionally other than one-dimensionally, as long as it is meaningful. However, 2D data arrangements can tend to offer more accessibility since there is more than one way to access the inforrmation (either dimension).

 Randomness is the lack of organization. It is often important when we're trying to build an experience that isn't necessarily easy (a perfectly legitimate endeavor as long as it's appropriate), for example as in a game.

The same organization (for instance a geographical or locational one) can be presented or *expressed* in several different forms, e.g., maps, written descriptions and directions, illustrated in graphs, charts, and timelines, or read to us audibly. The organization need not change through all of these forms and, thus, the meaning won't either. However, the presentation will still affect a person's ability to understand.

Data often has its own natural organization. It almost has a *will* to be organized in a particular way (still within one of the forms we've discussed). Experimenting with different organizations is often a process of uncovering the organization that exudes from the data, thereby informing its structure.

Each organization creates a new mental model of the data and can lead to new understandings of the data. These can sometimes revolutionize our understanding of even familiar subjects since they illuminate an aspect that might have been confusing or obscured before.

nathan shedroff **experience design**

Traffic signs are so common that we rarely stop to consider how effective
they are in alerting us to dangers or directing us to our destinations. The
context is what makes these signs effective, as well as the training we receive
when we reach driving age. Additionally, the effectiveness of these signs
relies upon the convention of using them, and the shared agreement about
their meaning.

experience design nathan shedroff

The transformation of information usually yields more information, and sometimes more than the original information itself.

Altavista's Babelfish is an online translator for text and Web pages. This is one of the dreams that developers and users of computers have had for decades. While the translation isn't as accurate as that completed by a native-speaker of the translated language, it is reasonably well translated and certainly good enough for casual correspondence.

The information inherent in the original message leads to new information in the translation, but introduces two kinds of other information: The first is what might be termed the "mis-translation" or unintended meaning; the second is the experience we get comparing the two messages, even casually, and the familiarization and exposure we get to the translation.

experience design nathan shedroff

plus d'information, et parfois plus que l'information

et les webpages. C'est un des rêves que les lotisseur
décennies. Tandis que la traduction n'est pas auss
langages fournis, elle est traduite raisonnablemen
occasionnelle.

und webpages. Dieses st
einer der Träume, die
Entwickler und Benutzer
der Computer für
Dekaden gewünscht
haben, während die
Übersetzung nicht so
genau wie die ist, die durch
ein menschliches
durchgeführt wird,
gebürtiges Sprechen der
hergestellten Sprachen,
ist sie recht wohles
übersetzt und zweifellos
gut genug für beiläufige
Korrespondenz.

dores han
discurso
lenguajes
er traducido
ciertamente

nathan shedroff **experience design**

The difference between information and knowledge is a difficult one to explain. Knowledge isn't just a more complex version of information—its use is different as well. Knowledge is a kind of meta-information that must be understood in a more general way. In fact, **a definition of knowledge could be "sufficiently generalized solutions gained through experience."**

This means that knowledge is something that is, necessarily, accessible in many and varied contexts and situations, and not merely descriptive of details in particular ones.

This generalization is important because it makes knowledge more useful, and it helps distinguish knowledge from information since its meaning must be distilled from information in order to be understood as knowledge and not information. In other words, **generalization is a criteria that helps us understand a meaning that is deeper or of a higher-order than information.** This is also possible only through experience since we cannot distinguish knowledge from information unless we can compare its use in several, different situations, each of which is an experience.

While we can help build knowledge for others (in pointing it out as well as designing the experiences to make it easier to understand), this is the beginning of the crossing of a threshold in which **people must build these kinds of understandings for themselves.** Wisdom, for example, is something people can only build for themselves and knowledge shares part of this characteristic.

Knowledge is increasingly personal in that

the processes in our minds that help define and understand knowledge rely increasingly on personal contexts, content, and previous understandings, and less on shared ones. Again, by the time we can build wisdom, the context is so personal that we are unable to share it. This process of internalization helps create knowledge and wisdom but at the same time makes it more difficult to share.

Context moves from the global (societal or cultural) to the local (shared among increasingly smaller groups and more idiosyncratic) to the personal (easily understood only to ourselves without explanation). **Knowledge, then, becomes more casual in its use. As it becomes more personal,** it cannot be used as formally with others; and formal situations often can make it more difficult to communicate knowledge.

experience design nathan shedroff

Knowledge also builds upon itself, making it increasingly easier to acquire more knowledge.

This is because it helps us use and organize our own contexts and understandings, and these structures help us more easily integrate new experiences, information, data, and, thus, knowledge into this system. The practice also gives us confidence and decreases fear about learning and understanding.

Because the experience is so critical to building knowledge, the richer the experience, the more likely it is to fit one of our contextual models and the more able we are to find meaning in it. However, just because it is rich, doesn't mean it is effective. Often, rich experiences offer only more stimulation and not more context. This stimulation can just as easily make it more difficult to decode and integrate any knowledge as make it more likely. This is why activities like storytelling and conversation are so powerful and necessary for creating knowledge. **They allow us to interact with the information in a way that helps us build personal context and integrate the information into our previous understandings.** Any valuable education or learning, therefore, cannot exist without building these processes into its models.

nathan shedroff **experience design**

Of course, there are many kinds of classes, but cooking classes are particularly exciting since the skills they teach are applicable to everyday life. The products created are delicious and are something in which most people can take pride. Every class is an opportunity to impart knowledge. Cooking classes make this easier since most allow students to cook themselves, and it is this experience that allows for knowledge to transfer more readily.

Actually performing an activity is almost always more memorable than simply watching. Because our whole body is involved in the activity, our kinetic, olfactory, and tactile memory is stimulated in addition to our visual and sonic memory. This creates a richer experience and binds our memories together, often in subconscious ways.

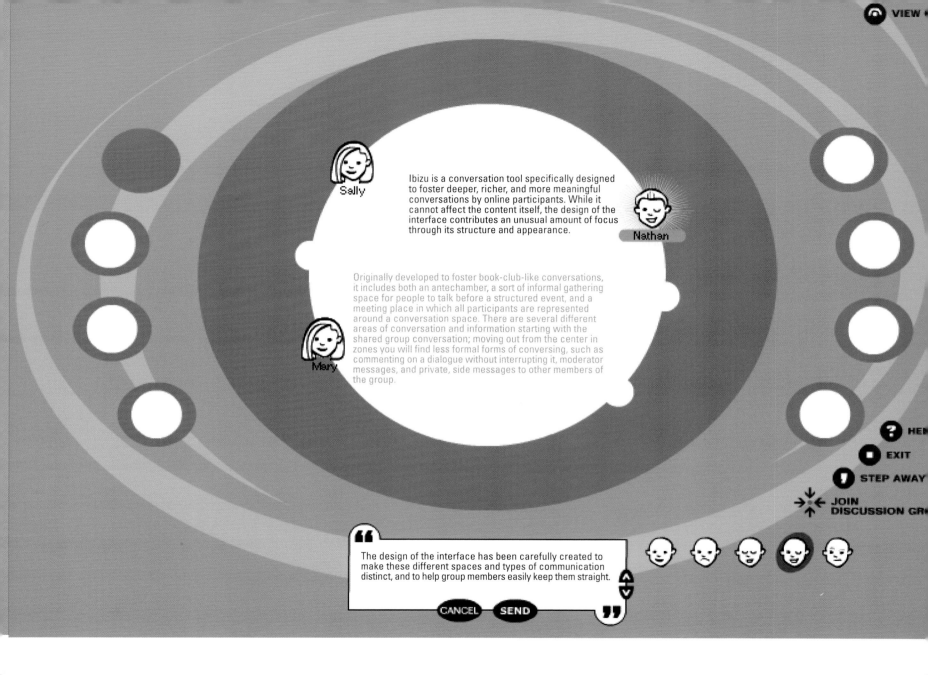

Ibizu is a conversation tool specifically designed to foster deeper, richer, and more meaningful conversations by online participants. While it cannot affect the content itself, the design of the interface contributes an unusual amount of focus through its structure and appearance.

Originally developed to foster book-club-like conversations, it includes both an antechamber, a sort of informal gathering space for people to talk before a structured event, and a meeting place in which all participants are represented around a conversation space. There are several different areas of conversation and information starting with the shared group conversation; moving out from the center in zones you will find less formal forms of conversing, such as commenting on a dialogue without interrupting it, moderator messages, and private, side messages to other members of the group.

The design of the interface has been carefully created to make these different spaces and types of communication distinct, and to help group members easily keep them straight.

CANCEL   SEND

www.ibizu.com

creators: Sal Arora, Leslie Carlson Vaughan, Rachel McNamara, and Anthony Pho

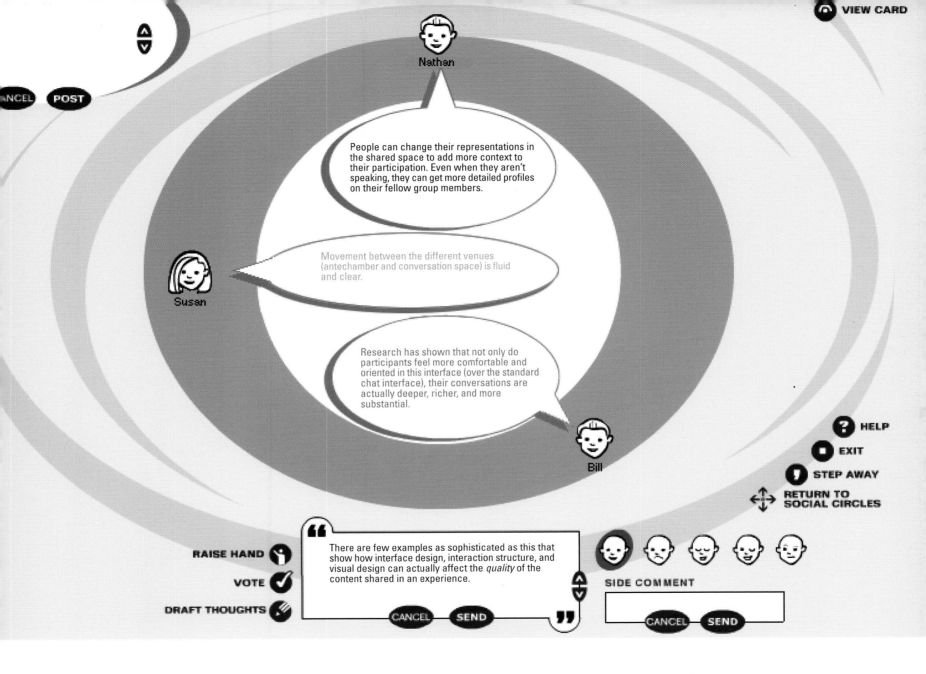

There are few examples as sophisticated as this that show how interface design, interaction structure, and visual design can actually affect the *quality* of the content shared in an experience.

Widsom is even more difficult to explain than knowledge since the levels of context become even more personal, and thus the higher-level nature of wisdom renders it much more obscure. Where knowledge is mainly sufficiently generalized solutions, **think of wisdom as "sufficiently generalized approaches and values that can be applied in many, varied situations."**

Wisdom cannot be created like data and information, and it cannot be shared with others like knowledge. Because the context is so personal it becomes almost exclusive to our own minds, and incompatible with the minds of others without extensive translation. This translation requires not only a base of knowledge and the opportunities for experiences that help create wisdom, but also the processes of introspection, retrospection, interpretation, and contemplation.

We can value wisdom in others but only we can create it for ourselves.

Because of this, it doesn't come naturally or accidentally; it is for the most part created deliberately. Exposing people, especially children, to wisdom and the concept of wisdom is critical in opening the door to becoming wise (or having common sense); however, the work cannot be done for us by others. It can only be done by ourselves and this requires an intimate understanding and relationship with ourselves.

It is quite possible that the path to wisdom is not even open until we approach understanding with an openness and tolerance for ambiguity. Fear and rigid tenets often create barriers to truly understanding experiences and situations and creating wisdom from them. This doesn't mean that we must be without principles, but that we must be constantly willing and open to challenging our principles and modifying them—even abandoning them—in the face of new experiences that prove more reliable or illuminating. Since wisdom is so personal, a fear or lack of understanding about yourself becomes one of the most extreme roadblocks to becoming wise. Since we are always striving to better understand ourselves, this becomes a continuous process that requires that we constantly evaluate ourselves as well as our previous understandings and functions.

experience design nathan shedroff

Dinner parties are hardly new experiences—they still satisfy our needs for entertainment, food, and company. This is especially true for Mary Jordan's annual fete honoring her experience in Burma. The 80 or so invitees this year not only bring sake and donations for a 35-foot carved Buddha to be presented as a gift to the people of Burma next year, but they must bring specific contributions to the performances and entertainment of the dinner party guests. These include probing questions to be answered (which are pulled at random from a bowl at Mary's whim), mysterious locations (also written on paper and relinquished to a different bowl), and appropriate (or approximate) dress to help make the experience special.

In addition to their own preparations, all guests are expected to perform and participate in the performance of others. Experience and performance are the operative themes here, and the pieces range from poetry readings to improvisation to music and dance to acts that defy description.

Guests are also made to perform rituals upon arrival, some of which include cleansing their thoughts and minds, fording streams, and submitting to a sonic massage by dijeridoo.

creator: Mary Jordan
held annually since 1998

The wisdom of the rituals and the preparations is that people need to purposefully and deliberately cross the boundary from the outside world to the inside world created by Mary. The rituals and performances subtly guide guests to contemplate the thoughts and offerings made by their fellow guests, consider their values and reactions to these experiences, and challenge their current beliefs in light of new knowledge.

Why did the Goddess create God?

Piano

06 Nov 1997 1:48 pm
Chicago, Illinois
source: Lunch

There is a piano (well, a keyboard) in my living room now. I'm staring at it as I write this - it's over by the window, slightly off to the side, a temporary chair in front of it.

My parents got it for Katrina, for her to learn to play. It's not quite a full-size keyboard, I notice now (though somehow I missed that in the beginning).

We're just staring each other down, really. I know I'll touch it eventually, in earnest, and that I won't stop after that. For now, we're in this strange state of detente. Waiting.

I've been here before, really. The last time I had a keyboard in my presence, I'd rented a piano in Salt Lake City. I was pregnant with Katrina, and that was many moons ago. I used to play when I thought no-one was listening... when the neighbors were gone, when Paul was asleep upstairs, when it was night, when it was dark, when it was quiet.

I used to play in the dark. Sometimes by candlelight.

Nothing monumental, you see. Nothing adapted. I never played to be good, really. I played for me, small melodies, old accompaniments, pieces I'd

Wisdom isn't something that's easy to find, and it may not be possible to have a wise experience online, but moments.org is, at least, a record of its creator's contemplation and introspection. Magdelena Donea records moments in her life—some ordinary, many extraordinary—so that she can remember and learn from them.

You won't necessarily become wiser by exploring her sites, but with the tools you are given, you may become wiser through example.

"I've seen things you people wouldn't believe. Attack ships on fire off the shoulder of Orion. I watched C-beams glitter in the dark near the Tannhauser gate. All those moments will be lost in time, like tears in rain..."

(Rutger Hauer, improvising as Roy Batty, *Blade Runner*, 1982)

M O M E N T S

ISO 400/27° 2   ISO 400/27° 2

17   18   19   20

I have this theory about myself, about my life and the way I choose to live it.

In my moments of weakness, I have a tendency to think that what I am is, by and large, defined by a very long and complicated set of memories. Those memories, in turn, are the retelling of past events as seen through the filter of my experience - a filter which, in and of itself, is shaped and colored by a set of other memories, older and newer alike, of yet bigger stories, of moments.

In the winter of 1983, I stood on a barren hillside hundreds of feet above the coast of the Black Sea, and I promised myself that yes, I would take care to record in my mind, and later remember, the time that was to come, each and every moment of it. It was a promise I kept well.

I just never stopped.

I've been recording my life and sharing it, in some form or another, ever since. I've done it on the web for almost four years now, having finally found an outlet, a space to tell my stories, a place where the chance of inconveniencing anyone with my chatter was minimal,

ACTIVITY LOG:

Date/Time: 4:46 AM SEP 10 2000
Place: Fairfax County, VA, USA

I'm flirting with the idea of getting N'Sync tickets for Katrina (and her two best friends) for Christmas. They'll be in town November 11th. Yours truly would accompany the bunch. No doubt, they would be talking about it for months.

Please talk me out of it.

Irregular updates. Occasional tidbits. Or, nothing new at all but it beats reloading this page for a year, no? It's MaggyMail! Subscribe again, please; I deleted the old list so as to not annoy anyone.

Pictures of the munchkins and the family have been known to exist at maxmcculler.com. Also... unbeknownst to me til this second, my husband's been updating his homepage! When did this happen?!

MOMENTS.ORG is sponsored in part by:

nathan shedroff **experience design**

The most important aspect of any design is how it is understood in the minds of the audience.

This concept, whether fully or partially formed, is a **cognitive model**. Everyone forms cognitive models for nearly everything they encounter—particularly those things they interact with repeatedly, or those things that we focus on because they are important to us. Some people are more adept at forming cognitive models than others, and these facilities also differ between people in their type of understanding—that is, some people form understandings textually, visually, aurally, temporally, geographically, and so forth. In any case, the form of the experience is what gives it meaning since this is what people experience directly.

Whether or not you focus on creating a cognitive model for your experience, your participants will nonetheless. They might form a mental map of the sequence or process or location. It might be of their feelings, or merely a randomly strung together list of memories of their experiences. What's important, however, is whether you want or need them to remember the experience well enough to follow directions, repeat it, recount it, or duplicate it. Much of education is about creating mental models for students to use and follow.

New cognitive models can often revolutionize an audience's understanding of data, information, or an experience by helping them understand and reorganize things they previously understood (or, perhaps, couldn't understand), in a way that illuminates the topic or experience.

To create meaningful cognitive models, consider the ways in which you want your audience to find meaning and what you want them to remember. In most cases, you will need to choose one form for the overall experience (like the sequence of a book, play, or music, or the layout of a party, theme park, or building). There are no *right* answers to this one form, but you would be wise to explore different forms before settling on one (see *Information* on page 42 and *Multiplicity* on page 72). Of course, this form won't work best for everybody, so when it's important—and possible—create other ways of moving through the experience that allows others to form a mental map in a way that better suits them. Also, be wary of mental models that constrain your experience or cause cognitive disonance (when the mental map formed doesn't conform well to the reality of the experience) for your participants (see *Metaphors* on page 102).

experience design nathan shedroff

nathan shedroff **experience design**

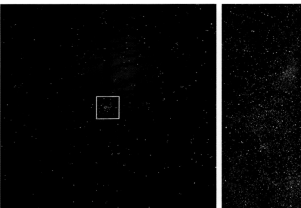 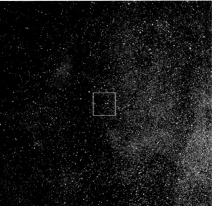 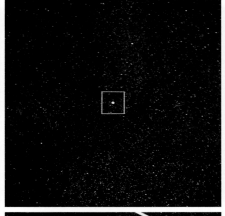 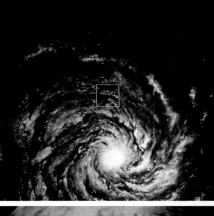

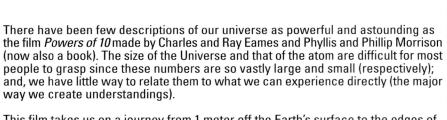 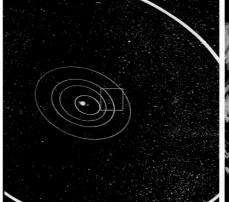 

There have been few descriptions of our universe as powerful and astounding as the film *Powers of 10* made by Charles and Ray Eames and Phyllis and Phillip Morrison (now also a book). The size of the Universe and that of the atom are difficult for most people to grasp since these numbers are so vastly large and small (respectively); and, we have little way to relate them to what we can experience directly (the major way we create understandings).

This film takes us on a journey from 1 meter off the Earth's surface to the edges of the Universe—not in a direct or algebraic line (a journey that would be impossibly long) but an exponential one. In other words, instead of presenting pictures back toward the Earth at every meter thereafter, we see views that increase exponentially from one meter to 10 to 100 to 1000 etc., finally stopping at nearly one billion light years from the Earth.

Likewise, the second half of this journey takes us into increasingly smaller views (starting at the same point one meter above the surface of the Earth) until we move inside the body, its organs, its cells, its organelles, its molecules, its atoms, and finally to the smallest edge of our understandings of the physical Universe: inside sub-atomic particles.

The film (and book) use this linear organization with constant intervals of distance to help us form a cognitive model of the relative sizes of the things we understand (and don't yet) in terms that we can begin to understand.

One of the most important, and unexpected, observations isn't how big or small things are, but that certain repeating patterns of vast emptiness and packed activity are almost constant from the sub-sub-sub atomic to the largest conceivable astronomical bodies. These kind of relationships draw conclusions about the nature of the Universe and even how we perceive, and these revelations also lead to a formation of a cognitive model for the Universe that anyone can understand.

isbn: 0716760088
www.eamesoffice.com/powers_of_ten/powers_of_ten.html

creators: Phillip and Phyllis Morrison and Charles and Ray Eames
first published in 1968

nathan shedroff **experience design**

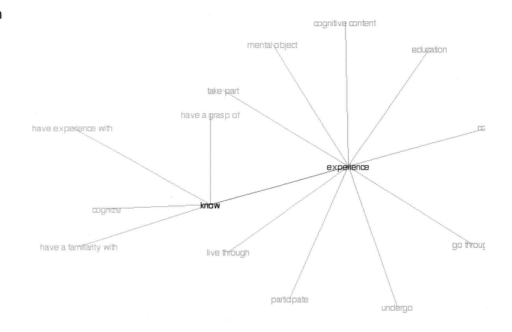

plumbdesign

cognitive content

mental object

education

take part

have a grasp of

have experience with

ос

experience

know

cognize

go throu

have a familiarity with

live through

participate

undergo

horizon

VISUAL THESAURUS

experience   know

DISPLAY : ○ AUTO-NAVIGATE
⦿ 2D   ○ 3D

CREATED USING THINKMAP   COPYRIGHT 1998 PLUMB DESIGN, INC

Sometimes the best cognitive models aren't aligned with known objects (as with metaphors) or environments (as with maps), but are abstract and reduce meaning to a more pure state. The Plumbdesign Thinkmap system is a diagramming system that relates terms, objects, or elements to each other in an abstract and cognitively reduced way. One of the effects of this is that there are no other meanings overlaid onto the cognitive space, and the cognitive model and presentation are aligned perfectly. Of course, this isn't necessarily the best solution for every use but, when it is, there are no more seductive presentations of these cognitive maps than the Thinkmap diagrams.

plumbdesign

cognitive content

live through
know

content

move

experience

go through

participate

take a step

take steps

take part

noun
adjective   verb
adverb

VISUAL THESAURUS

experience   know   participate   experience

horizon

DISPLAY : ○ AUTO-NAVIGATE
○ 2D   ◉ 3D

CREATED USING THINKMAP   COPYRIGHT 1998 PLUMB DESIGN, INC

One of the most difficult concepts for designers to understand is that **the presentation of an experience or design (its appearance) is separate from its organization.** Often, these are so tightly coupled or so commonly combined that we can't imagine a particular organization presented in any other way (geographic information, for example, presented as maps). However, the most common taxonomies for presenting information aren't always the most successful.

Almost any organization can be presented in a variety of ways. Textual data (words or numbers) can be presented in writing (such as a description), visually (as in any variety of charts), or aurally (as in live or recorded speaking), or in any combination.

Even map data can be presented in all of these ways. Consider driving directions to a house. The organization of the data most likely will be time and location (specifically, locations over time in an efficient route). However, these directions can be written into a descriptive paragraph, listed in a bulleted list, charted as a map in any of a variety of forms and projections, or recorded in sequence as an audio tape to be played in real time.

Often, the presentation itself affects our understanding so much that we can misunderstand or misinterpret the data. This is often the case with political or legal presentations in which it is more important to the presentation's creators to incite a particular opinion than it is to be accurate. This is how propaganda and disinformation are formed. Unfortunately, it's often the outcome of visual design work since most designers value visual style and appearance over understanding and accuracy (whether they realize it or not). While designers are *supposed* to bring something new and unique to the design process—often something unexpected or previously considered unrelated; sometimes these inspirational elements really aren't appropriate, or they are implemented in a way that obscures everything *but* the style.

experience design nathan shedroff

nathan shedroff experience design

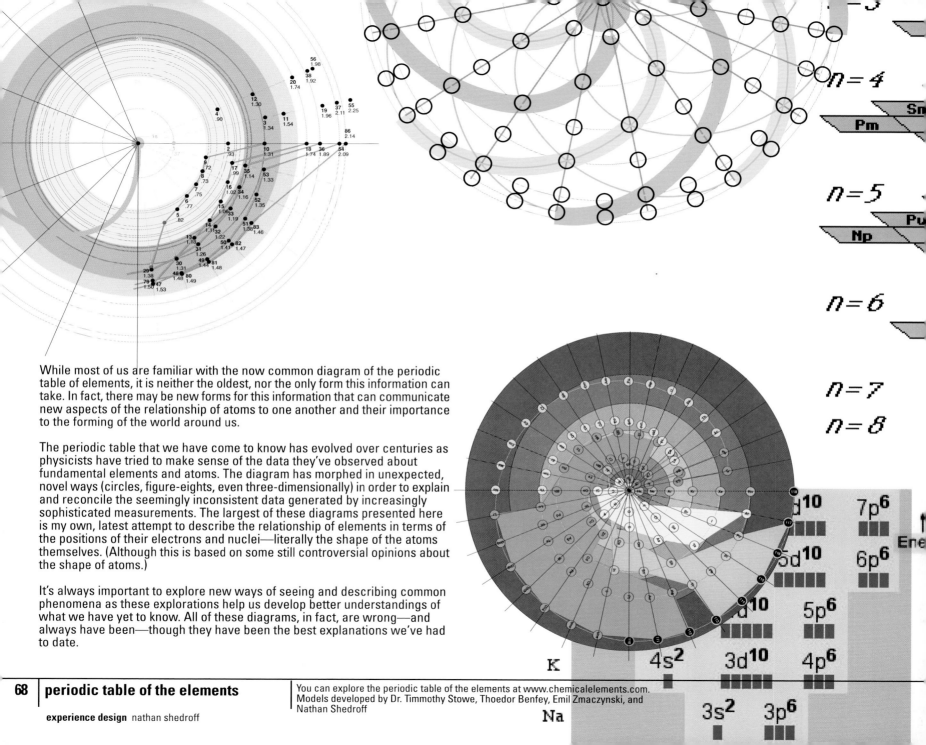

While most of us are familiar with the now common diagram of the periodic table of elements, it is neither the oldest, nor the only form this information can take. In fact, there may be new forms for this information that can communicate new aspects of the relationship of atoms to one another and their importance to the forming of the world around us.

The periodic table that we have come to know has evolved over centuries as physicists have tried to make sense of the data they've observed about fundamental elements and atoms. The diagram has morphed in unexpected, novel ways (circles, figure-eights, even three-dimensionally) in order to explain and reconcile the seemingly inconsistent data generated by increasingly sophisticated measurements. The largest of these diagrams presented here is my own, latest attempt to describe the relationship of elements in terms of the positions of their electrons and nuclei—literally the shape of the atoms themselves. (Although this is based on some still controversial opinions about the shape of atoms.)

It's always important to explore new ways of seeing and describing common phenomena as these explorations help us develop better understandings of what we have yet to know. All of these diagrams, in fact, are wrong—and always have been—though they have been the best explanations we've had to date.

experience design nathan shedroff

You can explore the periodic table of the elements at www.chemicalelements.com. Models developed by Dr. Timmothy Stowe, Thoedor Benfey, Emil Zmaczynski, and Nathan Shedroff

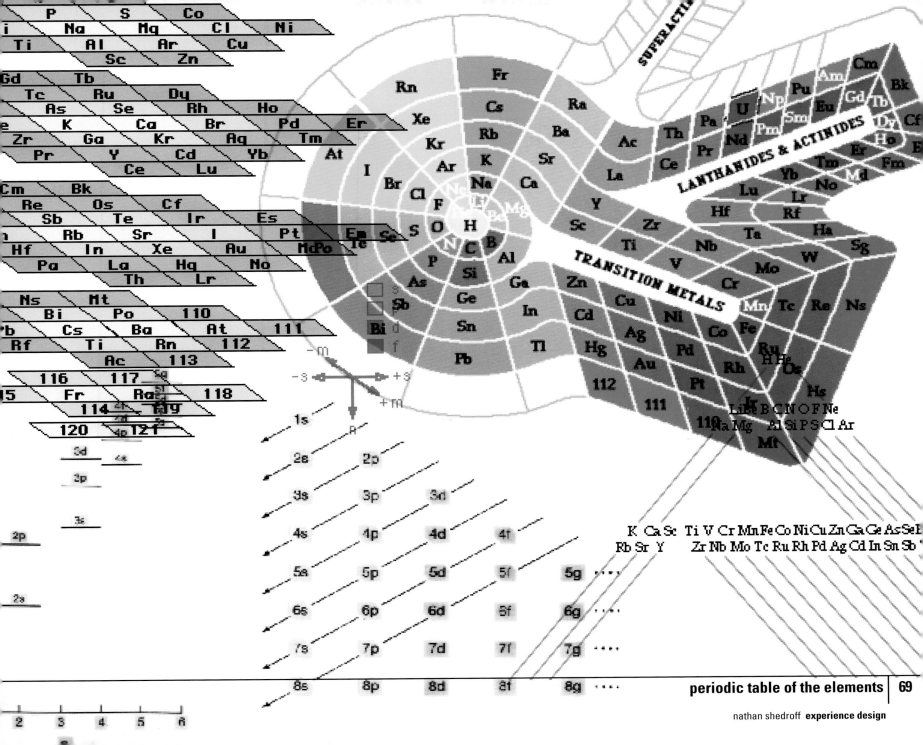

nathan shedroff **experience design**

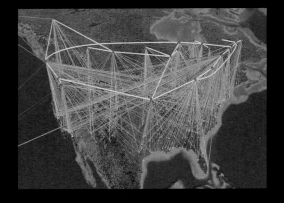

An Atlas Of Cyberspaces

Welcome to the Atlas of Cyberspaces

This is an atlas of maps and graphic representations of the geographies of the new electronic territories of the Internet, the World-Wide Web and other emerging Cyberspaces.

These maps of Cyberspaces — cybermaps — help us visualise and comprehend the new digital landscapes beyond our computer screen, in the wires of the global communications networks and vast online information resources. The cybermaps, like maps of the real-world, help us navigate the new information landscapes, as well being objects of aesthetic interest. They have been created by "cyber-explorers" of many different disciplines, and from all corners of the world.

Some of the maps you will see in the Atlas of Cyberspaces will appear familiar, using the cartographic conventions of real-world maps, however, many of the maps are much more abstract representations of electronic spaces, using new metaphors and grids. The atlas comprises separate pages, covering different types of cybermaps.

[Introduction | Conceptual | Artistic | Geographic | Cables & Satellites |
| Traceroutes | Census | Topology | Info Maps | Info Landscapes | Info Spaces |
| ISP Maps | Web Site Maps | Surf Maps | MUDs & Virtual Worlds | Historical]

Mapping Cyberspace
a new book by
Martin Dodge & Rob Kitchin
Published October 2000

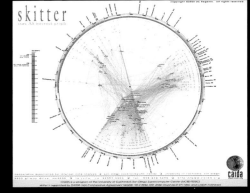

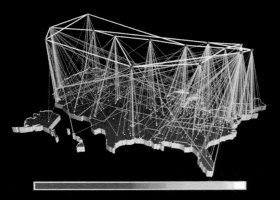

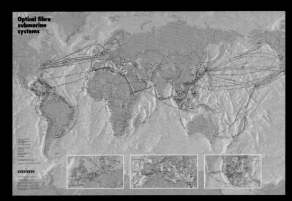

Optical fibre submarine systems

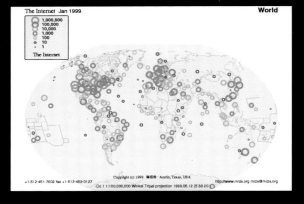

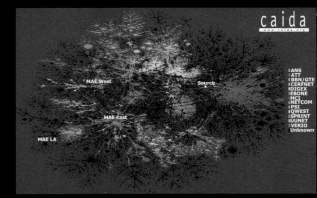

There are many ways to view the same thing, though we often become so accustomed to certain, standard views that we take the possibilities for granted and forget to even expect alternatives.

This site contains a wealth of maps in a variety of forms that all describe, essentially, the same thing: the size and activity of the Internet. This variety reminds us to search for new—and better—ways to visualize and describe what we're trying to communicate.

www.cybergeography.org/atlas/

book: *Mapping Cyberspace* by Martin Dodge and Robert Kitchin
isbn: 0-415-19884-4
www.mappingcyberspace.com

experience design nathan shedroff

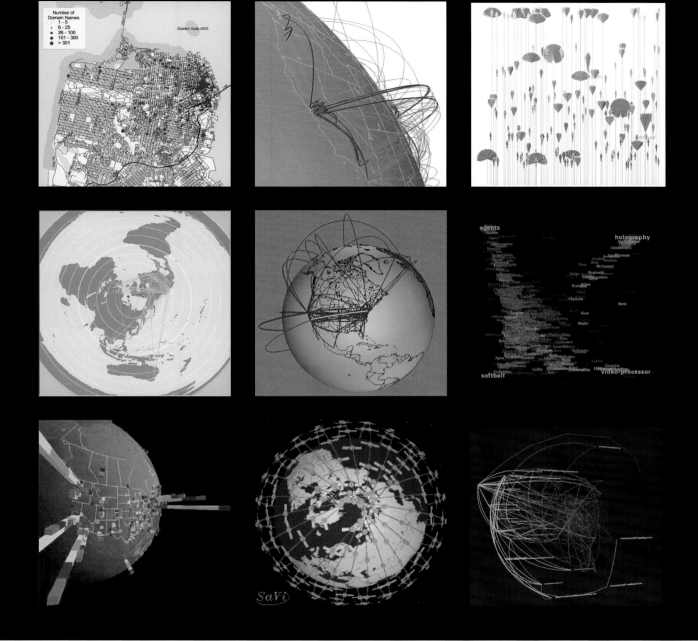

Key to the development of cognitive models is the diversity of people's learning styles and abilities, as well as the complexity and depth of data in many circumstances. This is what creates the need for multiplicity in organizational schemes, both in redundant and alternative organizations as well as in deeper levels of organization that are layered onto higher-level organization to make an experience clear.

Multiple views and other redundancies may seem like a waste of time and resources, but the duplication is critical to creating understanding for a variety of people.

Since everyone has different skills and experience, no one way organizing data is capable of creating understanding for everyon

Varying organizations and presentations allow each person to best find his or her way. Examples of these multiple points of entry into content are book indexes and building signage. In search interfaces, they allow for multiple search criteria, including browsing, which itself is an alternative to searching.

Multiple organizations also support multiple points of view. In some interfaces, different paths that support different organizations clearly allow and shape different understandings in a body of content. This can create an opportunity

for richer understanding since conflicting perspectives often can lead to deeper thought and more consideration when forming not only opinions and understandings, but cognitive models as well.

Most complex data require several levels of organization, varying the form of organization at each level to suit the content. Encyclopedia, guidebooks, and directories, for example, often nest their organizations. Directories might first list items by location, then by quality (or some other magnitude), and then alphabetically. These levels help break the data into meaningful chunks that can be navigated more easily. They also reflect and *create* hierarchies of importance and priorities, and thus, meaning.

Lastly, multiple levels of organization create a hierarchy for reading as well as importance. It's advisable, then, that the most important meaning (however this is deemed), also be the most evident (whether on a page or screen). In other words, importance should be reflected in obviousness, or at least, ease of reading. Likewise, the second level of importance should be reflected in the next apparent data and organization, and so on. Unfortunately, many designs often use style to mask the hierarchy of importance thereby decoupling this relationship, making it more difficult to navigate as well as understand the meaning of the content itself.

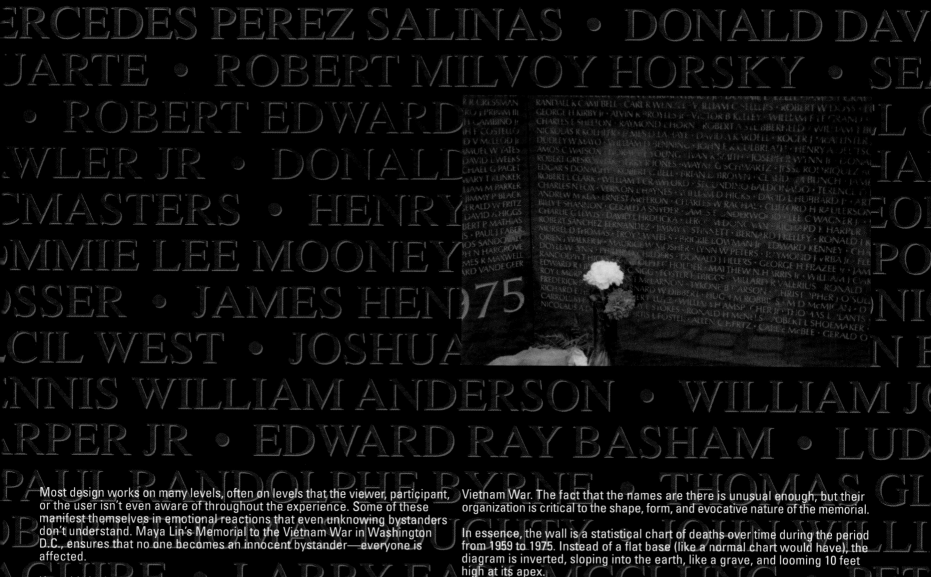

Most design works on many levels, often on levels that the viewer, participant, or the user isn't even aware of throughout the experience. Some of these manifest themselves in emotional reactions that even unknowing bystanders don't understand. Maya Lin's Memorial to the Vietnam War in Washington D.C., ensures that no one becomes an innocent bystander—everyone is affected.

How this is done is subtly but wonderfully perfected. By combining simple forms of organization with an understated, yet haunting, presentation, she has personalized what is normally impersonal about war memorials.

The monument is a seemingly simple nexus of two black granite walls, inscribed with the names of the 58,183 US men and women who officially died during the Vietnam War. The fact that the names are there is unusual enough, but their organization is critical to the shape, form, and evocative nature of the memorial.

In essence, the wall is a statistical chart of deaths over time during the period from 1959 to 1975. Instead of a flat base (like a normal chart would have), the diagram is inverted, sloping into the earth, like a grave, and looming 10 feet high at its apex.

What gives the monument its structure is the organization of names (deaths) over time as the deaths gradually build from the early years, and then decrease as the US pulls out of the region in the end. The actual graph has been simplified, of course, and the power traded for accuracy is more than worth the normalization of the graph.

www.virtualwall.org
Washington, D.C.

designer: Maya Lin

experience design nathan shedroff

Shortly after the monument was chosen as the winning design, the names were summarily reordered alphabetically because the jury felt that the chronological order would make it impossible for visitors to find loved ones—and they were correct. However, the power of the design—and the whole reason for its form—was suddenly diminished. In addition, the names themselves became less important as each of the 16 James Jones became indistinct. As originally conceived, the names of servicemen and women often would appear in relation to the others with whom they had died. Like any great work of art, the more one knows about the piece and its context (such as the names of soldiers of a battalion that suffered heavy loses at a particular battle), the more meaningful it becomes.

The answer was a multiplicity of organization that reordered the names as originally intended. Two podiums also were added at each side of the entrance to the monument that encased alphabetical directories of the names and locator panels. The addition not only restored the monument's original power and emotional potential, but the experience was made feasible in light of the needs of its visitors. The two organizations were essential in creating the necessary experiences.

Welcome to Herman Miller RED!

PRODUCT SEARCH [ ] **GO**   LOGIN   SHOPPING CART   HELP

SHOW ALL FURNITURE

Seating
Desks & Tables
Storage
Screens
Lighting
Accessories
More Cool Things

COOL. DOABLE.
Feisty furniture for companies big on attitude, but tight on cash.

OUR MOST POPULAR PRODUCTS

SEATING | DESKS | STORAGE | ACCESS.

SCREENS | LIGHTING

ROLLOVER IMAGE FOR LARGER VIEW.

We'll match any price on the web for the hottest chair on the globe.

REDROCKET
For companies that won't take slow for an answer.

Why Herman Miller RED
Privacy
HermanMiller.com

Everyone has a different need for the same things, and a different way of finding them. In this case, it's furniture. What's nice about this site is that the furniture is organized in multiple ways so that buyers can find what they want based on their needs, or what they already know about the furniture. In particular, the furniture is organized by category (seating, storage, accessories, and so forth). There is a product matrix that arranges all of the offerings not only by categories but also by product lines and, roughly, by price. While not all of this is immediately apparent to the user, it's inherent in the organization, and is an understanding that can emerge with use.

HermanMiller RED   Seating   PRODUCT SEARCH [ ] GO LOGIN SHOPPING CART HELP

SHOW ALL FURNITURE

Seating

Desks & Tables
Storage
Screens
Lighting
Accessories
More Cool Things

Why Herman Miller RED
Privacy
HermanMiller.com

SEATING

Think about your body.
You probably spend more time in your office chair than in bed. Ignore that fact, and sooner or later, various parts of your body will want to talk to you about it. Last year, Aeron was named *Design of the Decade* by *Business Week* and IDSA. And *Time Magazine* honored the Eames molded plywood chair as *Best Design of the 20th Century*. It's obvious that we respect the eye. Sit for a minute or two and you'll know how much we love the rest of you.

COMPARISON CHART

OFFICE CHAIRS	SIDE CHAIRS	OTHER SEATING
Aeron Highly Adjustable Work Chair	Eames Molded Plywood Side Chair	Eames Lounge Chair & Ottoman
Equa 2 Adjustable Work Chair	Aside Chair	Eames Sofa Compact
Reaction Highly Adjustable Work Chair	Limerick Stacking Chair	Eames Aluminum Lounge Chair
Reaction Adjustable Work Chair		Eames Walnut Stools
Avian Work Chair		Eames Aluminum Ottoman
Eames Aluminum Executive Chair		Eames Molded Plywood Lounge Chair
Eames Aluminum Management Chair		Eames Molded Plywood Chair
Eames Soft Pad Management Chair		Nelson Platform Bench
		Covey Stool

visual designer: Ryan Gagnard
builders: Xceed Corp., Dallas office
date launched: November 2000

experience design nathan shedroff

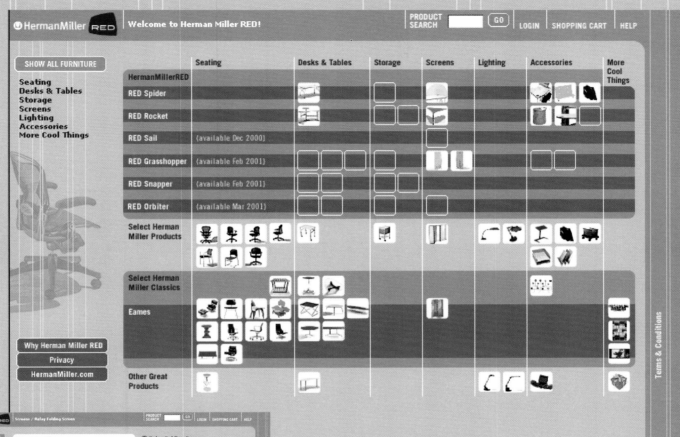

caveat:
Nathan Shedroff has worked on the experience design
for this site and this company.

There is no such thing as objectivity.

As much as we would like to believe otherwise and for all the repeating of this mantra in our educational system, it simply isn't true. Every part of the process of communicating is subject to the values, perspectives, and understandings of those creating the content.

This doesn't mean that we can't make a point of trying to be "objective,"
or more accurately, to present meaning with as little hyperbole and sensationalism as possible. Indeed, the best understandings are formed from presentations of differing, balanced views and opinions. What this means, however, is that even acts as simple and seemingly innocent as organizing data are subjective. Indeed, organizing data and the creating of information may have a profound impact on its meaning.

Even the documents that we think of as so basic that they are free of subjectivity, are actually rife with it. Dictionaries, for example, are organized simply (alphabetically), but the words themselves—as well as their meanings—are included through an often highly subjective process. This isn't necessarily bad. Subjectivity is necessary for the communication of opinion and personal stories. The problem arises only when we deny the existence of subjectivity at all levels (including the deepest and most "basic") of communication.

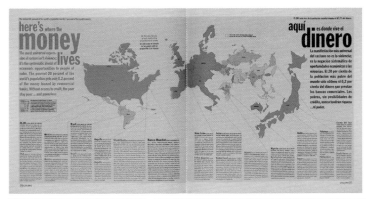

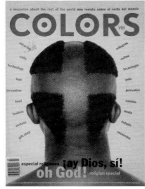

Most journalism seeks to ignore and even mask its own values and biases by decree of objectivity. This, of course, is a lie—but a common and generally accepted one. Instead of denouncing its role in the creation of opinion, COLORS makes this inevitability a cause to celebrate, and influence. Never denying its goals, it presents some of the most moving testimony to the complexity and wonder of cultures around the world.

Through photography and text, both wonderfully reflecting its point-of-view and consciousness of the power of juxtaposition, COLORS has created one of the most refreshing views on the world. And, astonishingly, those views are, in some ways, more "objective" and more powerful than those produced by the mainstream media.

www.benetton.com/colors

creator: Tibor Kalman

experience design nathan shedroff

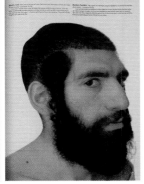
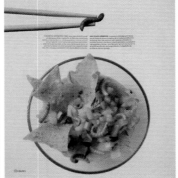

The quality of any knowledge depends on the quality of perspective, and the character of the information. Salon is a site that presents top-notch writing without leaving out the perspective. In fact, it is precisely this perspective that makes these stories so valuable.

salon.com

books @ amazon.com
SHOP HERE   SAVE UP TO 30%

SALON AUDIO
PAGAN BABIES
STEVE BUSCEMI READS
THE NEW ELMORE
LEONARD NOVEL

A&E   BOOKS   COMICS   MOTHERS   NEWS   PEOPLE   POLITICS   SEX   TECH & BUSINESS   AUDIO

ARTICLE FINDER

BOOKS

Search

○ All of Salon.com
○ Only Books
○ The Web with Ask Jeeves

[OK]

Directory

Hot Topics
Garrison Keillor
Laura Miller Audio
Hunter S. Thompson
Stephen King
Book Bag
Harry Potter
Book Reviews
Jack Kerouac
Gore Vidal
David Sedaris

Articles by date
● All of Salon.com
● By department

SALON.COM SITES

Arts & Entertainment
- The Movie Page
▶ Books
Comics
Mothers Who Think

▶ Recent Highlights

I was a captive of Xanth
Dragons! Centaurs! Sex!
Bad puns! A writer
confesses her
embarrassing love for
Piers Anthony's epic,
cheesy fantasy novels.
By Emily Jenkins
[12/07/00]

Freedom from choice
From short stories to
sports and science
writing, "Best of"
anthologies prove that
readers like their books
preselected.
By JoAnn Gutin
[12/06/00]

50

Older and better Critic
David Kipen talks about

book bag

Friday, Dec. 8, 2000

Small worlds
The author of "Election" and "Joe College" picks five great
books set in places where everyone knows everyone else's
business.
By Tom Perrotta

[In Audio]
The Paris Review
From the legendary literary journal: George Plimpton's exclusive
interviews with John Le Carré, Garrison Keillor, Hunter S.
Thompson and more.

Recently in Books

SHOP → We now
have three
books from Salon editors!
You'll find them in Salon
Shop: Books.

Hot gifts for
cold nights
from
RedEnvelope.

Watch the
film "Final
Approach"
at
Cinemanow.
com

LUXLOOK Fashion
Designer
Accessories Fall 2000

More great offers in
Salon Plus

amazon.com
Buy Books
On Health Here

Keyword Search:
○ Books ○ All [GO]

FREE
Step-By-Step
Stock Evaluation
www.quicken.com

salon.com

Arts & Entertainment click here
» TELEVISION

ENTER TO WIN click
DIGITAL CAMERA

salon.com

SALON AUDIO
PAGAN BABIES
STEVE BUSCEMI READS
THE NEW ELMORE
LEONARD NOVEL

A&E   BOOKS   COMICS   MOTHERS   NEWS   PEOPLE   POLITICS   SEX   TECH & BUSINESS   AUDIO

ARTICLE FINDER

Search

○ All of Salon.com
○ The Web with Ask Jeeves

[OK]

Directory

Hot Topics
The Beatles
Florida
Garrison Keillor
Wanderlust
David Blaine
Lynda Barry
Camille Paglia
Brilliant Careers
David Horowitz
Day Trading

Articles by date
● All of Salon.com
● By department

SALON.COM SITES

Arts & Entertainment
- The Movie Page
Books
Comics

▶ From the wires

Texas executions reach
40 this year

Rolling Stone retracts
Clinton quote

Jane Fonda among big
Gore donors

Nobel winner denounces
politics

Corzine spent $62 million
on Senate race

Napster hires Orrin
Hatch's chief advisor

Priceline.com scraps
expansion plans

Gender considered in new
asylum rule

Murder charge dropped;
victim found

Gore makes case to
Florida's Supreme Court

Intel warns of poor sales

Arafat: I want Mideast
peace

Friday, Dec. 8, 2000

The death of John Lennon

[In People]
The hero who never looked down
Young lion, musical genius, victim of an age of excess, the
slain Beatle still looms over the unsettled legacy of his time.
By Gary Kamiya

SHOP → Get your
"Recount
this!" T-shirt from
Salon.com.

amazon.com Free
shipping
on orders over $100 till
Sunday, December 10.

CINEMANOW
com

Watch the
film "Final
Approach"
at
Cinemanow.

nerve

Looking for
love? Salon
Nerve
personals

More great offers in
Salon Plus

BUSINESS 2.0

Tracking the Internet
Unionization Effort

Top European ISPs Merge

Will Games be the Killer

There's usually more than one way to get anywhere.

The same should be true with many experiences, at least with informing experiences as opposed to entertaining ones. Entertainment experiences, like stories or other narratives, tend to be one-way only because the story is told from a particular and deliberate point of view.

If possible, you should offer your audience several ways to navigate the experience, and this tends to be fairly easy with digital media. Even non-digital experiences, like books, can be more navigable with a bit of innovative thinking. Concepts like "links" or "jump words" can work just as well in print. However, they're often more difficult to implement and much more difficult to maintain and update, if at all, as they can be for CD-ROMs or online content. There are several examples of innovative books that try to link information throughout the book by concept and relationship. Indexes and directories are other, established ways of navigating static media and work just as well in digital experiences. Likewise, tables of content are merely another form of navigation already common to print media and accepted by audiences.

Many websites have a "site map" that, supposedly, is a visual way of accessing the entire site on one page. Of course, these are usually difficult to maintain—especially for larger, dynamic sites—so these "maps" are nothing more than lists (in other words, indexes). To compound the problem, many Web developers only put high-level links in these maps so that the index is only slightly more useful than the horizontal navigation throughout the site. The trick to making a useful site map is to organize as much of the site's content in one place and present it as clearly as possible.

Other forms of navigation also can use any kind of map or chart as a navigable presentation of a data set, when appropriate. Sometimes, these can orient people more easily than simple lists.

Wayfinding is an important, though subtle, aide to navigation. Wayfinding elements, or passive navigation, help orient users to where they are and where they can go. Technically, wayfinding elements, like street signs, don't actually need to function. In other words, they aren't the links and buttons themselves. Instead, they are the labels on pages and sections, the symbols, icons, or other visual elements that help orient people—even the rollover highlights that signal which of several options have been chosen.

Important to wayfinding is usually the persistence of all navigational choices at any level. Users usually find it easier to orient themselves if the navigational choices they haven't chosen don't disappear as they move through a site. This can be difficult if there are a lot of navigational choices (which may signal another problem anyway) since they will take space on the screen and can, potentially, add to the noise and clutter. However, it is common for sites to keep "horizontal" or categorical navigation persistent in the navigation on every page (usually at the top). These choices allow users to begin a new path in a new category if the one they have chosen happens to be unhelpful. The "vertical" or deep navigation can be represented in a number of ways—as long as it *is* represented. The reason for this is to allow people to backtrack easily without restarting from the beginning.

One convention for presenting vertical navigation is the **directory path**. This line of linked text is a representation of the steps between the homepage and wherever the user is at the moment, functioning as a kind of digital trail of breadcrumbs. This allows people to not only move between the pages represented in this path but simply to review the path to orient themselves if they find that they are lost.

Cascading menus are another convention that presents pop-up menu choices at each step in a navigational menu, allowing users to jump to any page in a site by rolling over the right combination of menu choices. These systems can be useful if the set of pages are applicable to a lot of people, but they can be confusing. If it's likely that users have use for only a few pages of a site (or certain sections), such a menu system is probably overkill.

Fish-eye views are another way to navigate data sets and websites. These views essentially show the entire set of data or pages but allow the user to focus on one section at a time. In this way, users get a sense of the whole data set (size and shape) but they aren't bombarded with so much data that they become confused. Users can then move the focus around the data set to explore and reveal what they're after. Inxight Software offers a tool for building and managing just this kind of view. These can be useful for large, disparate site maps, for example.

People often perform the role of navigational advisor. Some sites offer live customer service in which people can be consulted in real time, and pages can be pushed to users as needed to help them find that which they're interested in. Several companies offer tools to manage these types of services. These **guides** don't have to be real people. Some can be computational processes of the system that form a kind of consultative interface. *Guides 3.0* from Inxight is an experimental interface using the personification of data markers and algorithms as characters. These characters are composites of data and have no real personality, yet they can embody a point of view more clearly for most users. However, characters are difficult to create well and shouldn't be implemented merely to make an interface "cool."

nathan shedroff **experience design**

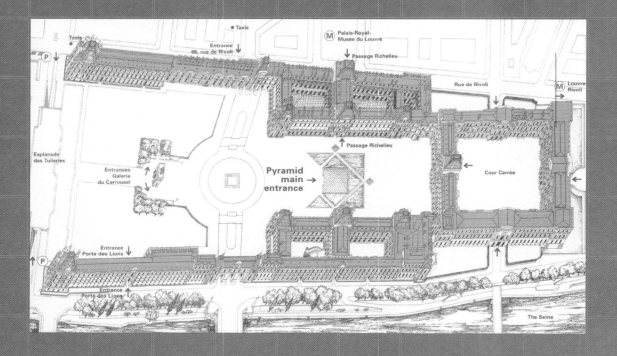

All signage systems are, essentially, about navigation and most are perfectly adequate—although too many are not. The Louvre's signage system is particularly successful, considering the complexity of the space it describes. The Louvre is a old building with irregularly shaped rooms and corridors. Most visitors find it daunting, if not for its overall shape then surely for its size.

The Louvre signage never abandons or abstracts the Louvre layout, rather it uses a grid system that overlays the actual building thereby regularizing the building without obscuring its detail. Then, each grid square can be referenced individually for location. Signage for each area quickly orients visitors to the three main wings of the museum. Highlights stand out in white against the gray background, the black building, and grid outlines.

This system isn't foolproof and I'm sure that people can still get lost or disoriented in the cavernous wings and rooms, but it does provide an outstanding way of orienting people in order to limit this problem.

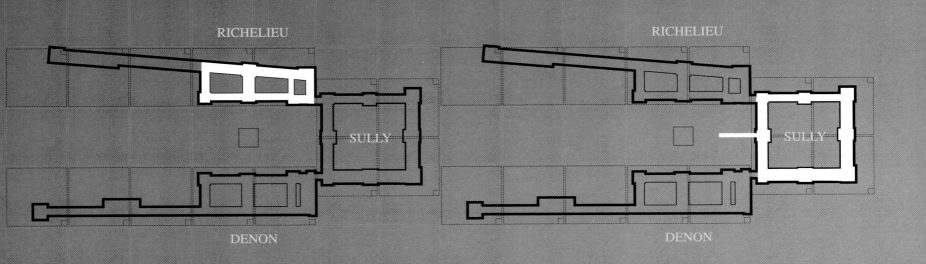

RICHELIEU

SULLY

DENON

RICHELIEU

SULLY

DENON

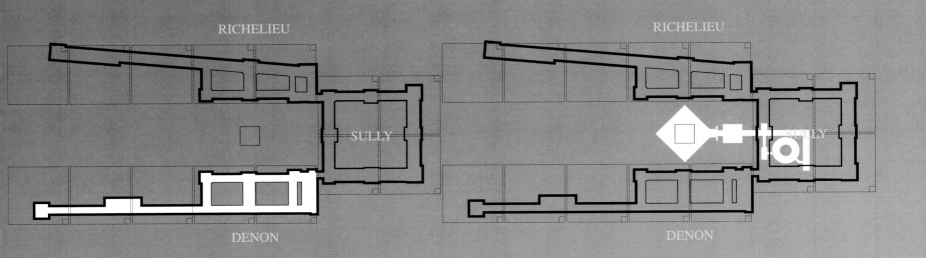

RICHELIEU

SULLY

DENON

RICHELIEU

SULLY

DENON

nathan shedroff **experience design**

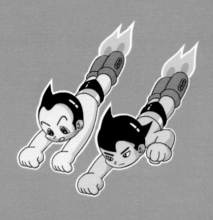

n 1997, Peter Spreenberg and Samuel Lising established FORK, communication design division of IDEO Product Development. In June 1998, they left IDEO to form MOVE Design. This site contains new portfolio work as well as projects completed while at FORK / IDEO.

Web site proposal for a technology consultant designed as a series of modular cards. Each card contains a small byte of information—clicking on a card links t page of more cards (and so on). View the Eobe Web Site.

whoismove?

INFO ← → PORTFOLIO

01 02 03 04 05 06 07 08 09 10 11 12 13 14 15 16

There are several examples of innovative navigation but none more seductive than movedesign's site. When a cursor rolls over the navigation bar at the bottom of the screen, the choices slide in that direction, visually reinforced by a counter-directional moving bar that makes the movement of the main bar more apparent.

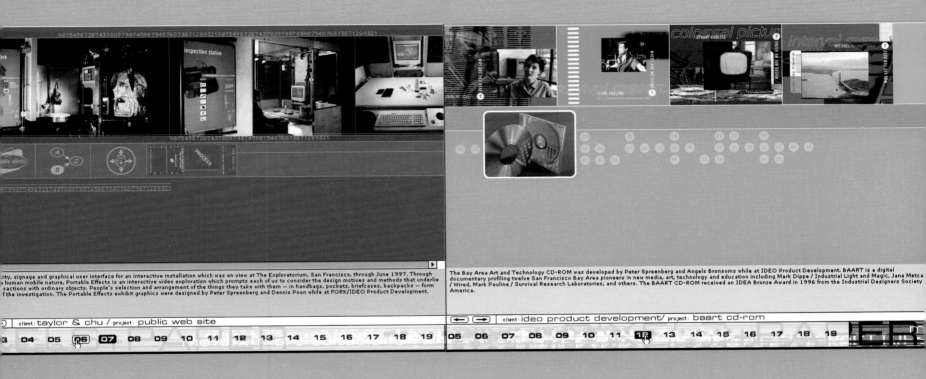

...city, signage and graphical user interface for an interactive installation which was on view at The Exploratorium, San Francisco, through June 1997. Through ...human mobile nature, Portable Effects is an interactive video exploration which prompts each of us to consider the design motives and methods that underlie ...sactions with ordinary objects. People's selection and arrangement of the things they take with them — in handbags, pockets, briefcases, backpacks — form ...f the investigation. The Portable Effects exhibit graphics were designed by Peter Spreenberg and Dennis Poon while at FORK/IDEO Product Development.

The Bay Area Art and Technology CD-ROM was developed by Peter Spreenberg and Angels Bronsoms while at IDEO Product Development. BAART is a digital documentary profiling twelve San Francisco Bay Area pioneers in new media, art, technology and education including Mark Dippe / Industrial Light and Magic, Jane Metca / Wired, Mark Pauline / Survival Research Laboratories, and others. The BAART CD-ROM received an IDEA Bronze Award in 1996 from the Industrial Designers Society America.

client: taylor & chu / project: public web site

client: ideo product development/ project: baart cd-rom

03 04 05 06 07 08 09 10 11 12 13 14 15 16 17 18 19

05 06 07 08 09 10 11 12 13 14 15 16 17 18 19

This immediate feedback helps make the navigation more easily understood and feel reactive. The movement also makes the navigation seem fluid.

nathan shedroff **experience design**

Visualization of understanding is much more important than merely making it look "good." The visualization is integral to the communication—as it *is* the organization made visible. Often, data and organization (and thus understanding) gets concealed when the type of visualization doesn't match the organization or the goals of the communication; or the visualization so highly distorts it that it is difficult to see.

Lists and diagrams come in a variety of types and forms and each has its best use. Timelines, maps, and charts (pie, bar, fever, and other types) are all types of diagrams that can illuminate—or obscure—meaning. Pie charts, for example, only work well when the number of data categories are few (no more than 10), and are varied in size (percentage); otherwise, bar charts are useful precisely when pie charts aren't. A good understanding of diagrams starts with exposure to the variety, as well as the realization that while almost any data can be presented in any style of diagram, like organizations, the results will vary in effectiveness.

Charts and maps are particularly useful for layering multiple data sets on top of each other to show relationships between the sets; in order to be effective, though, the scales and coordinates must be consistent and relative. This is

experience design nathan shedroff

especially true of three-dimensional (3D) diagrams as any problems of scale get more distorted (and inaccurate) with each dimension added. Generally, 3D diagrams and visualizations are used gratuitously and without an understanding or concern for the actual meaning of the data. Very few 3D charts actually illuminate data, but are used instead to fancify and "dress it up." This is *always* an inappropriate use of a technique.

Good visualizations pay special attention to **scale** (relative or absolute), **orientation**, **view**, **projection** (especially in the case of maps), **detail**, **generalization**, and **layers**. Some effective diagrams can use not only representations of three dimensions to represent three aspects of the data, but use color-coding and/or symbols to introduce from one to six more dimensions into the chart. The more dimensions, the more potential for clutter, but with careful consideration, some diagrams can be remarkably clear while displaying 8D data sets.

nathan shedroff **experience design**

Visualizing the data from the stock market has always been a concern of market traders, most of whom still prefer fast text-based interfaces and displays. The market wall at NASDAQ's Times Square lobby in New York City is an example of a visualization of the top-trading companies and market indicators displayed across a large wall that lets people quickly assess market conditions based on patterns and colors.

While this isn't a presentation that traders could probably use to watch specific stocks (as there's still a lot of noise), it's a successful overview for those who want overall impressions and market context. The color-coding of the companies is especially helpful as it allows for these quick impressions of overall conditions. Red is used to show declines, and the amount of red corresponds to the amount of decline. Likewise, green is used to show advances, and blue is the neutral color which is used to compare the ups and downs.

experience design nathan shedroff

National Association of Security Dealers, Inc.
4 Times Square, New York City, NY 10036
www.nasdaq.com

date opened: December 1999

nathan shedroff experience design

One of the most remarkable visualizations created in the last decade is the Map of the Market, a real-time map of the US stock market viewed as a graphical, colorful diagram where every part of the visualization has meaning and communicates information. What makes this most important isn't that it's new or even that it's innovative, but that it's *usable*. In fact, it's an incredible way to view a complex data set that is organized around the salient points of an investor's concerns.

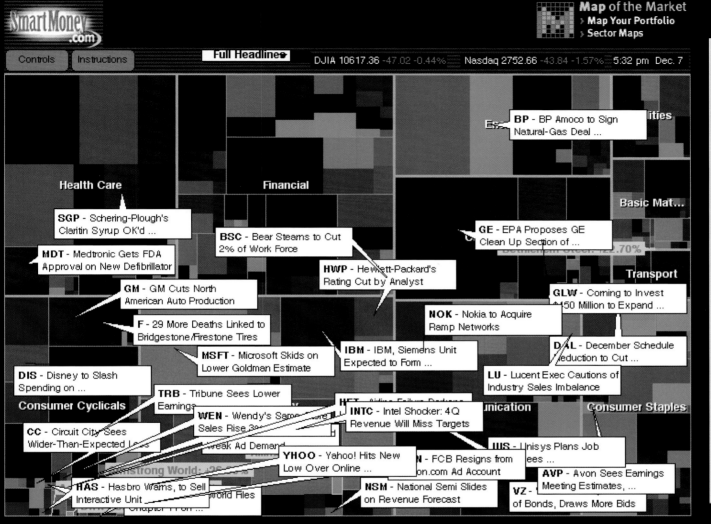

The map itself shows the entire market volume as a square, which is marked off into industries and companies by volume. The most important companies in a particular industry are grouped together and the size of their block is relative, in value, to their competitors. Each block is then color-coded based on its gain or loss at that moment. Lastly, company names and related headlines can appear when the cursor is placed on the blocks. There isn't much more to this map and that's important. (There doesn't need to be much more for it to be useful.) In fact, it is so stunningly clear, it's almost anticlimactic.

Consistency is often an end in itself. While it is always a good idea for elements of an experience—especially informational ones—to be consistent, sometimes it can actually get in the way. Because life experiences are often inconsistent, consistency can sometimes be confusing when it is incongruous with our experiences or expectations. Therefore, a good measure of when consistency works is to compare it with the expectations of the users for the intended behavior of the experience or system. Because consistency is a cognitive process, it is something that must work for us mentally, and the only way to check this is to test the experience with real users in situations as close to real as possible.

This is not a license to create inconsistent experiences—unless confusion or disorientation is the goal or challenge of the experience (as with some games). Like metaphors (see page 102), it's important to ease off on consistency only if it is actually interfering with users' assumptions, and a strict adherence to consistency shouldn't prevent designers from doing this.

Consistency is also important among related experiences. Branding is built successfully, for example, when different experiences, often in different media, feel consistent and connected. Again, what is important is the cognitive level of consistency—that is, that the experiences *feel* similar and related, even if the details are quite different. Because media differ greatly in their strengths, weaknesses, and how people perceive them, transmedia design must deliberately mutate in order to take advantage of these differences and to be successful in each. What is carried away from the different media types is the feeling of connection that comes when the overall experience and some elements are consistent overall. The mistake that many designers make is in trying to design once for all circumstances. While this is always an ideal goal, this is rarely possible and usually results in experiences that aren't quite successful in all media, though very much consistent overall.

experience design nathan shedroff

Tiffany Shlain, the founder of the Webby Awards, and her small but creative team make it a point to break the conventions of most awards ceremonies. For example, they limit acceptance speeches to five words (significantly enhancing the responses and shortening the ceremony itself). They also try to maintain a sense of humor and context throughout the awards, and the pace is fast with lots of unexpected turns.

The Webby team knows that the experience doesn't just begin when people walk into the auditorium. There is a series of celebrations the night of the awards (pre and post awards), and the exterior of the auditorium building itself becomes a canvas to be transformed. Last year's awards featured an elaborate altar inside (for nominees to presumably pray at), which included a hidden camera so that curious quests seeking a closer view of the altar were unaware that their faces were being broadcast 440 feet high inside the auditorium until they, too, were face-to-face with the broadcast.

The Webby also extends the experience before the ceremony in the form of elaborate, original invitations and announcements. At the awards, guests find a lunchbox with goodies inside, including an energy bar to help them make it through the ceremony.

Lastly, this multi-dimensional experience is extended onto the Web where the whole world can vote for its choice of best website in each category. Also the ceremony and parties are webcast simultaneously (in fact, one of the most appropriate examples of a webcasted event).

www.webbyawards.com

creator: Tiffany Shlain
date: held annually since 1996

nathan shedroff **experience design**

virgin atlantic

BOOK **NOW**
CLICK HERE

Book now!

This is Virgin Atlantic

Where and when

Frequent flyer

Our services

Join in

Virgin is known for creating a brand around its distinct values and personality. It's been adept at extending this brand throughout its many enterprises but none more effectively or consistently than its airline.

The heart of Virgin Atlantic's brand is to create opportunities for its customers to feel that they are special and to have a unique experience. Virgin recognizes that it has a special perspective on the world, and it makes every attempt to share this view.

freedom

Design is important to Virgin and the design of every element of its customer experience is carefully considered and purposely different. For example, the design of Virgin's airport lounges repeat the same stylish sense as the interior of its airplanes—especially in its Upper Class section. Likewise, the design of the tickets, website, and other points of contact with customers are all carefully considered and consistently aligned. Even the safety-instructions video on board the planes evokes the humor and the style that the company represents.

The Virgin Atlantic website attempts to make the standard tools and information special where it can, keeping it in step with the rest of the customer experience.

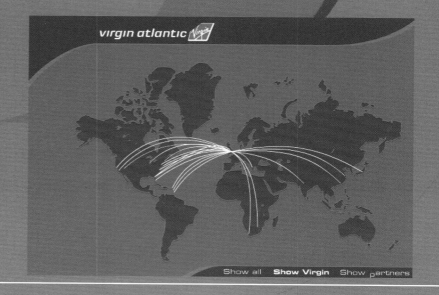

virgin atlantic

Show all   **Show Virgin**   Show partners

www.virgin-atlantic.com

experience design nathan shedroff

Route Network | Schedule | Our fleet | Airline alliances | Baggage allowance | Airport info

Search | Site map | Print

Our fleet

● ○ ●

New livery

▸ Click for 3D Model

If you see something glinting in the sky, chances are it's one of our fantastic new look silver aircraft - keep your eyes peeled: the proof is out there...

nathan shedroff **experience design**

Back to top

Metaphors are one way to build a *cognitive model* (see page 60), and they can be very powerful in orienting people to help them understand an experience; but they can be equally disastrous if they aren't applied well. Metaphors use references to already known experiences as clues to new ones. The "desktop" metaphor of most personal computer operating systems is an attempt to help people create and use files, store and arrange them, delete them, and work with them. It has mostly worked well, but only because the metaphor isn't totally consistent with the real experience—the operating system doesn't *really* work like a person's desk. Too close of an adherence to the theme either limits the functions of the system, or creates confusion when the two don't work together consistently.

In actuality, most metaphors used in this sense are actually similes. The difference is subtle but was astutely pointed out by Brenda Laurel in her book *Computers as Theater*. It's worth noting in the context of experience design because it is possible to design experiences that are true metaphors. New devices and unique, playful theater or product experiences can actually redirect interaction with one object into manipulations of another. Whereas before a computer interface might visually represent the directory file system on its hard drive *as if* it were a desktop, in reality the two were not the same. However, researchers and designers are experimenting with objects that can behave metaphorically. Your imagination can open you up to the possibilities. A theme park like Disney's *Epcot Center* is a metaphor for the whole world, as Disney's new *California Experience* theme park is for the State.

Metaphors are not required and can be crutches for poor ideas and design. Used well, however, they can be illuminating for users and quickly orient them to the functions and interactions of an experience.

Computers as Theater, Brenda Laurel, Addison-Wesley, 1991, isbn 081011313
disneyland.disney.go.com/disneylandresort/CaliforniaAdventure/
asp.disney.go.com/disneyworld/db/seetheworld/themeparks/facilities_epcot/index.asp?id=47

nathan shedroff **experience design**

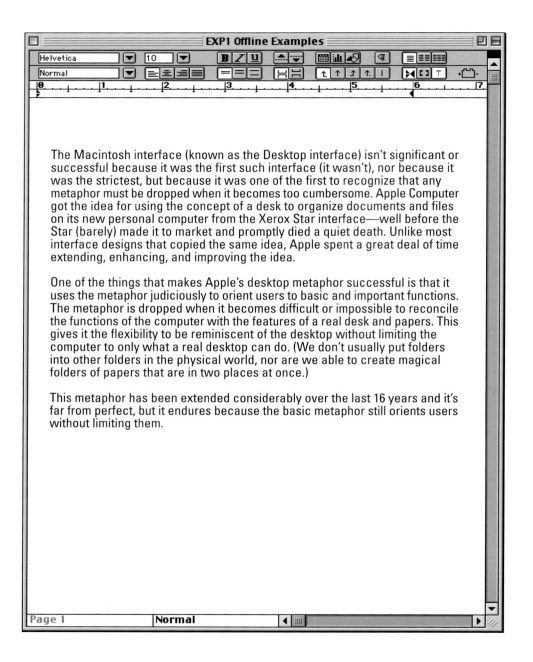

The Macintosh interface (known as the Desktop interface) isn't significant or successful because it was the first such interface (it wasn't), nor because it was the strictest, but because it was one of the first to recognize that any metaphor must be dropped when it becomes too cumbersome. Apple Computer got the idea for using the concept of a desk to organize documents and files on its new personal computer from the Xerox Star interface—well before the Star (barely) made it to market and promptly died a quiet death. Unlike most interface designs that copied the same idea, Apple spent a great deal of time extending, enhancing, and improving the idea.

One of the things that makes Apple's desktop metaphor successful is that it uses the metaphor judiciously to orient users to basic and important functions. The metaphor is dropped when it becomes difficult or impossible to reconcile the functions of the computer with the features of a real desk and papers. This gives it the flexibility to be reminiscent of the desktop without limiting the computer to only what a real desktop can do. (We don't usually put folders into other folders in the physical world, nor are we able to create magical folders of papers that are in two places at once.)

This metaphor has been extended considerably over the last 16 years and it's far from perfect, but it endures because the basic metaphor still orients users without limiting them.

experience design nathan shedroff

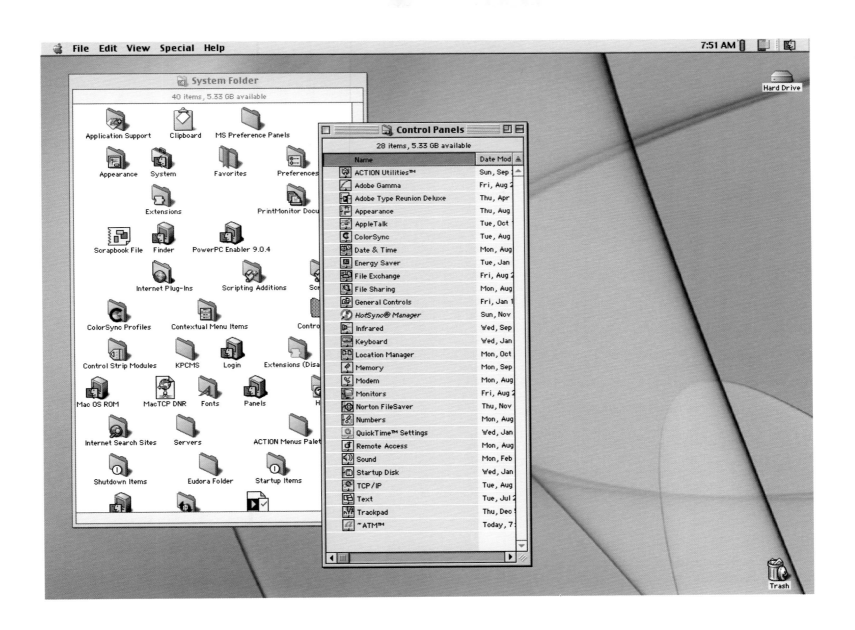

nathan shedroff **experience design**

Kvetch is more than merely a humorous place to complain. It's also a wonderful site to discover others' thoughts and emotions on the Web. Crucial to this site's function is the capability to enter your own kvetch and add it to the collection. The kvetches come up randomly so there's no way you can search for your own—nor can anyone else—and this, too, is deliberate.

Kvetch could have looked like anything, but designer Derek Powazek chose to model it as a retro-styled machine. His inspiration was old stereo equipment from the 1970s, and the site takes its cue from this theme. The site's navigation and functions also use this metaphor as their point of departure.

www.kvetch.com

designer: Derek Powazek
date: 1999

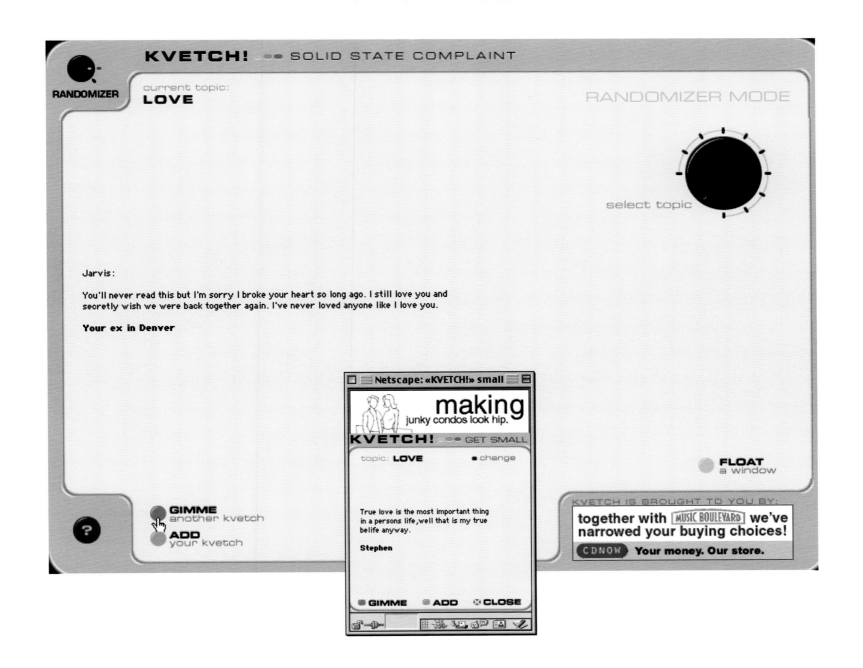

nathan shedroff **experience design**

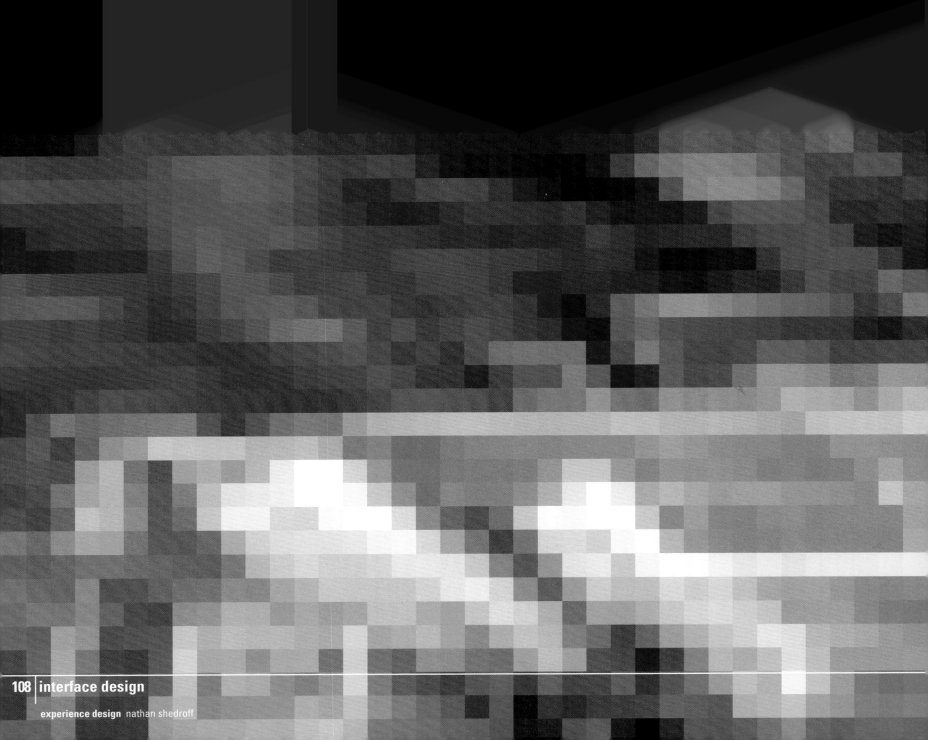

Interface design is only one of many terms used for the design of experiences. It's a term that originated in the 1970s specifically for software interface design. Over the years it has expanded a bit to include not only software applications, but kiosk and CD-ROM interfaces as well. To some extent, website interfaces have been embraced by the general interface community; however, interface designers have resisted the expansion of the term to include print-based interfaces and other non-digital experiences, even though most of the approaches serve experience design in a greater sense.

You can think of interface design as encompassing information design, interaction design, and some forms of sensorial design (mostly visual and auditory design, since most computers can only display sights and sounds). Typically interface designers have addressed the layout of screens, the design of screen elements like icons, and the flow among them.

There is a wealth of design knowledge and innovation within the interface design community, and most of it is not published on the Web. Many of the online industry's so-called innovations were already pioneered and developed within the interface community, and usually researched much better than the solutions created in the last few years.

Mostly, interface design is concerned with the effectiveness and usability of a software interface but this should also extend to the usefulness and purpose of the product too.

interface design

nathan shedroff **experience design**

Usability is one of the battle cries of the traditional interface designer, as well as for those designing websites—usability applies to all experiences on some level. Unfortunately, it has become somewhat hackneyed, though nonetheless important; and, in some cases, its proponents have misstated and misused the concerns, processes, and results of usability to such an extent that its reputation has been tarnished. For sure, the concern for a product or experience's ease of use often takes a back seat to the concerns of schedules, budgets, and even appearance. However, usability is sometimes also used to squash innovation or to enforce the status quo.

To be effective, usability principles should always be verified with **user testing**. This means that design solutions should be tested in a neutral manner with users as close to the target maket as possible, who have not been exposed to the design-process solution. Those conducting the user testing also need to be careful not to lead their users through the test (and therefore subtly help them), to interpret the results objectively, and to base the redesign on the results of the testing.

Usability is actually many factors. **Learnability** (the ease with which people can understand the experience/interface/product/service and begin using it), and **functionality** (how easy it is to use the experience once it is learned) are the two basic elements. These are often two very different and mutually exclusive phenomena. Designers may have to set their goals on one or another rather than expect to achieve both. The reason for this is that the cues necessary to help a novice easily learn what to do are usually exactly the things that get in the way of experienced participants in using the system quickly, easily, and efficiently. If possible, two different interfaces to the experience (one for each group) might be better than one.

One of the things that most impacts functionality is **memorability** (how easy is it to remember what to do and when to do it). Experiences that are memorable tend to be easier to repeat successfully—especially since people may *want* to repeat them more as a result. Memorability is directly affected by the cognitive model (see page 60) people build in their minds about the experience. Clearer, more natural cognitive models (or those standard with our expectations) are built more successfully and are easier to remember. These tend to reduce errors as well as raise confidence and satisfaction for the user. Easy **error recovery** is another consideration that, while not making the experience necessarily easier to learn or use, does increase satisfaction and decrease fear and frustration when errors do occur. Easily recovered errors are those that don't end the experience, or require it to restart from some prior point, or require previously finished work to be redone.

Usability (or a concern for "ease of use") is often the starting point of innovative design. When we approach preconceived solutions with fresh eyes—often those of our audience instead of our own—we open up the possibilities to create more satisfying experiences. Sometimes the roadblock to people being successful in an experience isn't that they don't understand how to use the experience but that they don't understand what to expect from it or why it might be valuable to them—concerns that designers almost never consider since they can't imagine their audience not understanding what they are trying to accomplish.

usability

nathan shedroff **experience design**

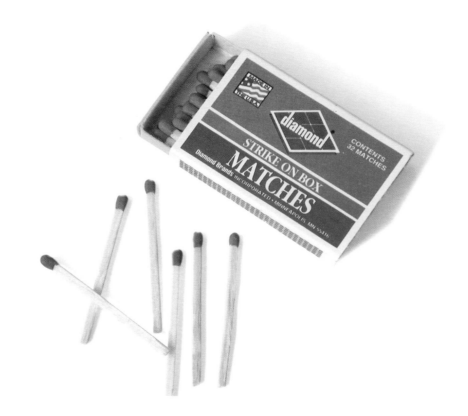

Matches are about as simple and as clear a device as you will find. Of course, they are only half the solution, requiring a suitable surface to strike them against. However, a match's operation has been reduced to a minimum of steps and a minimum of possible mistakes.

the kids AIDS site

Register & Give
Shop & Help
Be A Sponsor
More You Can Do
Donation Totals
Common Questions
About Us
About Pediatric AIDS
Home

1,800 children worldwide are infected with HIV each day.

♦ = 15 kids

DONATE FREE CARE
→ Click Here ←

Donate Free Care

the breast cancer site

Register & Give
Shop & Help
Be A Sponsor
More You Can Do
Donation Totals
Common Questions
About Us
About Breast Cancer
Home

43,300 mothers, sisters and friends will die from breast cancer this year.

Early detection saves lives.

DONATE FREE
MAMMOGRAMS
→ Click Here ←

Donate Free Mammograms

the rainforest site

Register & Give
Shop & Help
Be A Sponsor
More You Can Do
Donation Totals
Common Questions
About Us
About Rainforests
Home

Almost two acres of tropical rainforest disappear every second.

2005

DONATE LAND - FREE
→ Click Here ←

Donate Land - Free

One of the most frustrating things in our lives is dealing with the difficulty in reconciling our desire to help and improve things with the practicality of accomplishing something for a greater good. We aren't always sure if something will really improve a situation, if the money will be well spent, if the organization is credible, or if the people in need will really benefit.

The Hunger Site makes this effortlessly easy—so easy, in fact, it's a no-brainer. All you do is simply click a button, and a meal (or one of many other benefits like free mammograms or purchasing an acre in a rain forest) is sent to someone who needs it. Each click is small, but when combined, they can have a tremendous effect.

This only works because the site creators, owners, and sponsors have done all of the work, including establishing their credibility. The site's usefulness and its usability have made it as simple and as clear as possible to help one another.

Hunger Site | Rainforest Site | Kids AIDS Site | Child Survival Site | Breast Cancer Site | Landmine Site

the hunger site

Register & Give
Shop & Help
Be A Sponsor
More You Can Do
Donation Totals
Common Questions
About Us
About Hunger
Home

TRUST·e

Every 3.6 seconds someone dies of hunger.
75% are children.

When a country darkens on this map it represents a death from hunger.

December 07, 2000
21:59:28 GMT-0800

DONATE FREE FOOD
→ Click Here ←

Donate Free Food

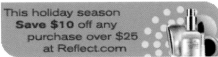

Thanks to CoolSavings for making The Hunger Site possible.

Create Custom Beauty Products at Reflect.com.

Home | Privacy | Contact Info | Translations

© 2000 The Hunger Site. All rights reserved. Patent Pending. Operated by GreaterGood.com

Users interact with experiences in different ways, and this interaction can be a source of information for customizing the experience so that it responds differently for each user. **Experiences should, ultimately, change and modify themselves to be more appropriate for users.**

It's conceivable, though undoubtedly difficult, for an experience to know a lot about its audience. For example, with computer-based experiences, computers can tell a lot about users, such as whether someone is present, how fast they are moving through the experience, whether or not they are running several programs, and whether they are splitting their attention among several programs. With real-time experiences, people controlling the experience can usually see how many people are present, if they're engaged sufficiently, how they're interacting, and whether or not they're understanding the experience, and so

forth. Storytellers have been modifying their stories in real time for as long as stories have been told. It's the behavior of their audiences that allows them to adjust their stories to get the effects they're seeking.

There's no reason why an experience can't be designed to change based on how people react to it, whether the experience is digital, theatrical, or occurs in real space. Even small changes to only a few characteristics can make an experience feel more interactive (see *Adaptivity*, page184).

experience design nathan shedroff

The best restaurants (those with outstanding cuisine and outstanding service) try to adapt as much as possible to their customers' needs, desires, and cultures. For example, the staff at Emeril's Delmonico in New Orleans is known to adjust their behavior to the culture of the diners at any given table.

Perhaps an older traditional couple at one table might be celebrating their anniversary and, as a result, expect to be distracted as little as possible and treated with the utmost respect that their age and experience suggest. Another table might be filled with younger diners who have no need, in fact a dislike, for pretense or tradition and prefer a waiter that smiles, laughs, and intrudes in a friendly way, possibly offering suggestions, making jokes, or engaging in personal conversation. These tables might be served by the same person, who adjusts and adapts his or her behavior based on whatever cues he can read from his customers (such as dress, demeanor, body language, conversation, tone, and so forth).

experience design nathan shedroff

1300 St. Charles Ave, New Orleans, LA 70130 TEL 504 525 4937   creator: Emeril Lagasse
The Venetian, Las Vegas Blvd. S., Las Vegas, NV 89109 TEL 702 414 3737   opened in 1997
www.emerils.com/restaurants/delmonico

Not only does the chef willingly make substitutions on-the-spot to compensate for diners' food allergies, preferences, or customs (seeing it almost as a professional challenge), the restaurant even has been known to reconfigure a room during the course of a meal to position a group under the stunning chandelier in the Crystal Room when all of the other patrons have left. This commitment to adaptively building experiences creates moments of surprise and comfort and makes each diner feel special.

All experiences should strive to adapt themselves to the differences each customer or participant engenders.

Osmose is one of the most beautiful and successful experiments in virtual reality. Its beauty, however, can distract from some of the sophistication of the experience. At its heart, Osmose is a truly immersive environment: visually, aurally, and physically as well. The 3D stereoscopic goggles—typical of most sophisticated VR experiences—are augmented by 3D sound that reinforces the illusion of a spatial environment. However, one of the most unique features of this project is that users move by controlling their breathing, rising and falling with exhales and inhales as a SCUBA diver would do. This actually forces participants to move more slowly, adjust their expectations, and relax.

One of the interesting features of Osmose is that it responds to the different behaviors of the participant. In particular, there are objects and events within the system that only trigger when approached slowly, versus quickly.

experience design nathan shedroff

www.immersence.com/osmose.htm
principal designer: Char Davies

programmers and engineers: Georges Mauro, John Harrison, Rick Bidlack, and Dorota Blaszczak

nathan shedroff **experience design**

**People find meaning in experiences and things based on a wide variety of personal values.
That people find meaning in things is, perhaps, the only constant that can be relied upon.**

To this end, it's important to design experiences so that audiences or participants *can* find meaning in them by making connections to their own lives and values— that is, if we want these experiences to have lasting impact.

Meaning is often built by objects and experiences that allow us to grow or experience intense emotions. Not every experience should, necessarily, have this as a goal but, often, the distinction of a successful or memorable experience is that it transforms us or makes us feel something. **Artifacts** of an experience (physical objects from the experience that serve as reminders of what we experienced, such as photographs and souvenirs) become valuable to us because they serve to remind us and help us relive those experiences.

Certainly, art does this and often with varying results. While older forms of art often relied on technical capabilities (e.g., photography) to stimulate our interest by reproducing nature, modern art (e.g., videography) must stimulate our thoughts with ideas in order to leave a lasting impression. These experiences have their most success when they have the most meaning for us. I'm sure you've seen art that you couldn't understand or didn't find accessible. These artworks fail for us because they haven't created meaning. It is the bane of an artist or designer to try to touch all people on a personal level since everyone's context is so varied and intimate. However, it is the best artists and designers that, at least, attempt to communicate with their audiences on this level.

meaning

nathan shedroff **experience design**

People have always used many different ways to search for and establish meaning in their lives. Tarot cards just tend to be one of the more interesting and beautiful. Whether or not you believe in their abilities to foretell the future, the fact that they have endured for so long attests to our need to find meaning in our lives, to make meaning out of the experiences we have, and to use symbols to express the abstractions we find difficult to describe otherwise.

experience design nathan shedroff

Thoth Tarot Card Deck
U.S. Games Systems, Inc.
isbn: 0913866156

designer: Aleistar Crowley
illustrator: Lady Frieda Harris
date: November 1988

One of the best uses of the Internet is to connect people across distances and cultures in support of common values or needs. USENET, the oldest collection of discussion groups online, has hundreds of forums dedicated to sharing stories, problems, and triumphs in the face of adverse conditions and illnesses. In particular, alt.support.alzhiemers is a group of caregivers to friends and family of people with Alzhiemer's disease. What they talk about is what you would expect: problems and solutions, news about the disease and its treatment, advice, and stories. While most of these people have never met and have little free time, they have still formed an important connection in each other's lives and helping each other in an important and direct way.

It has been a long time and I have not been keeping up with the news group. Seems my time is so limited. In any event my mom has been in a govt care home for almost a year and is in the "middle stages?" of AD.
My question: Has anyone had troubles getting their loved ones settled in to the home. It seems that Mom is always totally agitated and even with changes of Meds this agitation remains the same. It bothers me because when I look around in the home so many of the residence seem quite content. Mom never really seems content. She is given Adavan (sic) when she gets agitated and that just seems to put her out (was the drug to calm her and any more trouble). She is on ...

I haven't posted much lately so I just thought I would say Happy Holidays to everyone and post a story about Rosie.

This past Thursday she got into my wife's handbag and found a child's Social Security card...(said the Lord told her to look in there)...I mean...good grief...we need it to get her medical treatment. Well...then she pitched a fit about people steal everything she gets and she was just going to move to a nursing home where she could get decent treatment. This rant lasted about two hours and then she went back to bed, later in the day she said she wasn't going to stay with us anymore else and that she might just go out in the road and stand in front of a truck (luckily she can't get the door open). Friday she was pretty quiet and wanted me and my wife to bathe her...then some family members visited her and brought her some presents...after that she was cheerful and happy like nothing ever happened. Today she had her bath an we all went to our Daughter's house for Christmas dinner and presents and Rosie had more fun than the grand-kids. I guess in some ways it's a blessing that she *doesn't* remember everything...Rosie's happy...and we're happy...maybe she'll be calm for a while now. I've got my fingers crossed.
*

Hi, all and Merry Christmas
Haven't posted in awhile because so much happened since Mom's hip surgery. We did bring her home a couple of days before Thanksgiving and at first all was okay. I stayed home that week and my husband the second week. The week I went back to work Mom's mood really changed, became quite nasty. Sometimes she would remember to use walker other times we'd catch her without it. We had put up hospital rails to deter her from getting up and not using walker, however, she found ways get out (unreal)!!! Then after she'd been home for 8 days she got really really abusive and for the first combative with me. I turned to my husband told him I could no er do this and we weren't doing her any favors by keeping her with us, we couldn't keep her safe.

experience design nathan shedroff

bringing my mom home for Christmas day. I'm a little nervous about
she is unstable in her walking and it will be a crowded house with
ly my wife's family.

her home a couple weeks ago, but luckily the home health aid I hired
her stuff. When I was trying to get mom out of the car, mom wouldn't
but the aid coaxed her into walking. I think I might have to look into a
soon.

her thing that scares me is my wife is 43, and seems to be showing
ptoms of Alzheimer's. She doesn't think so. latest events, lost her
hone, $250 to replace, lost her keys and got her car hit in the street
use she parked it where it didn't belong, but couldn't move it without
eys even though we had a spare set in the house, I came home from
ol the other night, and found her car do open-says she had to bring in
sometimes leaves the car windows open in the rain, spills sodas in
ar and doesn't clean up the mess, leaves portable phone 'off hook',
ts to wash her hands sometimes before cooking dinner, lost her check
put a stop payment on a series of checks, found the check book, then
to write checks that had the stop payment on them-the one that got
ht was one to of my mom's home health aids, obesity getting worse and

had a doctor's appt, so I called the doc in advance to explain what I
observed, but she canceled the appt...she says she made a new appt. for
month.

this be Alz or just holiday depression. We are getting hit with some
or my mom's private pay, and I have asked my wife to increase her
ime hours at work, but that falls on deaf ears. I can't even get her
e coupons.

I want to tell you my grandfather's story,

I don't even want it like he could.

My pop (grandfather) is my hero. He was born in the '21ts

He had been my "father figure" for most my life. He has seen the most abominable and horrible things ever done to a group of human beings (Nagasaki '45) unclose, and in person.

Hi everyone. I'm new this group.

My mum was diagnosed with AD about 2 years ago when she was 53. She's still fairly good although she's definitely deteriorating slowly but steadily.

What's worrying me are all the headaches she's getting. She's never been the sort of person to complain but I reckon she gets headaches about 3-4 days a week. Worse still, she gets occasional darting pains in her head which cause her to visibly wince. I mentioned it to the doctor and he

Alzheimer's Vaccine Effective in Animal Model

WESTPORT, CT (Reuters Health) Dec 20 - In murine m
disease, amyloid-beta peptide immunization reduces be
plaques and prevents memory loss, according to two re
December 21st issue of Nature.

In one study, Dr. Peter St. George-Hyslop, from the Uni
and colleagues evaluated the impact of immunization w
of amyloid plaque formation and behavior in th
Alzheimer's disease

Using a water maze test, the researchers found that im
si...ntly reduced the cognitive impairment of test mi
total brain levels of amyloid-beta. Deposition of cerebra
amyloid-beta was also reduced, they note.

These findings suggest that either an approximate '50%
dense-cored amyloid-beta plaques is sufficient to affect
vaccination may modulate the activity/abundance of a s
...ically toxic amyloid-beta species."

In another study, Dr. Dave Morgan, from the University
Tampa and colleagues assessed the cognitive protectiv
amyloid-beta immunization in transgenic mice engineer
deficits as amyloid accumulates.

At the onset, immunized and nonimmunized mice perfo
arm water-maze test of working memory. This finding in
no harmful effect related to immunization. Later, when
began showing cognitive impairment, immunized mice
cognitive function that was comparable to nontransgeni
report. A partial reduction in amyloid burden was also n
mice at the end of the study.

In a related editorial, Dr. Paul F. Chapman, from Cardiff
UK, notes that while these studies support previous find
id deposition, "they go further, to show that immunizatio
the [?] 'spatial' learning deficits
accompany plaque formation."

While... Chapman is optimistic about the findings, he
of behaviors tested was rather narrow, and the mecha
beta-amyloid vaccine is not yet fully understood."

nathan shedroff **experience design**

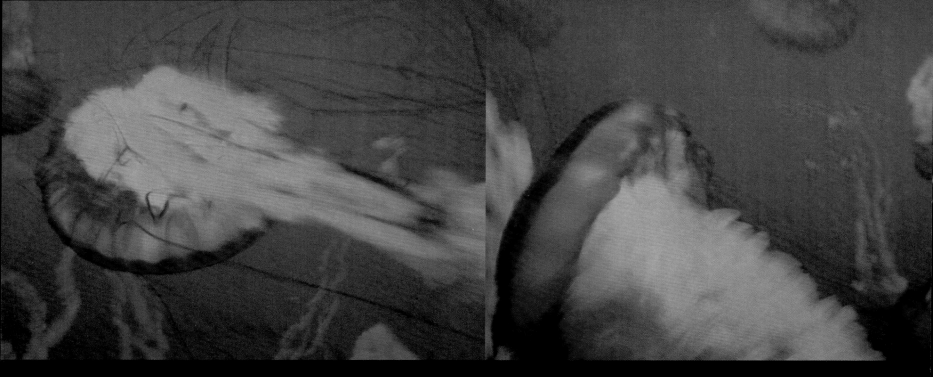

Like user behavior, experiences can be modified through an awareness of their users and their environments. In particular, experiences that modify themselves based on behavior seem more sophisticated. These changes might be environmental (temperature, humidity, ambient sounds, light, time of day, and so forth), technological (bandwidth, compatibility, or performance), as well as social (number of participants, types of relationships, subject matter, interaction with others, among other factors).

Awareness isn't necessary for experiences to be successful but it can be a vital component of sophisticated and more personal experiences.

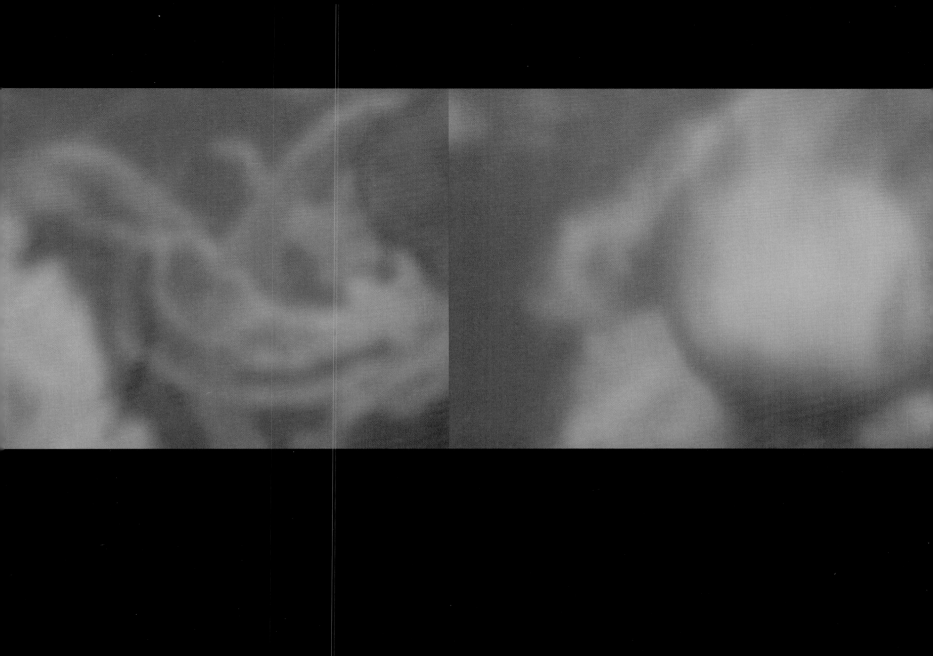

There are few consumer products that we revere simply because of their behavior. Mostly we value products because of their features, either the number of features or their specific capabilities. Most consumer products, though lively, don't ever feel alive or animate, which is mostly due to the lack of awareness they have of their environments and the people around them. Even computers, which are endlessly flexible, capable, and configurable, haven't been programmed to be aware of their surroundings or of the people who use them regularly.

Some exceptions to this condition are some simple home media products from Bang & Olufsen, a company renowned for its stunningly beautiful products as well as their relatively clear and easy operation—and now, their responsiveness to their owners.

One example is a B&O stereo that opens itself when a hand is poised in front of it (reacting to the presence of someone with the intent to play a tape or CD). Another is a television that turns itself toward the direction from which the remote control signal is coming, in order to position the screen toward the

viewer no matter where he or she is sitting in a room. Another is a volume control that continuously monitors the ambient sound in a room and adjusts the volume of the stereo or television to remain consistently audible.

Any object can be built to be aware of its surroundings and the behavior of its users, but few have been. Indeed, computers and other products (like our homes themselves) know a great deal about us, but have made little or no use of this information so far.

Although it is extremely simply, the goodwill generated (as well as orientation and personal feedback) by the simple "Hello, ..." message at the top of Amazon's site is one of the key reasons the experience of shopping at this online retailer is so satisfying to its customers. These messages are nothing new. However, Amazon was one of the first to make use of them (combined with its other customer service features such as 1-Click® ordering, suggestions based on past purchases, and reader reviews), and nowhere are these features put to better use than on this site.

These features have a direct correspondence to the physical world of shopping. Decades ago, when customers tended to shop repeatedly at the same local stores, store owners recognized these customers and treated them more like trusted friends. A welcome when they entered, and a recognition that they had visited before was only "common courtesy," and went a long way in establishing and maintaining a relationship.

While Amazon's offerings have ballooned, they have managed to present a plethora of choices (not just of products, but also of features) in a reasonably clear and accessible way.

www.amazon.com

Interaction design is a discipline that specifically focuses on the interactivity between an experience and its audience. It's not that interaction designers ignore information design, visual design, or other principles, it is that they specifically focus on experiences with complex interactions that tax users. Interaction design is relatively new and undocumented but growing as more interaction designers tackle and document their success and failures.

Overall experiences are usually more all encompassing than we first recognized. For example, consider the experience of shopping. To understand it from the perspective technologists usually take, shopping is merely the act of comparing product specifications until we're ready to make a purchase. But shopping as we know it in the real world is a complex, much more rewarding experience. In fact, the act of shopping usually begins before we even realize it—often before we perceive the need for something—and doesn't end until we finally discard and/or replace the product. Interaction designers are concerned with this distinction and are interested in exploring the complexity of real experiences in order to create new interactions that compare in richness and complexity, not merely in features.

experience design nathan shedroff

Technology is so seductive that those who work with it too often forget that the purpose of technology is to serve people's interests and needs. Ultimately,

what's important is not the technology but the people served by it.

Technological problems, in fact, are usually easy to solve (although economic viability is usually the limiting factor). Meeting people's needs, however, is much more difficult—whether solved with technology or not. In fact, technology has become so sufficiently sophisticated that the limiting factors are less and less technical, and are now more social, cultural, and often political.

Technology should not be ignored—whether the technology in question is high-tech and computer-related or more traditional. Indeed, technology both enables and limits the experience that can be implemented, often creating an aesthetic of its own, the way art media are influenced by their technologies (compare, for example, tempera, oil, and watercolor paints). Rather, technologies need to be understood and implemented *after* the overall experience is designed.

nathan shedroff **experience design**

This is one of the most technically advanced shows you'll ever see, but you won't see the technology. Like all of Cirque de Soliel's® works, the staging, timing, rigging, lighting, and music is a technological masterpiece—like a true work of theater; however, the audience is only aware of the performers, the story, and the spectacle. Even more than other performances from Cirque du Soliel (such as *Mystère*® featured on page 280), *O*™ breaks new ground since the entire performance happens in, above, under, and around water.

At times, it seems like the water itself is yet another character, changing colors with the moods of the sets and music. It transforms magically from solid to liquid so subtly that the audience is unclear as to what is solid and what is not.

O is only made possible through a specially designed theater that allows the directors to control all aspects of the climate—in the water, on and behind the stage, and throughout the audience. The water needs to be maintained at a temperature of 88° for the performers to feel comfortable, and their costumes need to shed water immediately in order to look dry again and to allow easy

Cirque du Soleil
http://www.cirquedusoleil.com/en/piste/o/
Bellagio Hotel, Las Vegas, NV

Duo Trapèze and Banquine acts from *O*
costumes: Dominique Lemieux

experience design nathan shedroff

movement. However, the audience is only going to be comfortable at a standard room temperature of 72° and it would be disastrous for condensation or other moisture to form in the theater. These needs led to the creation of a sophisticated environmental system with ducts under almost every seat, which can control the ambient environment so precisely that if the producers wanted to they could form rain clouds above the seats and move them around in the theater.

None of this, of course, is visible to the audience and this is why *O* seems so magical. Performers emerge out of the water seemingly from nowhere. Others retreat into the water and are not seen resurfacing. They are helped by scuba divers hidden at the bottom, who are exposed only for one moment as they flop about like fish out of water. Even this purposeful exposure of the technology and process is handled as a humorous metaphor, as well as a nod to the tip of the technological iceberg that is used to create such magic for people.

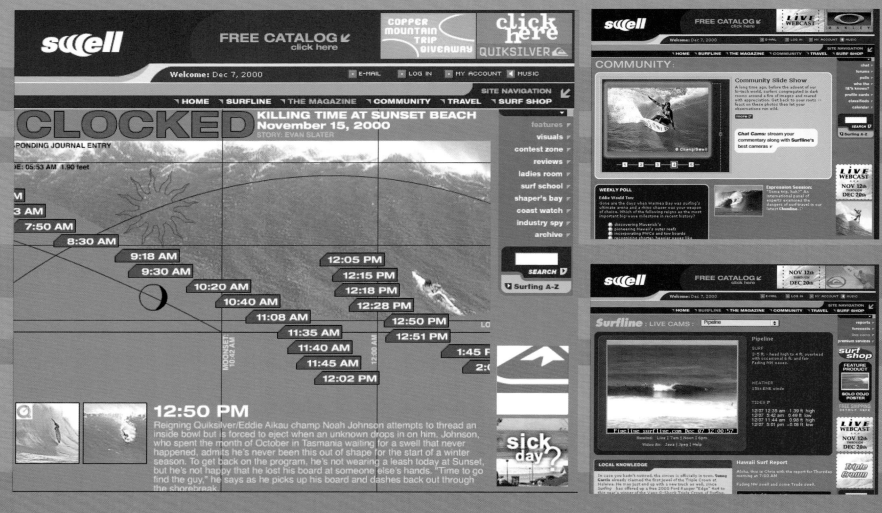

Swell has quickly become the dominant website for surfing—real surfing in water, not Web surfing. What's important to this community isn't the latest technology or the medium itself, but the information and tools that allow them to do what they love—surf. Surfing is a sport that is very much about personal achievement and not statistics or team performance (unlike professional football, for example). While some surfers are interested in surf competitions and "gnarly" photos or great waves and rides, most are focused on getting into the water and doing what they love.

The developers of the Swell site understand this. There are lots of tools that take advantage of various technologies (wave cams, faxed surf reports, community tools, etc.), but the technologies are never center-stage. In fact, the focus never shifts from surfing. The site never asks for plug-ins or diverts the attention to "cool, new" technologies because the site creators know that no one here cares about how they're viewing the site or what it took to build it, just that they've got the best and latest information to help them do what they like best.

principal designers: Claudy Niesen and Tom Rohrer,
vivid studios/Modem Media
date launched: October 2000

**swell**

Welcome: Dec 7, 2000 ▪ E-MAIL ▪ LOG IN ▪ MY ACCOUNT ◀ MUSIC

SITE NAVIGATION ↙

↘ SURFLINE ↘ THE MAGAZINE ↘ COMMUNITY ↘ TRAVEL ↘ SURF SHOP

▪ Peter Mel, Maverick's. November 24, 2000. Photo: Doug Acton/Swell

surf shop

FEATURE PRODUCT
REEF 2001 CALENDAR

2001 calendar
KEEP TRACK of all those HOT DATES
◆ REEF

TAN AND SULTRY FOR 2001

BROWSE NEW ITEMS
• VIDEOS & POSTERS
• SWEATSHIRTS & FLEECE
• WINTER WETSUITS

WEEKLY TOP SELLERS
• YEAR OF THE DRAG-IN
• OAM BOARD BAGS
• KALIS SHOE FROM DC
• BILLABONG ABSOLUTE

FLAT RATE SHIPPING ON ALMOST ANY ORDER!*
★ $5.50 ★

Free World Wide Waves **VIDEO** WITH ANY PURCHASE*

NEW ON SWELL•SURFLINE

▪ **LIVE WEBCAST OF THE VANS G-SHOCK TRIPLE CROWN**
Real Time on the North Shore: the only Hawaii coverage with no waiting period

▪ Dec. 7 **LAST MAN STANDING**
Sunny Garcia outlasts Sunset and a host of challengers at the Rip Curl Cup

▪ Dec. 7 **TIME FOR A LICKING**
Aussies team up to wrestle tour dominance back from America

▪ Dec. 6 **CLOCKED**
Dawn till dusk on a 10-foot day at Sunset Beach

BIG WAVE AWARDS
i XXL: BIGGEST WAVE WINS

▪ CHECK OUT THE LATEST ENTRIES
▪ WHO ARE THE TOP CONTENDERS?
▪ CHECK OUT THE TOP 5 SPOTS
▪ BIG WAVE STUFF

LAUNCH PARTNERS:

QUIKSILVER

SEARCH ▷

Interactivity is nothing new.

People have been interacting for as long as they've existed. What *is* new is that we consider it possible for computers to be interactive—that is, people can truly interact with computers and related technologies, rather than just use them.

Interactivity is not so much a definable thing as it is a nebulous concept. It is a spectrum from passive to interactive; and, there's no distinct point along the continuum where an experience switches from passive to interactive. In fact, it's probably only possible to compare experiences as being more or less interactive, rather than interactive in and of themselves.

In an interactive medium, it would seem that interactivity would be important, but the issues over the past few years have revolved around almost everything *but* interaction: content, technology, bandwidth, connectivity, politics, security, and so on. Even those who claim to understand interaction usually produce merely dynamic media (such as animation) rather than interactive experiences.

<<<passive

Interactivity is *the* differentiable advantage of interactive media.

We have had multimedia for a long time (in print and television, for example), but what is different now is **interactivity**. Technologies are not inherently or automatically interactive. They must be made so through a careful development process that makes a place for the audience (users) to take part in the action. Products and experiences in these media that aren't truly interactive won't be successful because the medium isn't being used to its advantage. (For example, using the interactive media to broadcast content or recreate traditional passive media experiences like television.) Television will always be better at being television than the Web or any other interactive media.

The biggest problem with the term *interactive* is that it has been misused by too many companies and people, as the term has been generally accepted as meaning either animation (which is an old passive medium), or anything that appears on a computer or on the Web since these are "interactive media." Unfortunately, these definitions are not only incorrect but misguided in how narrowly they look at activities. Interactivity encompasses everything that we do, not just that which we do on or with computers. In fact, most interactive experiences in our lives have nothing to do with technology. Playing sports or other games, hobbies, and work are more interactive than computers have been able to address. Probably the most interactive experiences in your life will be great conversations.

What's important to understand is that **everyone already creates interaction** for themselves and others, we just don't think about it. However, we already know a great deal about interactivity from which we can draw experiences, processes, and techniques for creating computer-based interactivity.

Interactivity is also comprised of many other attributes. Some of these include feedback, control, creativity, adaptivity, productivity, communications, and so forth. Many of these attributes are also valuable experiences (certainly creativity and productivity); and, correspondingly, interactive experiences that contain these attributes are highly valued when designed well. Interactivity isn't necessarily better, but it usually does correspond with higher involvement by an audience.

On a philosophical level, **interaction** is a process of continual **action** and **reaction** between two parties (whether living or machine). It is debatable whether or not a computer is capable of actually initiating action rather than merely reacting through its programming. This controversy about action and initiation is one of the deepest issues for interactivity, and may represent one of the key differences between animals (including humans) and machines. As we continue to explore this issue, the answers we find may guide us in creating experiences that are more interactive and successful than what has been created to date.

experience design nathan shedroff

feedback

control

creativity

interactive >>>

productivity

communications

adaptivity

interaction: a cyclic process in which two actors
alternately listen, think, and speak. -Chris Crawford

Understanding Interactivity
www.erasmatazz.com/book.html

nathan shedroff **experience design**

The Actimates were the first stuffed animals (or plush toys) that interacted with children, both directly through physical contact as well as through the computer (when its CD-ROM is inserted). The result of these simple, yet prophetic features is that a magical character seems so responsive that it's hard for children not to regard it as alive—at least in some way.

The Barney Actimate satisfies many of the characteristics that make a device seem interactive. It is very responsive—especially to touch (like squeezing its hands or covering its eyes)—and it can be used to play games and sing both alone and in conjunction with the CD-ROM. What's truly remarkable about the Actimates is that they seem so much more aware of their surroundings than other toys. Via a wireless transmitter and receiver (radio frequency), it can tell which part of the CD-ROM game is active and sing along with kids perfectly in sync, as well as play along with the games as an independent player.

Surely, these toys will only grow more sophisticated, but this is one of the ground-breaking products that will have paved the way.

Microsoft Actimates
www.microsoft.com/Actimates/

experience design nathan shedroff

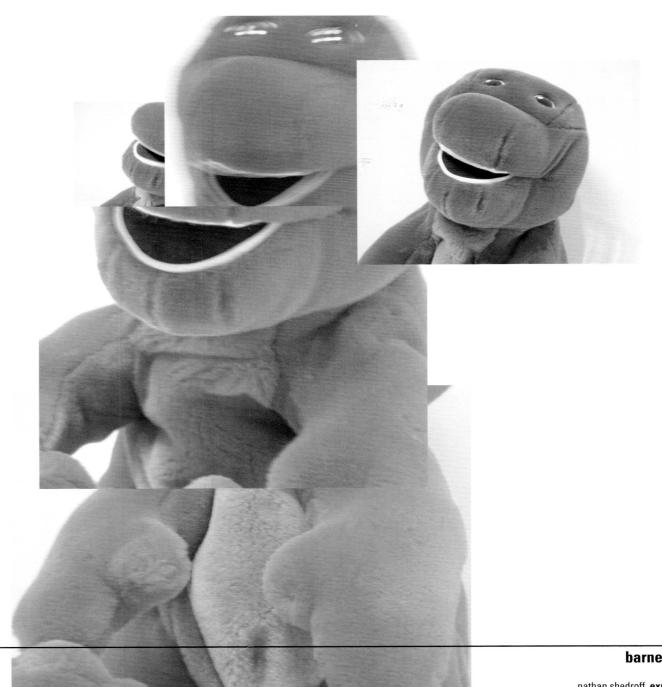

One of the most interesting aspects of the Internet is the explosion of webcams around the world. Cameras are increasingly pointed at people, at work, and at the home; they are even pointed at dogs, famous vistas or places, as well as objects such as vending and coffee machines. There are several services for chatting with others visually (basically, the realization of the video phone) and, of course, lots of live pornography online.

EarthCam is a site that attempts to link to every webcam pointed at a place or object. Just about every major city in the world has at least one camera pointed somewhere 24 hours a day, and this site will help you find it. There are probably as many reasons to use the site as there are cameras. Some people want to check the weather before they travel, others want to see a familiar sight from their home. Others use it as a form of virtual travel; if they can't be in Hawaii right now, at least the can get a quick reminder or view of the sunset.

Most aren't terribly interactive (since all you can do is view what's being filmed), but some actually allow viewers to control the camera, rotating it to see different perspectives. Nonetheless, their lack of interactivity doesn't make them unsatisfying experiences—particularly since the expectations for interactivity are already low.

www.earthcam.com

experience design nathan shedroff

09/11/00 02:34:59 PM

anhattan surfline.com Jan 31 12:22:4

15:49:50 23-JAN-2001   ALT.COM.BR

This is an archive pictu
Click to connect LIVE

www.centraldotempo.com.br 31.01.01 18:34:53

02:34:53 PM

Fri Jan 05 11:51:35 01

GOYA

NABANA

Jan. 31, 2001 at 10:40

reetings From Herrington Horbou

nathan shedroff experience design

Designers are often afraid of what their audiences or users may do with their designs. If possible, most designers would love to prevent audiences from changing (or "ruining," in their minds) their designs—whether they are designed products, experiences, books, or websites. Other designers welcome audience participation in order to understand how well the solution works, and whether it improves with use, like a good wine does with age.

Experience designers must regard their audiences as active participants—not passive viewers. Many real-space experiences (such as parties and other events versus art displays or theater) require participation in order to be successful. These are often the most satisfying experiences for us.

While *participant* is probably the best word to describe your audience for such interactions, any instance where *customer, user, actor,* or *consumer* is used, you should regard them in the same way.

Imagine a room filled with messages left by the people who've visited the room, which were wrapped and sealed into thousands of little bottles. Aside from the metaphor, the room itself was beautiful and mysterious.

The Museum Of... isn't so much a museum as it is an installation space. Each installation explores a different theme that allows the audience to explore aspects of themselves, their feelings, their ideals, and their experiences. The Museum Of Me opened in 1999 for four months, and challenged people to participate with the environment. The audience could leave behind either the artifacts of their own participation or keep them as a reminder of their experience. In these exhibits, the audience participates not only in the experience, but in the creation of the space. As more and more people interact, the artifacts grow and the evidence left behind changes the nature of the exhibit. This isn't, however, an exhibit of audience participation only. The concepts, environments,

challenges, and artifacts were all created by the museum staff. They were created in such a way that the audience could not only interact with, but also add to, the experience for others.

At the beginning of the exhibit, each participant is given an empty soup can and a partitioned sheet of paper for responses in different rooms of the exhibit. Each room prompts participants to think about their identities and what's important to them. Each response can be left in the room (such as tying a dream to a white balloon and letting it float to the ceiling after lying on a white bed thinking about your dreams), or saved in the can to be sealed at the end of the experience, and then included in a time capsule.

Most of the messages aren't visible to subsequent participants, but many are. This serves as a kind of one-way sharing between participants, and spurs further participation.

The Museum Of...
OXO Tower, London UK
www.museumof.org

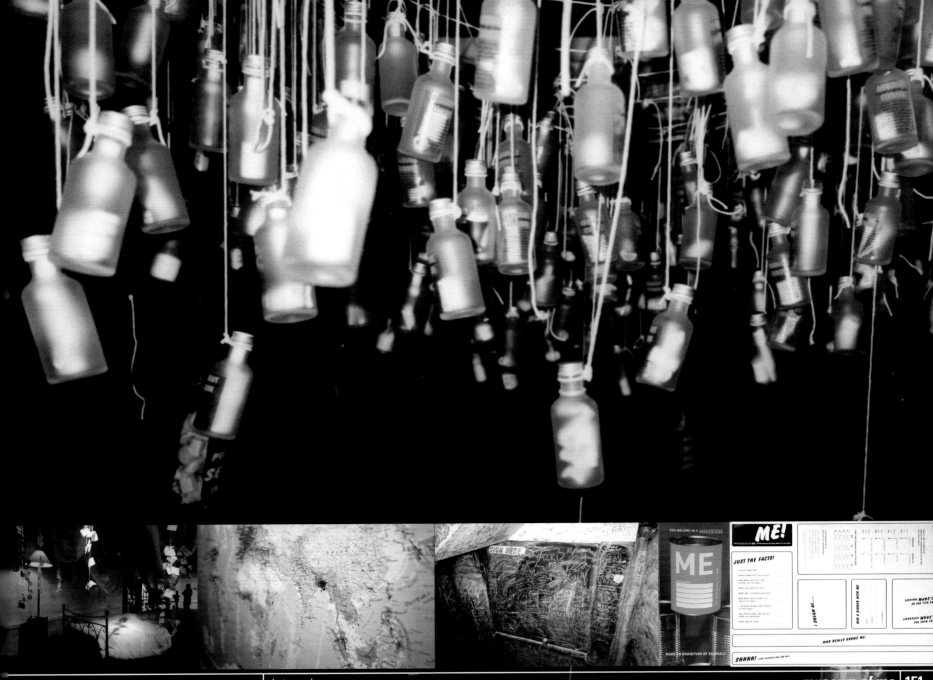

Multi-User Dungeons (known as "MUDs," or the newer name, Multi-User Domains) have been in operation on the Internet for at least 10 years. These are text-based stories that are written by the very people who play in the story space. Story may be an inappropriate word since the narrative isn't decided upon beforehand. Rather, these are a type of simulation space wherein participants create the story by interacting with each other. Think of this medium like the Holodeck™ in Star Trek™ (see page 286), only in text rather than fully immersive sights, sounds, and other senses.

MUDs are also known as MOOs (Multi-user domains Object-Oriented), MUSHs (Multi-User Shared Hallucinations), and a variety of other terms, but they are all similar in principle.

Because MUDs are simply text, many people are often unimpressed. Indeed, navigating a MUD can be confusing and sparse. What few realize is that they have the ability to create the action and construct the MUD's environment. Experienced users can create characters, rooms, houses, ships, or whatever other objects and environments may be appropriate. While MUDs can seem a bit spartan and lonely at first, when many people are in the space concurrently, they can be lively stories that reveal their origins in role-playing games like Dungeons & Dragons. Like those text-based games, MUDs can be infinitely evolving based on the ideas and participation of the very people in the MUD. Think of a MUD as a story that you write as a collective with others.

Most MUDs create a narrative around which the story develops. They might be based on a familiar theme (such as the Star Trek universe, or super heroes), or they might be entirely original. Few MUDs are neutral or have no narrative. Discovering and understanding these narratives (what's appropriate and what's not) is one of the confusing experiences within a MUD for novices.

Not everyone in a MUD is a person either. Some are populated with "bots" that interact automatically with participants, using algorithms that create and respond to conversation. The best bots can be difficult to distinguish from real people—at least at first—and many are designed to act as guardians or helpers in the MUD.

There are many MUDs out there; most must be accessed via TelNet software and not the Web. This can make these experiences even more confusing and difficult, though this may change with time as more MUDs migrate to the Web.

excerpts from the Ancient Anguish MUD
ancient.anguish.org:2222

```
                                                          <\
            _____>\        _
Welcome to...          <_____<  >ZZZZZZZ(_)
                                                          >/
                 /|              /|              </
             /~| N C I E N T /~| N G U I S H
         /\
   _       )(  _____           LPMud 3.2.1@141
  |_|NNNNN<()>_____>           (Native Mode)
         )(
         \/      A Realtime Multiuser Adventure Game

This world is Pueblo 1.0 enhanced.
Use Guest if you just want to look around.

            Welcome back to YOUR /\_ncient /\_nguish

  --== Archwizards: Adinos, Argeld, Arpeggio, Jerusulum, Malire, Paldin ==--
  --== Senators: Buxley, Bytre, Dale, Dawg, Drake, Florin, Greyson, Piper ==--

*** Ancient Anguish has added much new material to the game. Please
    read 'help newstuff' for details.
Orian the adept magician (nice).
Visitor the guest (neutral).
A stone statue of Epictetus.
A stone statue of Elfaeril.
A stone statue of Bertrande.
A stone statue of Guest.
Krom is looking at you!!! (Demonised).
A player usage graph hanging on the wall.
> Visitor turns into a stone statue.
> look
You stand in the common room of the Ancient Inn of Tantallon.  There are a
number of chairs and tables scattered around the room, and there are two
booths where people can go for private conversation.  There is a large desk
at the north end of the room, over which hangs an ornate clock.  A doorway
leads south into the world of Ancient Anguish and the adventure it has to
offer.
 Obvious directions are:
   north, south.
Orian the adept magician (nice).
A stone statue of Visitor.
A stone statue of Epictetus.
A stone statue of Elfaeril.
A stone statue of Bertrande.
A stone statue of Guest.
Krom is looking at you!!! (Demonised).
A player usage graph hanging on the wall.
> north
You are at a small room north of the inn's common room.  A large firepit is
the dominating feature here, casting warmth and powerful shadows across the
tables and chairs arranged around the room.  A large window to the northwest
displays the forest outside.
 The only obvious exit is south.
> BuDHa arrives.
> south
You stand in the common room of the Ancient Inn of Tantallon.  There are a
number of chairs and tables scattered around the room, and there are two
booths where people can go for private conversation.  There is a large desk
at the north end of the room, over which hangs an ornate clock.  A doorway
leads south into the world of Ancient Anguish and the adventure it has to
offer. Outside, a heavy fog obscures sight.
 Obvious directions are:
   north, south.
Orian the adept magician (nice).
A stone statue of Visitor.
A stone statue of Epictetus.
A stone statue of Elfaeril.
A stone statue of Bertrande.
A stone statue of Guest.
Krom is looking at you!!! (Demonised).
A player usage graph hanging on the wall.
```

An experience that tells us something about itself tends to feel more interactive than ones that don't. Whether the feedback is a simple explanation about why you are waiting, a reaction to some user action, or a detailed accounting of the system's performance, most people expect experiences to acknowledge their actions in some way. It's important to give just the right amount of feedback because too little may not be helpful or frustrating, and too much may be overbearing and distracting.

If your participants become confused about what's happening, they probably need some feedback to their actions—unless, of course, confusion is the goal of the experience.

Different experiences demand different rates of feedback. Games, for example (whether computer-based or not), require a great deal of feedback to keep the action moving. Relaxing experiences, on the other hand, require very little feedback in order to be successful. When designing experiences, it's always best to keep in mind real-world, physical experiences among people and use

experience design nathan shedroff

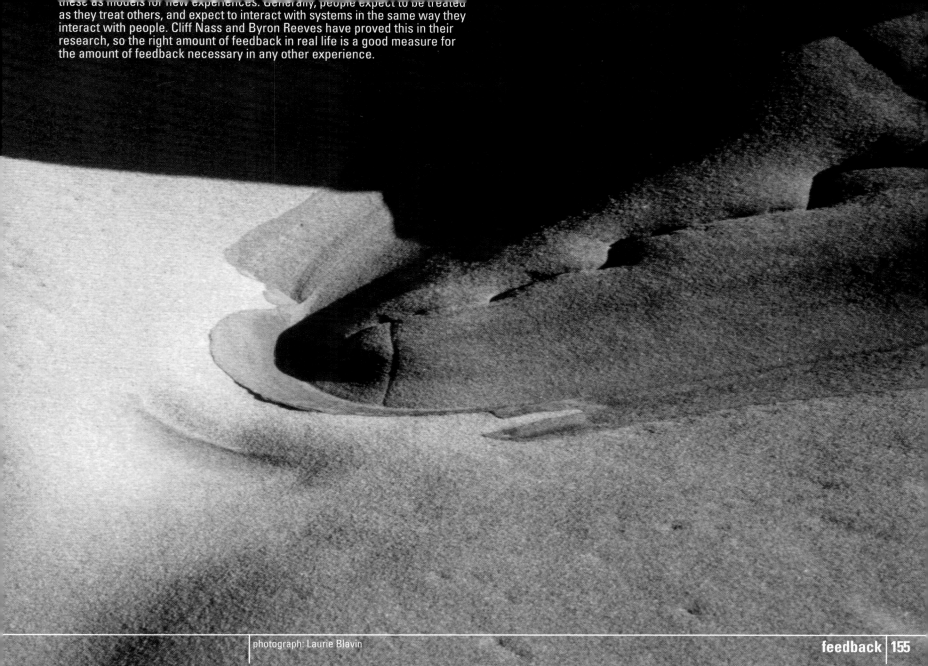

these as models for new experiences. Generally, people expect to be treated as they treat others, and expect to interact with systems in the same way they interact with people. Cliff Nass and Byron Reeves have proved this in their research, so the right amount of feedback in real life is a good measure for the amount of feedback necessary in any other experience.

photograph: Laurie Blavin

nathan shedroff **experience design**

The wooden mirror is a simple and astounding device. Its wooden chips are arranged in a matrix that covers an entire circle. Each wooden chip can rotate independently and is controlled by a computer. Through each angle of rotation, the chips reflect more or less light, turning the whole array of chips into a monochromatic, pixelated matrix.

Under computer control, the image in front of the array (that being the viewer as he or she approaches) is converted, and then played back onto these rather large pixels. The result is an eerie mirror that seems almost alive as it mimics the movements of the viewer, who also is providing the necessary stimulus for its actions. In addition, the sounds of the fast-turning wood chips add an extra and unexpected element to the experience, as it isn't a sound that we would otherwise associate with something digital or even electronic.

fargo.itp.tsoa.nyu.edu/~danny/mirror.html

creator: Danny Rozin
date: 1999

experience design nathan shedroff

This simple feedback machine confronts our expectations about physical media and creates an experience that makes us reconsider what materials other than computer displays can do in our environment.

Eliza is a computer program originally written by Joseph Weizenbaum in 1965. It is a simple program that reacts to the text written by the user by asking additional questions, in the style of a Rogerian psychologist. There are many instances of the program now online but its functionality remains, essentially, the same. Eliza turns statements back into questions following some simple grammatical rules. When stuck, it has a set of stock phrases to throw out in order to keep the conversation going.

Many people mistake this reactive questioning for intelligence, but there is no real intelligence to the program. In fact, it's fairly easy to trip up the program. (Try making nonsense sentences or changing the subject drastically.) However, when you stick to the rules of the game, Eliza can be fairly disarming and at the same time natural to use. In fact, to Mr. Weizenbaum's initial dismay, many people regard Eliza almost as a real person in whom they can confide.

Ultimately, Eliza is a pretty unfullfilling experience since it doesn't offer any resolution or advice. It's merely a way of talking through problems and eliciting our own thoughts.

experience design nathan shedroff

you can find a version of Eliza at:
www.manifestation.com/neurotoys/eliza.php3

creator: Joseph Weizenbaum
date: 1965

How do you do. Please state your problem.

>> I was just thinking about my lack of time and how I feel like I'm always falling behind.

In what way ?

>> Well, I never seem to have enough time to do all the things I want to.

What would it mean to you if you got to ?

>> Well, I would feel like I was getting more out of life and accomplishing more.

Were you really ?

>> Yes.

You seem to be quite positive.

>> Well, for the most part, yes, but I feel anxious about having so many responsibilities.

You are sure.

>> Of course.

I'm not sure I understand you fully.

>> What don't you understand?

Why do you ask ?

>> Because you just asked me!

Is that the real reason ?

>> Of course it is!

Please go on.

>> Because you just asked me!

>> Of course it is!

>> Well, you're not really helping much

>> ...you're not programmed to be very eff...

>> Because you aren't.

>> The fact that you're not offering any advic...

>> No, in fact it makes me mad.

>> ...saying no because you're starting

>> Well, I wasn't before I started to talk to yo...

>> Not in my fantasies at all. In reality.

>> ...h, forget it.

As with feedback, comparing the amount of control in real-world experiences gives us a good starting point for designing other kinds of experiences. People expect to have some degree of control over their experiences. This control usually makes them feel more comfortable and respected. It might be controlling the rate of interaction, the sequence of steps, the type of action or features, or even how much feedback they desire. The only way to know how much control is important is to question participants about their needs and desires, and then test the experiences to see how well they work.

nathan shedroff **experience design**

This virtual space is alive with animated characters that interact with the visitor as well as each other to create an interesting, immersive environment. This experience is based on a West African concept about our souls and how they interact with each other (including animals) and our environment. The system provides landscapes to explore, and characters whose behavior depends on how we interact with them. In this way, we can control a bit of the experience, changing it based on how we interact with the landscape and characters. For example, there are characters that only emerge at night, or only if they are approached slowly. Characters interact based on how they've been programmed to regard visitors, objects, actions, or other characters. These interactions occur via sound, gestures, and touch (the control for the experience includes a haptic, force-feedback joystick that allows visitors to feel vibrations that represent the energy of special places).

Creator Rebecca Allen envisions the experience as the exploration of the "soul" within us all—made visible through the system.

experience design nathan shedroff

emergence.design.ucla.edu
principal creator: Rebecca Allen
date: 1997

programmers and designers: Loren McQuade, Eitan Mendelowitz, John Ying, Daniel Shiplacoff, Damon Seeley, Karen Yoo, Vanessa Zuloaga, Jino Ok, Pete Conolly, Josh Nimoy, Mark Mothersbaugh-Mutato Muzika, Franz Keller, Jay Flood, and Maroun Harb

nathan shedroff experience design

The navigation panel for this movie promotional site is unusual not because it takes the form of a hanging shield, but because browsers can wrest its attributes quickly and easily.

The shield can be moved around the screen (only within the frame of the Flash movie, however) to reposition it. Also, the shield can be collapsed or expanded by clicking on the bar from which it hangs. Menus of options unfold from each of the shield's quadrants so all of the navigation for the site can be contained in a small space.

While this isn't a solution every site could use (the Flash technology itself can pose compatibility and performance problems for many visitors), it is an example of innovative thinking that can contribute to a better experience in the appropriate context.

www.spe.sony.com/movies/joanofarc/

developer: Gaumont Multimedia
www.gaumont.fr
date: 1999

experience design nathan shedroff

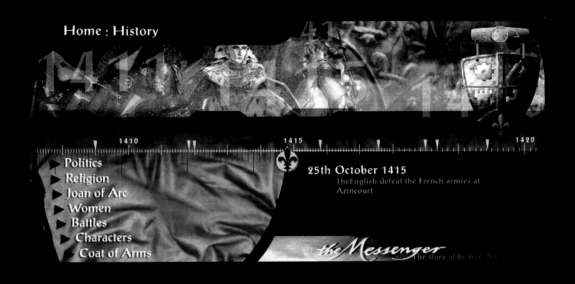

1410   1415   1420

- ► Politics
- ► Religion
- ► Joan of Arc
- ► Women
- ► Battles
- ► Characters
- ► Coat of Arms

25th October 1415
TheEnglish defeat the French armies at
Azincourt.

the Messenger
The story of Joan of Arc

Home : History : Joan's childhood

► Milla Jovovich

1.Joan's childhood : The call
2.Joan's battles
3. Joan's trial

**Joan's childhood
the call**

Joan of Arc was born in Domremy, in Champagne, in
north-eastern France, on January 6th, 1412.
 Domremy was part of the huge territory over which
the Duke of Burgundy ruled. He was an ally of the
English, but always remained loyal to the party of the
King of France.

Joan's parents were Christian peasants, and her
childhood was poor and pious: Joan certainly did not
partake in the local superstitious cults,but rather knelt
and prayed in the village church. In the Summer of
1424, Joan heard voices for the first time. According
to her, the "Archangel Michael" in person came down
and urged her to come to the aid of Charles, King of
France, whose sovereignty over the kingdom of

the Messenger
The story of Joan of Arc

One attribute that distinguishes us as humans is the ability to create things.
While not all of us think of ourselves as creative, we create things all the time.

Humans are inherently creative creatures and when we have a chance to create we feel more satisfied and valuable.

In fact, the products of our creation have a great deal of value to us, at least on a personal level.

Unfortunately, our culture tends to convince us that, mostly, we're not good enough to be creative—we can't sing well enough, we don't know how to paint or write well, our homemade gifts aren't nice enough, and our home-cooked food just doesn't compare. This is mostly true in terms of professional or commercial products. In reality, though, homemade gifts are often valued much more than manufactured ones. Likewise, home-cooked meals can usually beat all but the most expensive store-bought foods, and the products of your imagination have a great deal of value to those who know and love you.

Often, creativity is an end unto itself, whether anyone else ever sees, experiences, or appreciates the output. We feel proud of our own creations—even if we covet them in seclusion. Therefore, experiences which allow us to be creative give us feelings of satisfaction and accomplishment.

To counter our fears and reluctance at being creative, as well as our worries that we may not be good enough, many experiences offer advice to help us make decisions and to feel more confident. **Co-creative** (a term coined by consultant and designer Abbe Don) technologies are those that either offer assistance in the creation process or actually participate in the process by making some of the decisions and handling some of the details for the user. The anxiety that many people can experience when confronted with unfamiliar tools or techniques can be lessened by utilizing co-creative techniques such as recommendations, guidelines, advice, online help or actually performing operations for users.

Creativity is often thought of in terms of artistic expression and hobbies, while productivity is most commonly associated with work and value creation. In truth, there is no difference as each set of activities involves the creation of something. Those who identify primarily with the word *creativity* tend to abhor structure and look upon *work* as a limiting factor to their self-expression. Conversely, those more comfortable with the term *productivity* tend to regard it as an efficient and valuable endeavor and are suspicious of "creative types" who, in their eyes, waste time being abstract, unproductive, and frivolous. The truth is that both groups are involved in the same activity, whether they perceive it or not. Both find value in spending time creating something.

Abbe Don: www.abbedon.com

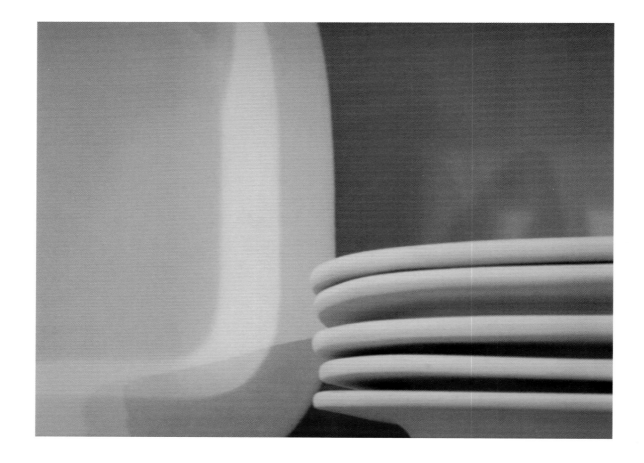

What makes the Terra Mia store so successful for its customers is that the process of creating personal ceramics is streamlined. Everything necessary for painting and decorating pre-made raw ceramics (from pots to plates to dog dishes) is ready for a customer to walk-in off the street and start. While there isn't a lot of variation in forms to use as a canvas (you can imagine the variety if your threw your own pots) there are certainly enough to satisfy most people, and almost anything that can be imagined in terms of painting on the surfaces is still possible.

What makes this a valuable experience is that more people can satisfy their creative urges, despite their lack of expertise, and can leave the shop having created an artifact of their handiwork. (The pieces are fired by the store and customers can pick them up when they're ready—usually in a few days.) These are exactly the kind of works that also make valuable gifts, not because of financial value, but the personal value that comes from items created by the giver for the recipient.

1314 Castro Street at 24th Street, San Francisco, CA 94114
TEL 415 642 9911
www.terramia.net

Owner Christine Simmons describes how customers who come in timid and unconfident, often leave with not only a newfound hobby, but with a new perspective on their own creative abilities. One customer was so inspired that she now paints pottery full-time.

There isn't anything new about online coloring books. Some of the first toys and visual experiments on the Web allowed people to draw or color. Haring Kids uses the drawings and style of deceased artist Keith Haring, known for his bold, graphic style and unique, quirky imagery. Elsewhere in the site, there's information about the site, the artist, and the Foundation's programs for kids.

Haring Kids allows kids (its target audience) to choose drawings, color, resize, and rotate them, as well as drag them around to form a new drawing. None of this is groundbreaking, but it is pretty easy for kids to do. There aren't a lot of options to choose from but, like all design, the challenge is making something wonderful within the boundaries established. It's actually possible to build complex images from these simple elements.

www.haringkids.com
Keith Haring Foundation

designers: Riverbed Multimedia (www.riverbed.com) in collaboration with Daniel Wiener

Productive experiences are so valuable that we spend more money on them—and the tools to perform them—than on almost any other experiences. For example, compare the prices of application software used to create things to the price of games and other entertainment programs (like CD-ROM titles).

If you can create opportunities for participants in an experience to make something, it's likely that the participants will both value the experience more and regard any artifacts that they create with fond memories. **Artifacts** aren't always necessary to productive or creative experiences, but they do serve to remind people of their experience and help them relive it. The artifacts themselves often have more than just emotional or mnemonic value.

experience design nathan shedroff

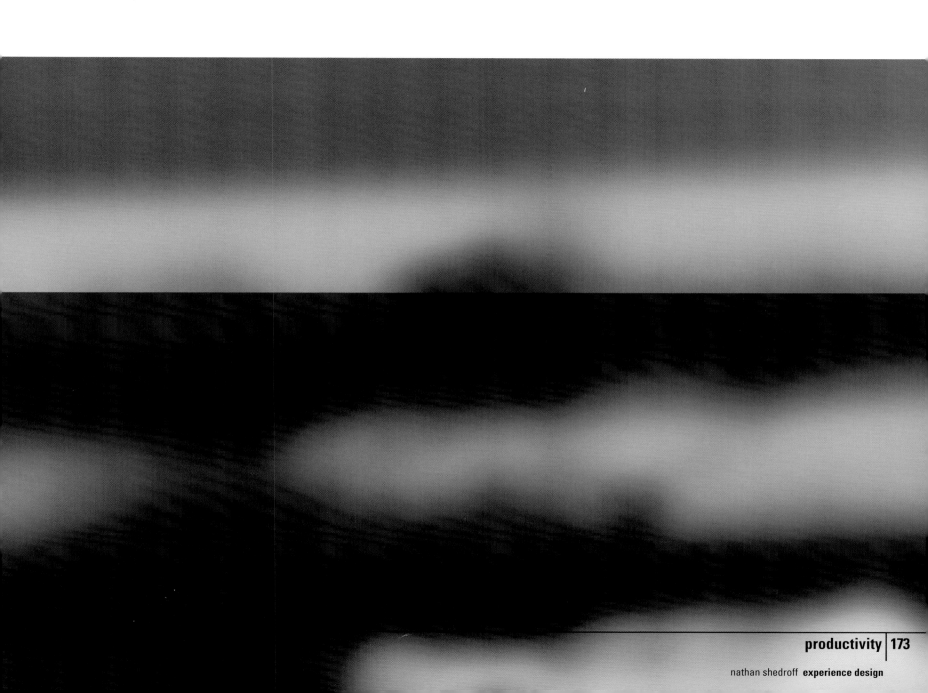

The (line 6) is less than $50,000.
end of 2000.

...ied state tuition program earnings, ...taxable scholarship or fellowship grants, unemployment or an education credit.

...your taxable interest was not over $400. **But** if you earned tips, including allocated tips, ...that are not included in box 5 and box 7 of your W-2, you may not be able to use Form or Alaska Permanent Fund dividends, 1040EZ. See page 13. If you are planning to use Form 1040EZ for a child who received Alaska Permanent Fund dividends, see page 14.

- You did not receive any advance earned income credit payments.

If you are not sure about your filing status, see page 11. If you have questions about dependents, use TeleTax topic 354 (see page 6). If you **cannot use this form,** use TeleTax topic 352 (see page 6).

Filling in your return

For tips on how to avoid common mistakes, see page 30.

Enter your (and your spouse 's if married) social security number on the front. Because this form is read by a machine, please print your numbers inside the boxes like this:

9 8 7 6 5 4 3 2 1 0

Do not type your numbers. Do not use dollar signs.

If you received a scholarship or fellowship grant or tax-exempt interest income, such as on municipal bonds, see the booklet before filling in the form. Also, see the booklet if you received a Form 1099-INT showing Federal income tax withheld or if Federal income tax was withheld from your unemployment compensation or Alaska Permanent Fund dividends.

Remember, you must report all wages, salaries, and tips even if you do not get a W-2 form from your employer. You must also report all your taxable interest, including interest from banks, savings and loans, credit unions, etc., even if you do not get a Form 1099-INT.

Worksheet for dependents who checked "Yes" on line 5

(keep a copy for your records)

Use this worksheet to figure the amount to enter on line 5 if someone can claim you (or your spouse if married) as a dependent, even if that person chooses not to do so. To find out if someone can claim you as a dependent, use TeleTax topic 354 (see page 6).

A. Amount, if any, from line 1 on front

B. Minimum standard deduction

C. Enter the **larger** of line A or line B here . . . . + 250.00 Enter total ▶ A. _____

D. Maximum standard deduction. If **single,** enter 4,400.00; if **married,** enter 7,350.00. . . . . B. _____

E. Enter the **smaller** of line C or line D here. This is your standard deduction . . . . . C. ___700.00___

F. Exemption amount.
☐ If single, enter 0.
☐ If married and—
— both you and your spouse can be claimed as dependents, ...
— only one of you can be claimed as a depen...

G. Add lines E and F. Enter the tota...

D. _____

E. _____

If you checked "No"...

While all forms (tax or otherwise) qualify as productivity tools, the 1040EZ deserves special note. Created by Siegel & Gale, it is a model of clarity. The firm, which among other things specializes in redesigning forms and legal documents so as to be easily understood, reduced the very complex and otherwise confusing process of filing taxes (even for complex processes like income averaging), into an exceedingly clear, one-page form that nearly anyone could use. Admittedly, its use is limited to the less complicated tax returns and the US Internal Revenue Service never implemented the design in its complete form (they reduced the features to further "simplify" it), it's still a model of clarified productivity.

experience design nathan shedroff

US Government Printing Office: 2000-460-502
United States Department of the Treasury–Internal Revenue Service
www.irs.gov

creator: prototype by Siegel & Gale

Department of the Treasury—Internal Revenue Service

Income Tax Return for Single and Joint Filers With No Dependents

0EZ

2000   OMB No. 1545-0675

Your first name and initial

Last name

Use the IRS label here

If a joint return, spouse's first name and initial

Last name

Home address (number and street). If you have a P.O. box, see page 12.

Apt. no.

City, town or post office, state, and ZIP code. If you have a foreign address, see page 12.

Your social security number

Spouse's social security number

Presidential Campaign (p.12)

Note. Checking "Yes" will not change your tax or reduce your refund.
Do you, or spouse if a joint return, want $3 to go to this fund?

You   Yes   No   Spouse   Yes   No

Income

Attach Form(s) W-2 here. Enclose, but do not attach, any payment.

1 Total wages, salaries, and tips. This should be shown in box 1 of your W-2 form(s). Attach your W-2 form(s).   **1**

2 Taxable interest. If the total is over $400, you cannot use Form 1040EZ.   **2**

3 Unemployment compensation, qualified state tuition program earnings, and Alaska Permanent Fund dividends (see page 14).   **3**

4 Add lines 1, 2, and 3. This is your **adjusted gross income**.   **4**

Note. You **must** check Yes or No.

5 Can your parents (or someone else) claim you on their return?
Yes. Enter amount from worksheet on back.
No. If **single**, enter 7,200.00. If **married**, enter 12,950.00. See back for explanation.   **5**

6 Subtract line 5 from line 4. If line 5 is larger than line 4, enter 0. This is your **taxable income**.   ▶ **6**

Payments and tax

7 Enter your Federal income tax withheld from box 2 of your W-2 form(s).   **7**

8a Earned income credit (EIC). See page 15.
b Nontaxable earned income: enter type and amount below.   **8a**

$

Type

9 Add lines 7 and 8a. These are your **total payments.**   **9**

10 Tax. Use the amount on **line 6 above** to find your tax in the tax table on pages 24–28 of the booklet. Then, enter the tax from the table on this line.   **10**

Refund

11a If line 9 is larger than line 10, subtract line 10 from line 9. This is your **refund.**   **11a**

Have it directly deposited! See page 20 and

b Routing number

c Type: Checking   Savings

d Account number

MUBU℠
MUSIC BUDDHA

The path to discovering new music starts here.

PALM

IN THE NEWS

CHOOSE A GENRE OF MUSIC BELOW

ROCK   POP   COUNTRY   ELECTRONIC   JAZZ   URBA

You are about to experience Music Buddha-- a sound-based, intelligent music recommendation service completely based on your personal moods and tastes.

Take a deep breath, clear your mind, and let Music Buddha enlighten you. Begin by choosing a genre of music above.

Music recommendation engines aren't terribly new. In the first year of the Web's ascendance, several affinity engines (for example, firefly) were started online. However, none of them were more interesting than the Music Buddha, where music is categorized into genres; within each genre, the site asks the user to listen and rate songs. This gives the engine enough information to start recommending music it thinks the user would also enjoy.

Click on the type of JAZZ music you'd like to explore...

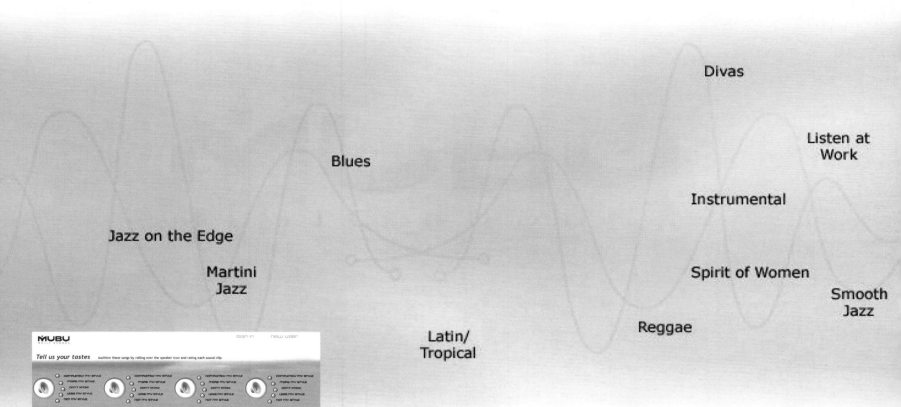

Divas

Listen at Work

Blues

Instrumental

IZZ

Jazz on the Edge

Spirit of Women

Smooth Jazz

Martini Jazz

Reggae

Latin/ Tropical

BEGIN AGAIN

People have an inherent need to express themselves.

Experiences that allow people to communicate with each other or simply to be heard tend to be rewarding, satisfying ones.

There are many different ways to communicate, whether through text, gesture, or speech. The results can be recorded in sound, on paper, as data, or not at all. Communications among people can be monologues, conversations, speeches, presentations, arguments, or discussions between one, two, or among many people. Communications between a person and a machine can be typed, spoken (employing speech recognition and speech synthesis), or gestured (using a variety of input devices like mice). However, machine responses will, most likely, be limited to algorithmic ones within a narrow field of appropriate or possible responses. This is because machines are very unsophisticated, not at all intelligent, and mostly are incapable of dealing with ambiguity—trying to have a conversation with one quickly reveals a computer's conversational limitations.

Like productive and creative experiences, opportunities to meet others, talk with them, and share personal stories and opinions are always viewed as valuable and interesting. Because these experiences involve two or more people, they also inherently involve high levels of control, feedback, and adaptivity. The telephone is an excellent example of a communicative experience, as are chat lines, discussion boards, and cocktail parties. Some of these are so valuable and enjoyable for some people that they have become virtually indispensable.

There are several types of communication, each with distinct strengths and weaknesses: Some are time-synchronized; others are time-shifted. Some are more private than others. However, even taken together, they still do not reach the rich diversity of traditional forms of communication.

experience design nathan shedroff

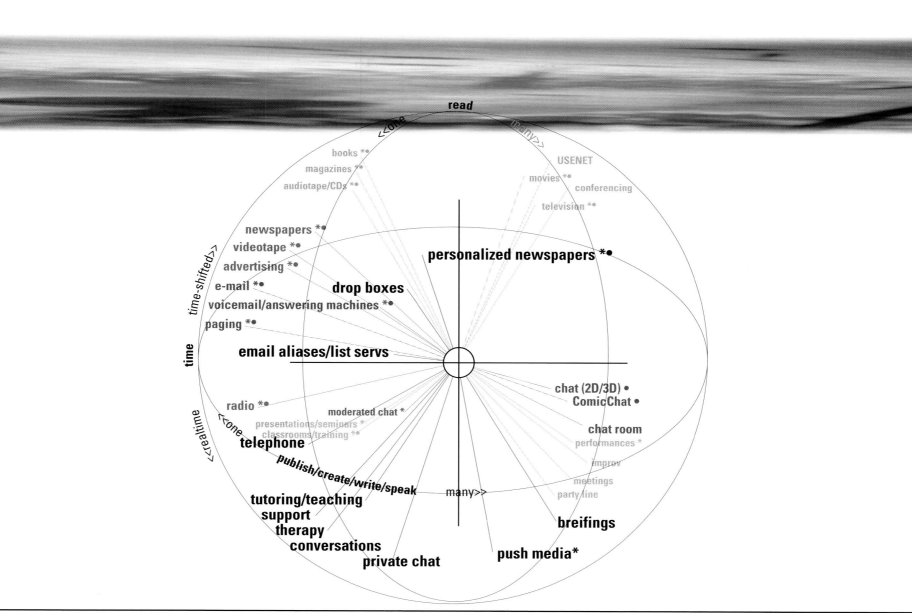

read

<<one   many>>

books *•
magazines *•
audiotape/CDs *•

USENET
movies *•
conferencing
television *•

newspapers *•
videotape *•
advertising *•
e-mail *•
voicemail/answering machines *•
paging *•

time-shifted>>

personalized newspapers *•

drop boxes

email aliases/list servs

time

chat (2D/3D) •
ComicChat •

radio *•
moderated chat *
presentations/seminars *
classrooms/training *•

chat room
performances *

<<one

telephone
publish/create/write/speak

<<realtime

improv
meetings
party line

many>>

tutoring/teaching
support
therapy
conversations
private chat

breifings

push media*

* moderated
• captured record/archive

In your life, you probably never will have a more interactive experience than a conversation with someone—especially if he or she is in front of you (as opposed to conversing over the phone or via a computer). The richness of a face-to-face conversation, the gestures, expressions, intonations, and other cues and feedback create opportunities for adaptive interactions.

Conversations are one of the most important ways we learn. Conversations allow us to be comfortable and conscious of the content, and to forget the form and means of transmission almost entirely.

Blogger is an easy way for anyone to quickly start a conversation on their site. Whether the conversation is between site owners and visitors or simply a way to keep a public diary, Blogger is one tool that will allow people to manage more complex interactions without reverting to programming themselves.

A blog (or weblog) is nothing more than a linear list of messages. What Blogger does is let site owners manage these messages easily, and then have them posted automatically to a specified page.

Cynthia's Life

"It's only when we truly know and understand that we have limited time on earth - that we have no way of knowing when our time is up - that we will begin to live each day to the fullest, as if it were the only one we had."
—Elisabeth Kubler-Ross

"Become so wrapped up in something that you forget to be afraid."
—Lady Bird Johnson

"He's no failure. He's not dead yet." --W. L. George

"Far away in the sunshine are my highest inspirations. I may not reach them, but I can look up and see the beauty, believe in them and try to follow where they lead." --Louisa May Alcott

"Happiness in this world, when it comes, comes incidentally. Make it the object of pursuit, and it leads us on a wild-goose chase, and is never attained. Follow some other object, and very

Friday, December 08, 2000

the weather is amazing......im talking light snow that has covered the whole city. it almost like the whole world is covered in perfection. that harshness out of footsteps is,, gone its alost like god put a blanket on the ground and told us all to calm down. theres just somethign about it that just mystifies me. just the fact that every snow flake is different baffles me. i cant imagine who has all the time to cut them out. i think i would like the job though:)
posted by Cynthia Castiglione 12:42 AM

Monday, December 04, 2000

i threw this party on saturday in my basement and it was awesome i think the reason that i had such a blast was because i didn't care about what happened to the place and i was playing every song i knew and singing at the top of my lungs. there wasn't a crowd just like 30 or 40 people all having a great time. this is definantly something i'm gogint o do more often.
posted by Cynthia Castiglione 1:22 PM

Friday, December 01, 2000

so the holidays are here......yeah and as you can tell by my excited tone that im stoked. the thing is nobody's really around and schools empty and ive been working non-stop ,way to much for any sane human being but as we all know I'm not very sane :) with all the pre holiday rush you think a restaurant in the middle of the bigest shopping area in chicago would be busy and so it is but the most ghetto fabulous people keep coming in, im talking minks and sweatpants people. but the other night this guy who was sitting at the bar for like ever comes up to me in the middle of me singing a song to myself way not the key the woman on the piano was playing it but still the same song it was lets call the whole thing off, you know that one from with when harry met sally , at least i think it was anyways so he overheard me singing and makes some smart ass comment and i look up to shoot one back but the moment ous eyes met it was like a pop or a boom or something , this click withit his total stranger, who by the way was gorgeous. i utter some uncomprehenible sound and he asks where the bathroom is and i manage to tell him. i watch him walk away for like two seconds untill someone interupts me and i have to do my job, by the timei get back from seating them i just catch him walking out the door. it was so weird because i totally cant get him out of my head and it was like some sappy movie when they meet and its only for two seconds but years later......we all have seen sliding doors ....i so wanted to run after him, if it had been any other place but work...... anyways other then that nothing new. im got asked to help with steel magnolias at the theater school so with what down time i have with work I've been doing that. nothing like a room full of woman to make you feel better about yourself.
posted by Cynthia Castiglione 8:18 PM

Saturday, November 11, 2000

so whats new with my life, nothing. nothing. i have tried and failed to make any advances as far as men or

182 | blogger
www.blogger.com
creators: Pyra Software: Evan Williams, Meg Hourihan, Paul Bausch, Matt Hamer, Matt Haughey, and Jack Saturn

experience design nathan shedroff

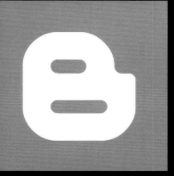

BLOGGER™

AMPHETAMINES FOR YOUR WEBSITE

CREATE YOUR OWN BLOG!

Blogger offers you instant communication power by letting you post your thoughts to the web whenever the urge strikes. **Learn more about it.** Or: [Start Now!]

◄ HOME
▸ ABOUT
▸ PRODUCTS
▸ HOW TO
▸ DIRECTORY
▸ SEARCH
▸ DISCUSS

RECENTLY ▾UPDATED ▸CREATED

THE 10 MOST RECENTLY UPDATED BLOGS

10:52 PM surreally.com
Kalam Kudus Web Log
angelwithoutwing...
Footnotes at
Joelavin.com
Melting Pot
Intenslee Personal
Reese's World
10:51 PM Neural Rot
M O R O N I C.org
Miscellaneous Graffiti

More Fresh Blogs >>>

BLOG OF THE WEEK

OSIL8

The latest episode of OSIL8 is called

WHAT'S UP

Media Web Logs For Fun and No Profit: "It's freakin' addictive. So, if you write for a living, don't read this, and don't try the Web-log game. It's too easy, and it will Suck Your Soul Away." We don't like to think of it as sucking your soul away. We like to think of it as giving a little soul to the web. [Thanks for the link GirlHacker!]
— pb [12/7/2000 4:49:00 PM]

Welcome WIRED readers! (Blogger is in the Street Cred section of the January issue.) You can check out our about page for more information about Blogger and weblogs. But the best way to learn is to try it out for yourself. Have fun!
— pb [12/6/2000 8:24:00 PM]

Inc. Magazine's Logging On the Web
— mathowie. [11/30/2000 11:47:45 PM]

O'Reilly Network: 24 Hours With a Wireless Palm Vx: "A copy of the Blogger Wireless Edition was also pre-installed. This innovative PDA app allows you to post and read blogs on your Palm. With the wireless edition, you could literally blog while commuting on public

SIGN IN

If you have a Blogger account, please sign in.

username [   ]

password [   ]

■ Remember me [?]

[sign in]

Forgot your password?

SIGN UP

If you don't have a Blogger account, sign up!

username [   ]

password [   ]

Experiences that seem to adapt to our interests and behaviors (whether real or merely simulated) always feel more sophisticated and personal. Though these experiences, necessarily, take more energy and planning and are significantly more difficult to accomplish, they are more valuable to the participants.

Customization is one form of adaptivity that allows people to overtly choose options to tailor an experience to their needs and desires. Customization is easier to develop than personalization since the options are always finite and controllable.

Personalization requires a more sophisticated level of interaction and planning, as choices and options cannot always be anticipated. Personalization allows people to create more unique experiences that are adapted even more to their needs and desires.

It is possible for experiences to adapt to participants in a variety of ways. The experience can change based on the behavior of the user, reader, participant, actor, or to a user's interests, needs, goals or desires (stated or inferred from behavior), experience or skill level, or even to the time or day or year, or even location (or experience or participant). It's important for designers to understand which attributes will make an experience more successful and valuable to users (which attributes are most appropriate), and balance these with those that are possible to create with the system, resources, budget, or schedule.

For example, many games become more difficult as the player becomes more proficient, constantly challenging the player in new ways. In other systems, content might change to be more detailed or simple based on the point of view, level of proficiency required, or amount of detail inferred from the user's behavior or location (such as a university versus a grade school).

The best experts and most proficient communicators are always adapting their interactions on-the-fly to suit the reactions they perceive in their audiences from body language, statements, answers to questions, and so forth. Because we are accustomed to this kind of behavior from people, it is natural to expect systems to respond in kind.

Many fine restaurants claim to customize their food and service to meet the needs of their customers. However, few go to the extent Arun's, a one-of-a-kind restaurant in Chicago, will go. Rather than merely checking to see if its guests have any special dietary needs, the waiters at Arun's ask you about your tastes, and the chef creates a meal just for you, customized with the ingredients you like—well, within reason, of course.

Aside from the custom preparations, the courses themselves are as elaborately decorated and as beautiful as any food I've ever seen—not to mention delicious. In fact, the courses are so exquisite that the restaurant has special containers so that diners can take home the decorations as perishable works of art.

4156 N Kedzie Ave, Chicago, IL 60618
TEL 773 539 1909
http://chicago.citysearch.com/profile?id=3685975

owner and executive chef: Arun Sampanthavivat

experience design nathan shedroff

Like other brands of personal start pages, My Yahoo is a customizable page
that summarizes, in one place, many of the things that might interest you. Not
only are the pieces of content customizable (if you don't like sports, you don't
have to see any), but the layout, colors, and priorities can also be changed to
suit individual preferences.

While this is a form of customization, and not personalization (since you can
only really choose among mostly predetermined options), it is merely the
beginning of the adaptivity that these services will someday offer.

With all of the attention being given to the creation of online communities, you would think that there would be more successful examples. However, most companies have approached the idea of community as merely another way to sell more products and services, without much regard as to why people would want to be a part of a community. Indeed, most discussions of community show a sad lack of understanding of what a community is, why it's valuable for people, of what is required to build a community. Most importantly, community designers need to realize that the community itself must serve the members of that community first and foremost, rather than a sponsoring or supporting a company's need to sell products.

The most successful communities excel in at least four considerations…

- **The ability of members to create persistent identities.**
- **Appropriate ways of communicating with others.**
- **Meaningful topics (whether content or context) around which to congregate and interact.**
- **The ability of members to actually share in the creation and expansion of the community, at the very least by helping to generate the content for the community.**

Abbe Don, a freelance designer with much experience in creating online communities, adds that a **successful community also requires strong leaders to guide the community and to offer help, to set examples, and establish standards of behavior since emotions are often amplified online.**

These principles underlie the need for communities to be developed over time. Communities cannot be expected to launch into full-blown activity immediately.

All communities, whether online or not, take time to develop their cultures, and in the
process, they change considerably as people leave and join, and the conversation evolves. Anyone interested in creating a community of some kind must be prepared for the length of time it takes for a community to come into its own.

Identity (see page 196) is important because communities require personal involvement, and that requires a sense of personal expression; identity is also important so that there is some persistence in participation. If anyone can say anything under any identity, then no one person's communications are important, and there will only be confusion as to who said what. Surely, a meaningful conversation cannot arise under such conditions.

Most important, members must feel some **sense of ownership** of the community or they will not participate, care about, or defend the community. This sense of ownership is the most difficult thing for companies and sponsors to come to grips with, as it often requires that they have less than total control over the community and what gets said there. However, organizations that set and enforce clear, fair rules for conduct and trust people to express themselves are almost always pleased with the results.

Abbe Don: www.abbedon.com

This sense of ownership often extends to the creation of key content around which the community congregates. For simple discussion systems, this is obvious because the discussion itself is the content. However, few communities can be successful unless members can, at least, start new topics of conversation, and few can survive merely on the strength of their conversations. Most require some form of content to stimulate discussions. Many successful communities allow their members to create this kind of content in order to provoke conversation. Some physical communities allow their members to help construct the community—even to bring their personal artifacts into the space and leave them there to add familiarity. These are the strongest communities of all and there's no reason why online communities can't achieve the same level of commitment.

When Heath Row approached his bosses, the founders of *Fast Company* magazine, about building an active community from their readership around the US, at first they were doubtful. They couldn't imagine how to do it, what the costs would be, and they couldn't see any benefit. They still thought of their readers in traditional publishing terms—passive customers who waited each month for the next installment of ideas, information, and advice. However, the readership wasn't sitting and doing nothing in between the issues, they were living their lives and trying to improve their work worlds. *Fast Company's* market,

in fact, was even more active in restructuring their careers than most, as this is a magazine that concentrates on these issues.

With a minimal budget and a tentative nod from his superiors, Heath first put together a network that allowed readers to find each other wherever they lived. He created the first networking opportunities as suggestions for meetings in coffeehouses and pot-luck dinners. Once the community could locate and contact each other (the most important requirement), they were the ones that

Fast Company magazine
www.fastcompany.com/cof

creator: Heath Row
date launched: 1999

| HOME | MAGAZINE | NEWSLETTERS | FC LEARNING | EVENTS | COMPANY OF FRIENDS | DISCUSSIONS | FC 2 GO |

Subscribe | Advertise | Membership | Customer Service | Search [____] Go

COMPANY OF FRIENDS

you are not signed in as a registered member of the company of friends

You can sign up here, or visit these demo pages to see what you can do when you register and sign in:
- my local cell
- other members
- discussions
- calendar
- notes
- group email

- my personal page
- edit my profile
- invite a friend
- coordinators

- CoF HOME
- visit other groups
- search for people
- community news

- the handbook
- CoF roadshows
- help
- f.a.q

Welcome to Company of Friends

 first time here? sign up now!   members sign in here

The Company of Friends is Fast Company magazine's global readers' network.

More than 25,000 business people, thought leaders, and change agents have signed up in more than 150 urban areas around the world. From Auckland, New Zealand, to Washington, D.C., Fast Company readers are self-organizing local discussion groups, mentoring and networking organizations, and creative problem-solving teams.

Through the Company of Friends, readers are taking the tools we offer in the magazine and using them to make change in their careers, companies, and communities.

To see how widespread the CoF is, see the list. The directory lists all of the cells we know about — and who you can contact to get involved locally as well as online.

As a member of the Company of Friends, you'll be able to contact cell coordinators and other participants via email, their Fast Company in boxes on the Web, and local discussion forums and mailing lists online.

You can meet the people associated with the cell in your area. And as a member of the readers' network, you can build your own personal profile online. Use your digital business card to network with other CoF members in your area — and to find people with whom you can connect, communicate, and collaborate.

Take the quick guided tour
or use the demo menu on the left
to see what the CoF can offer you.

 guided tour

engineered new ideas on how to help and support one another, make the most of their time together, and serve as resources for each other. Rather than Heath building the community himself, he built the means for the community to create itself with its own energy and enthusiasm. The community has grown to over 36,000 people in 150 locations around the world, and now it's a full-time job just trying to stay informed about what the community is doing, and visiting from time-to-time, in person, to see firsthand how people are changing the world of work.

WHISTLING PINES
CLASS PHOTO

www.purple-moon.com

founder: Brenda Laurel
date launched: 1998

experience design nathan shedroff

One of the most successful communities on the Internet (certainly for young girls), Purple Moon has been wildly active despite intentionally making it difficult to communicate. Because parents and site managers were concerned for their young and sometimes vulnerable audience's safety (in light of possible inappropriate adult interactions), the tools with which girls could express themselves were severely limited in their abilities.

Purple Moon's site offered most of what is necessary for a community to develop, including a rudimentary identity tool, and a very simple communications tool (in the form of postcards with optional attachments). While there was no opportunity for user-generated content (the girls could not contribute to the site as a whole), and really no context or topics to spur conversations, what made the site successful was that the girls themselves were so energetic and active that they didn't need the site itself to suggest topics to discuss, or context from which to start conversations.

In particular, the girls found innovative uses for the postcard since it wasn't really a conversation tool at all. To augment the fact that they could send only small pieces of text a little at a time, they started posting clubs that would meet at specified times, and then they would post the same message to everyone in the group in rapid succession, thereby creating a time-delayed chat system from the simple tools.

The identity tool, also, was purposely limited. Aside from choosing a pseudonym for themselves, girls could only choose between predetermined options to describe themselves. However, this was sufficient enough to meet each other and initiate conversations and interactions. Girls would search for others with similar responses (favorite foods, colors, sports, animals, etc.); these basic attributes were enough to create contact, while the conversations and messages were enough to tie them together.

The creation of identity is one of the most important aspects of our lives—certainly a key part of our personalities. Experiences that allow us to contribute to this creation—or help us form bonds with the creators or other participants—are often more meaningful and memorable.

Authenticity is usually one of the defining characteristics in identity. We tend to discount people we don't feel are "real" or authentic. The same goes for companies and organizations. When identities feel forced or otherwise disingenuous, we don't take them as seriously or give them as much respect, nor do we form strong, lasting bonds.

While identity is critical to successful communities, it is also critical to our own self expression. Experiences that allow us to express ourselves are some of the most valuable of all. Personal websites, in particular, are one of the newest forms of personal expression and one of the most powerful.

Personal expression is something experience designers often fear as they can never be sure exactly what might be expressed. Compounding this, many traditional media companies and pundits look upon personal expression with disdain and deride the attempts people make at expressing themselves simply because of a lack of professional quality. Indeed, personal photo albums, stories, and opinions are often only meant for those we know and not a wider audience, and their level of quality is perfectly appropriate and acceptable—spelling errors and lighting problems included. What's interesting about these attacks is that traditional media find it so threatening; and, indeed, the diverting of our attentions to each others' stories, concerns, and works does use attention that might otherwise be spent on the products of traditional broadcast media. However, serious, quality sources of valuable content have nothing to fear from growth in self expression. Instead, traditional media might take the opportunity to learn from personal media and make their own products more personally meaningful as a result.

There are a lot of cellular phones (just from Nokia alone). However, Nokia's 3210 has become *the* phone throughout Europe and Asia—so much so that it has become nearly ubiquitous. One of the features that makes it so successful is that it is customizable. The covers, sounds, screens, and even keypads can be customized to reflect our identities. There is a huge market in Japan alone for customized rings, as well as a popular and almost maniacal subscription rate to a ring-of-the-day service that doles out new rings everyday.

While many products allow fashion statements (for example, jewelry), the 3210 creates identity statements via its changeable appearances— more so than other personal electronics products (such as PDAs, MP3 players, and other cellular phones). Nokia's Xpress-On™ covers are quick and easy to change, allowing the phone to take on any number of styles to make it more personal. Many owners have more than one set of covers, changing them daily, weekly, or for particular events—like we might change clothes. It's easily the most customizable phone ever made.

The 3210 is *the* phone of choice for hipsters, teens, and others to express themselves. The small size and cost (it's less expensive than other models and even free with many services) make it affordable for these markets as well. GSM technology (a standard telecommunications technology across Europe and Asia) allows the phone's usage to roam everywhere *except* the USA without modification; and, the SMS messaging (something only now becoming available in the USA) allows people to quickly send short text messages to each other (now accounting for at least 50 percent of all cell traffic).

The 3210 is now discontinued but you can see some of the variations at: www.l8shop.co.uk/

nathan shedroff **experience design**

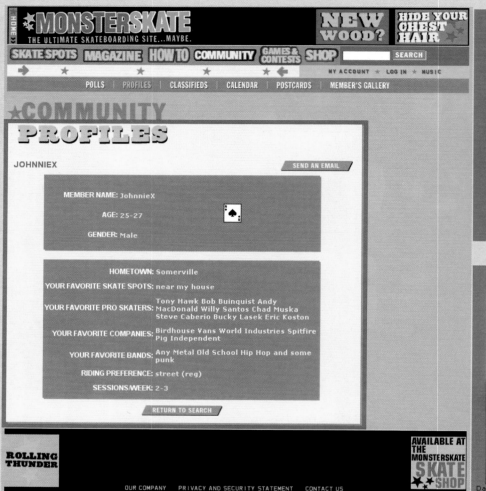

MEMBER'S GALLERY: PHOTO

Rutherford County Sun Skatepark in Murfreesboro, Tennessee, hasn't seen the last of Casey Daley. Kickflip over a folding chair.

MEMBER'S GALLERY: PHOTO

David Adamson checks himself on a backside 5-0 in Aberuthven, Scotland

Monsterskate is *the* skateboarding site, and like the skateboarding community, it's an active, in-your-face website that reflects the community's culture. What makes it such a rich community isn't just the site's demographic, it's the community's ability to build lasting identities for themselves. Skateboarders aren't given a lot of options—and this may be a good idea in this case—but, it doesn't stop them from expressing themselves. Even without a picture of the person—and maybe because there's no picture—you can quickly get a sense of the user's persona from responses to questions, and the name they've chosen for themselves.

Elsewhere in the Monsterskate site, members can send in pictures of themselves skateboarding—the operative activity here—rather than those cheesy head-shots that you might find in a personal profile.

The rest of the site is a well-designed resource for the activity and culture of skateboarding, including geographical and travel information (where the best skate parks are, for example), articles, and, of course, a store.

experience design nathan shedroff

www.monsterskate.com

principal designers: Matt Kipp, Danny Morrow, Tom Rohrer, and Victor Barclay,
vivid studios/Modem Media
date launched: December 2000

MONSTERSKATE

THE ULTIMATE SKATEBOARDING SITE...MAYBE.

DECEMBER 2000

SIGNED BOOK

SKATE SPOTS | **MAGAZINE** | **HOW TO** | **COMMUNITY** | **GAMES & CONTESTS** | **SHOP** | [SEARCH]

MY ACCOUNT ★ LOG IN ★ MUSIC

WELCOME TO MONSTERSKATE

★ ★ ★ ★ ★ ★ ★ ★

BIG BIRD

★ ★ ★ ★ ★ ★ ★ ★

TONY HAWK

FEATURE ARTICLE BY SEAN MORTIMER

Full Story

What do the best skaters in the world have to say about T Hawk? Will he get fat? Can he cook? Is skating hard for him? Josh Kalis, Jamie Thomas, Muska, Sean Sheffey, Bob Burnquist and others all throw in their two bits in an exclusive profile on the world's most famous skater. Hawk explains everything from his domestic skills to what his hardest trick to learn was. Check out videos and pictures and his personal board collection.

Danny Gonzales back from the operating table

TALL TALES

Dead people, exploding vehicles, machine guns -- what does all this have to do with Alou

WATCH THE NEW EPISODE
THE

Participation is the key to many successful experiences—certainly those that are intentionally designed in such a way that they couldn't exist without the participation of their audience. Participation makes experience more meaningful because it taps into our desires to be creative and communicate. Whether we are merely sharing our ideas and opinions or creating and displaying our works of art, it is gratifying to almost everyone to express themselves creatively and work with others to build an experience.

Many experiences couldn't survive—or even exist—without the involvement of their audiences. Most experiences could also be made better by redesigning them to include opportunities for participation on the part of the audience.

experience design nathan shedroff

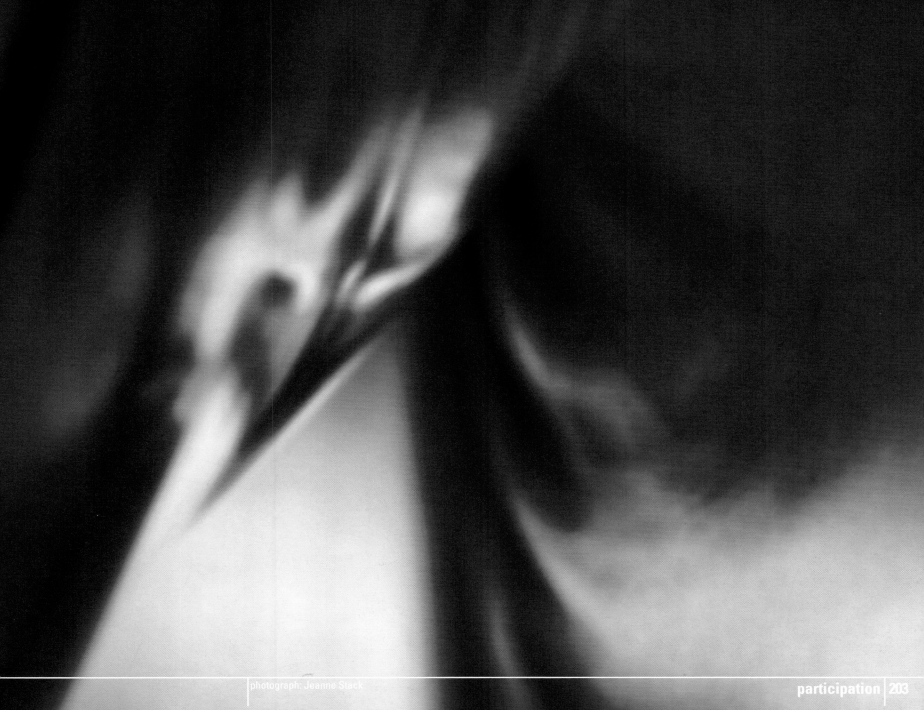

photograph: Jeanne Stack

nathan shedroff experience design

Now an infamous annual festival in the Nevada desert, Burning Man has managed to keep (for as many changes the festival has gone through over the past 10 years) its most important tenet in place—that is, a time and place primarily for participants, not spectators.

Burning Man only exists because of the participation by nearly all attendees, who create inconceivable spectacles of creative energy and imagination. Walking through the make-shift and temporary streets and among the artworks farther out on the playa, you are enveloped in the imaginations of other people made real. As self-motoring couches and teams of bicyclists roll by, you come to realize what potential we have for outlandishness, originality, weirdness, and fun.

It is the few spectators without spectacle, who haven't bothered to contribute to the experience, who feel out of place in this world turned inside out. Usually, our society is exactly the opposite—we are afraid and uncomfortable to create a scene, to be outlandish, or to portray a character that is neither prepared for us nor pre-approved by the whole. This leads us to consume entertainment and creativity prepared and preprocessed for us by the larger corporate world—often promoted beyond its relevance or importance.

Burning Man is a place that reminds us that we can make our own art, music, and spectacle, and the weight of 10,000 others there for that week prods—if not commands—us to participate.

NEVADA
23273 L

204 | burning man

Black Rock Desert, Nevada, Memorial Day weekend, annually
www.burningman.com

originator: Larry Harvey
date: held annually since 1990

NO SPECTATORS

Yahoo! Clubs

Home > Health & Wellness

[Search Clubs] [All Clubs ▼]

- Advice (105) NEW!
- Alternative Medicine (487) NEW!
- Beauty (436) NEW!
- Children's (148) NEW!
- Drugs and Medications (466) NEW!
- First Aid (22)
- Fitness and Nutrition (861) NEW!
- Health Care (180) NEW!
- Men's (72) NEW!
- Pet Health@
- Professional (1435) NEW!
- Reproductive (108) NEW!
- Seniors (34) NEW!
- Stress Management (111) NEW!
- Support (4640) NEW!
- Teens (69) NEW!
- Women's (450) NEW!
- Other (319) NEW!

Popular Clubs in All Categories Under *Health & Wellness*

Rank	Club Names	Description	Members
1.	BODY FOR LIFE USA	Body For Life INTERNATIONAL FITNESS CLUB	4276
2.	HerpesSingles	Your one-stop herpes dating site	2925
3.	Body for Life Women's Club	A place for "girl talk" about fitness :o)	2865
4.	Body For Life	Helping you Build your best Body for LIFE	2567
5.	hpv	Support 4 people w/HPV (genital warts & dysplasia)	2402
6.	Alcoholic Anonymous	A place where one Alcoholic can talk with another.	2383
7.	BFL Photo Gallery	"A place to share your Challenge photos."	2193
8.	PUMP	Let's get pumped!	2167
9.	Hardcore Muscle and Fitness	Discussion on training, nutrition, steroids, supps	2024
10.	Body For Life Recipes	Nutrition For Life	1978
11.	BFL USA East Coast	BODY FOR LIFE Eastern USA	1782
12.	WeightLossAndFitness	A place to discuss Weight Loss and Fitness	1768
13.	Fitness and Health Club	A place to talk to get motivated to get in shape.	1666
14.	Black Hair Super Grow Out	Take the 365 day challenge, grow longer hair	1589
15.	GETTING FAT	A place to talk about gaining weight	1491
16.	IBS Self Help Group	Irritable Bowel Syndrome Self Help Group	1488
17.	Stretching 101		1368
18.	Depression	For anyone suffering from depression.	1359
19.	Hempsters	Legalize Marijuana!!!	1343
20.	NonStop Makeover	Bumpy roads! Solution New Attitudes	1334
21.	hair extensions and dreadlocks	dream it and we will make it	1324
22.	Women4Sobriety	An Alternative Recovery Program for Women	1304
23.	Bald by Choice Men	The club for men who shave their heads BALD!	1294
24.	The EAS Challenge	The Challenge to Transform Your Physique for LIFE	1240
25.	BarbershopHaircuts	A club for guys who enjoy short or shaved haircuts	1221
26.	The Body for LIFE Club	The Official Yahoo! Club for Body for LIFE	1218
27.	Cut that Hair Girl	Women with short/shaved hair...share stories!	1201
28.	Severe female helmet haircuts	Blunt lines, shaved sides and lovely shaved napes	1182
29.	Obsessive Compulsive Disorder	Support and information for those with OCD.	1172
30.	Richard's Angels	"Never give up, never surrender!"	1164
31.	MouthWear Braces Club	The Braces Resources Centre	1161
32.	Miracle of Birth	A place to share the miracle of birth.	1153
33.	Orthognathic Surgery Support	A place to learn, grow and heal	1142
34.	Keepitshort	Short or buzzed hairstyles on women	1121

Yahoo! Clubs   [Create a Club]

Home > Health & Wellness > Children's (147)

[Search Clubs] [All Clubs ▼]

- Circumcision@
- View Most Popular Clubs Including Categories Above

Clubs for *Children's* (147)		Most Popular	A-Z Index	New Clubs

Rank	Club Names	Description	Members
1.	Kids With Braces	A Place Where Kids Can Unite Who Have Braces	486
2.	preteens drynites	preteens in nappies	469
3.	Boy's GoodNites	If you are a boy and wear GoodNites	467
4.	Windelwerbung und Diaperads		445
5.	girl's in goodnites	a place to talk about girl's in goodnites	342
6.	Early onset of puberty	A place for support on early puberty	227
6.	MomoMuscleBoys 1 NEW!	The place to post your muscleboy pics.	227
7.	Children with ADHD or Depression	Gentle conversation, management and guidance	155
8.	Parents of Little People	Somewhere 2 Share About Our Kids with Dwarfism:)	150
8.	Surport For BedwettingKids	Surport Page (for preteens - teens & parents.)	150
9.	Baby Boys with Earrings	Is it Right to Pierce Baby Boys Ears ?	135
10.	Help with Potty Training	A place to go for help with pottytraining	102
11.	Kids With Asthma@	Parents sharing about childhood asthma	87
12.	PARENTS OF CEREBRAL PALSY KIDS@	A place for parents with children with CP	82
13.	Potty Talk	children who just won't train and are over 5	81
14.	Strong kids		76
14.	The Best of Bowlcuts for Boys	The Best Pictures from the Best Yahoo! Club!	76
15.	kids with epilepsy@	place for kids with epilepsy	73
16.	Parents of Diabetic Children@	Supportive place for parents of diabetic children	71
17.	TALKING ABOUT BIRDS AND THE BEES	give and recieve tips on talking to kids about sex	70
18.	Autism and Fun Message Board	Support and Friendship in dealing with autism	62
19.	Vaccinations and Children	vaccine, vaccination, immunization: educate first	53
20.	preemies	a place for parents of premature babies	47
21.	Heart Babies	Chat with parents of children with heart defects.	44
22.	Parents Support for ADHD and ODD		42
23.	Touched An Angel Club	To Remember Your Lost Angels	39
24.	Juvinile Diabetes SUPPORT@	You can do this! It's a day by day thing... :)	37
25.	CMV and CP Parent Link		36
25.	Pediatric Leukemia@	Talk with specialists about childhood leukemia.	36
26.	Children's Cancer Club@	Discussions & News Dealing With Children's Cancer	35
27.	Special Kids	Support for Parents of chronically ill children	34
28.	Enuresis Support Club	Advice /support to families troubled by bedwetting	31
28.	For Kids Sake Keep Them Healthy	How your child can be toxic free and healthy too.	31
29.	Hearts with CHD	Congenital Heart Defects Support Group	30
30.	CHILDREN WITH ALLERGIES		25
30.	sick children	a place to talk about your sick child	25
30.	SNK Parent Support	Support and help for Parents Of Special Needs Kids	25
31.	Feeding and Tubes Issues	Place for chit chat about feeding and tubes.	22
31.	Nederlandse Perthes Supportgroep		22

www.clubs.yahoo.com

Yahoo! Clubs

Home > Hobbies & Crafts

[Search Clubs] [All Clubs ▼]

- Collecting *(3810)* NEW!
- Crafts *(1283)* NEW!
- Hobbies *(2009)* NEW!

- Home Repair and Remodeling@
- Models *(900)* NEW!
- Other *(975)* NEW!

Popular Clubs in All Categories Under *Hobbies & Crafts*

Rank	Club Names	Description	Members
1.	Craftalk And Craftideas	"A place to find craft projects and friends."	3633
2.	antique collector	A place to talk about antiques	2761
3.	John Deere Garden Tractor Club	"THE" Place For John Deere L&G and Compact Info	2275
4.	krafty kreations	Teaching club!! Have fun teaching and chatting!!	2152
5.	Cross Stitchers	Cross Stitch and needleworking tips, exchanges, etc	1963
6.	Home Shop Woodworking	A place for Home Woodworkers to share info	1891
7.	Boy Scout Collectors Society	Largest collector club in Scouting history -	1748
8.	WORLD STAMPS	THE CLUB FOR ALL STAMP COLLECTORS	1674
9.	Scroll Sawing	A meeting place for all Scroll Sawyers !!	1566
10.	Cards and collectibles center	"1400"+ members & more than 325,000 page views!!!!	1461
11.	Bolens Tractors Club	Club for owners and restorers of Bolens Tractors	1412
12.	COINS CLUB	A PLACE FOR EXCHANGE (tips for collectors)	1408
13.	Rubber Stamping	Rubberstampers always make good impressions.	1372
14.	Crazy Quilters and Friends	Friendly place for quilters & fabric addicts :-)	1367
14.	JD GARDEN TRACTOR CLASSIFIEDS	CLASSIFIED ADS ONLY - JD L&G equipment & parts	1367
15.	Wheel Horse Garden Tractors	A site for true Wheel Horse fans.	1248
16.	Candlemaking	Candlemaking for the beginner to the expert.	1233
16.	The Ham Shack	A place to talk and meet other hams and nonhams.	1233
17.	the baseball card palace	a place to trade/buy/sell cards	1231
18.	Antique Garden Tractor	A place to talk about Antique Garden Tractors.	1210
19.	Scrapbooking	A place to share scrapbooking ideas.	1199
20.	Sports Cards 7	1035 Members 216,000 Page Views. Why not join?	1147
21.	Teen Boy Fighters	Club for Boy Fighters, Wrestlers, Boxers, Storys	1130
22.	Real Snail Mail Address's	Leave your snail mail address for penpals	1079
23.	HO Trains	Everything HO. Period.	1047
24.	A 1 Autographs	EVERYTHING FROM ADULT FILM STARS TO SPORTS STAR'S!!	1007
25.	Yanmar tractor owners group	A valuable source for owners of Yanmar tractors.	971
26.	Ashley's PenPals Galore 4 Ever	Get PenPals & More Have A Happy Valentine's Day	962
27.	Rubber Stampers Tea Room	Rubber Stamping Chats, Links; Techs Sharing Ideas	928
28.	Teen Fighting		927
29.	The Sears Garden Tractor Club	THE Yahoo and Internet authority on Sears tractors	907
30.	Maximaphily	Maximaphily - Maximum Cards, Stamps and Postcards	901
31.	Rug Hookers	This is a place for rug hookers to talk together.	887
32.	Antique Dealers Forum	A VERY Helpful Club For All Collectibles Fans	882
33.	The Real Fight Club	A club to chat about gutpunching and fighting.	871
34.	Soap Crafters	Let's talk candles/soaps/toiletries!!	868
35.	A Noble Needle	with diligence she set color with a noble needle	865
36.	Snail Mailers United	Use a stamp - Go postal for a change!	860
37.	X Stichers	Home for X Stitch tips, tricks, & trades!	855
38.	Dan's Crochet Corner	A place for crochet minded people to mingle.	851

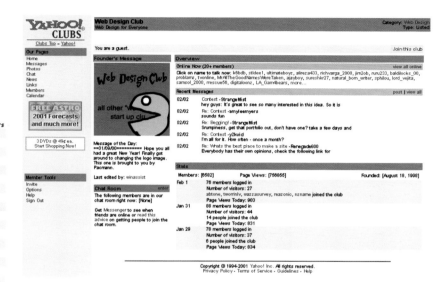

Any true community site can only exist when its members are the ones creating the majority of its content. Yahoo Clubs is one of the most vibrant communities—or more accurately, collection of communities—you currently will find on the Web. Communities of interest on any conceivable subject exist here, with members expressing themselves through message boards and chat, sharing photos and other files, and describing themselves through use of adequate identity tools.

If you can't find a club already formed around one of your interests (and the likelihood is low, indeed), you should start one (which is *very* easy to do), and see who else is out there interested in the same things.

Some of the most compelling and involving experiences are organized around the telling of stories—whether these are from the experience creators or the audience.

Storytelling is one of the oldest experiences and still one of the most powerful

because it organizes information in a way that allows us, usually, to draw *personal meaning* and create *knowledge* (see page 48).

There are as many different ways to tell a story as there are storytellers. The two most important characteristics of successful stories are that they are **authentic** (this doesn't mean that they cannot be fictional), and that they are **relevant** to the audience. Additionally, many stories are successful when they can evolve to fit the circumstance and take into account the reaction of the audience. This doesn't mean that the story must be told or created cooperatively (in fact, this form of storytelling can be fun or silly, but isn't usually fulfilling).

Storytelling must take into account **perspective**—whether the story is told from the first person (as something that happened to the storyteller personally), the second person (a difficult perspective to use for most stories), or the third person (a very common perspective).

Most stories require at least a **beginning** (to understand the context), a **middle** (the story itself), and some form of **end** (to draw the story to a satisfactory close and, often, to point out the meaning, moral, or lesson if there is one). Settings, characters, styles, dramatic purpose, and themes are all important, but without the basis of purpose and flow, no story can be told well.

Innovative experiments in storytelling have tried to incorporate multiple points of view in the telling, offer non-linear or branching stories, or provide improvisational story building. Some of these have been successful, but it takes a particularly skilled storyteller to do these well. More often than not, simple, linear story structures allow storytellers to concentrate on the meaning and emotional content as well as the careful development of action and characters in order to arrive at a satisfying conclusion. Storytelling is so difficult for most people that the less variables they need to control, the more successful the stories they create.

Stories can be used not just as entertainment but as a way to make difficult concepts, information, or instructions more accessible.

Again, because we are so familiar with stories, the structure allows us to concentrate and order the information more easily than many other forms. As long as the story doesn't get in the way of the purpose or use of the information, there's no reason why stories can't be used to make instructions, directions, reports, or guidelines of any kind easier to understand and remember. Politicians have been using stories to illustrate their positions for a long time.

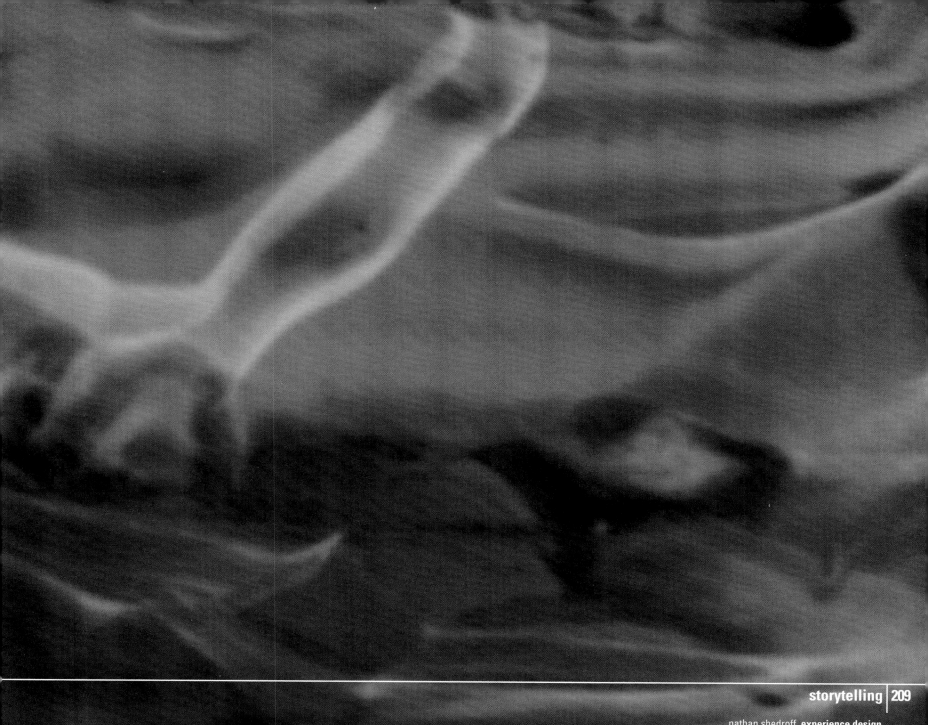

My Grandmother, Myself
by Rosalind Glazer

Grandma Bobbie Green   Rosalind Glazer

I was a colicky baby but Grandma Bobbie alone knew how to get me to stop crying. This was a huge relief to my exhausted mother. She would cradle me in her arms and sing to me in Yiddish. Her father, my great grandfather was a chazzan--and a rabbi--and I still love to sing Jewish songs.

I loved visiting her apartment in Yonkers, NY. Her giant potted plants had marbles and shells which I used to pick out and play with. The carpeted hallways had plastic runners and the living room had plastic couch covers. I can still smell it. The asphalt playground outside her red brick building had the best seesaw around.

As a child I loved her excellent Hungarian kosher cooking, but when she got too tired to cook she took to eating Chinese food and Burger King. My mother told me how grandma taught her to eat shrimp cocktail and lobster. But that was only out of the house.

Grand Central Aunt
by Deborah Gar Reichman

The hippest, most interesting relative I have is 90 years old. She's my grand aunt, my mother's aunt. But to tell you the truth, I always found her more compelling than any of the relatives closer to my age. I owe to her my independence, my feminism, and the fact that I grew up in the very metropolitan New York Area, while the rest of the family clan stayed in Michigan. See, she was my mom's favorite aunt too. And when my mom was of "moving age," she went to visit Becky in New York and like her aunt, never turned back.

Mom and I, her biggest fans.

Aunt Becky has lived her entire life as a single woman during a time when it wasn't so acceptable to do so. She grew up in Detroit, Michigan but ached for excitement, independence and culture. While her sisters, brothers and friends all married and settled down in the Jewish enclave of Detroit, she dreamed of places beyond. She wanted to experience art and music. She wanted to drink coffee on gold furniture. She wanted to wake up in the center of a great city. She wanted to really, truly live, and her definition of doing so was quite different than that which was expected of women at the time.

At the age of 40, upon her father's death (for she was his sole caretaker), she said goodbye to her family, and took a train from Detroit to New York City. She found a tiny studio on East 57th street, with a view of a brick wall, around the corner from Bloomingdales and down the street from the Museum of Modern Art. She bought a wooden table and chairs which she spray painted gold. For $60 a month she began her life. For the next 40 years she would live there, on a block that would become the most coveted real estate in the greatest city in the world.

Aunt Becky

In My Mother's House
by Liz Rudey

Bertha and daughter Thelma   Thelma c. 1910

My mother, Thelma Barasch was born on January 20, 1907 in New York City. She w the daughter of Bertha Hirschdorfer and Morris Barasch. They lived on East 10th Str accross the street from Tompkins Square Park.

Bertha was born in Milwaukee, Wisconsin in the early 1880's and moved with her fa to New York's Lower East Side. Bertha and her half sister Anna Bikel married two Austrian brothers, Morris and Sigmund. The men opened a bank on Delancey Stree Bertha and Morris had five children. (The first died for lack of antibiotics). Thelma ofte spent time with her Aunt Anna and Uncle Sigmund, and spoke German for the first of her life. The family moved to Williamsburg where Thelma and her siblings went to school.

Bertha helped her husband in the bank as an accountant. Her exercise included wa over the Williamsburg Bridge each day with a basket of hot lunch for her husband. S

As part of her quest to teach others how to create and share their personal stories using online and interactive media, Abbe Don, an artist and producer, periodically holds digital Story Bees. These events allow people to discuss the nature of storytelling and identify the most important moments in the stories; they also teach at these events how to use the tools that are necessary to tell their stories.

The story bees, like their inspiration quilting bees, are very social events. They start with a discussion of materials (family photos, stories, and so on). This is where the stories begin to form. Starting with oral storytelling is more natural for people and helps them to focus on the best elements of the stories they have to tell. In essence, the stories are "written" during the discussion so that the production of the story online goes quickly and easily for novices.

story excerpts:

Laura Jacobs, **Tel Aviv**
My grandmother came from a very small town just north of Warsaw, Poland. She once told me the story of why she had poor vision in one eye. When she was a very young child she was quite beautiful and a woman who lived in her village was quite jealous of her good looks. One day my grandmother walked past this women who "cast an evil eye on her" and from that time on she was not able to see clearly in one eye. Even though her mother took her to a Rabbi in the town to "remove the evil eye" this problem persisted all her life. Because of this experience my grandmother never complimented her grandchildren on their

What is a digital story bee?

Well, it's a little something I cooked up in response to people asking me how I do what I do or if I can teach them to do what I do so they can share their stories here at my place, Bubbe's Back Porch. Nothing makes me kvell more than seeing people connect with a dormant part of themselves or their past. Ever since I began putting stories on the web, I realized there's something about stories that enable us to learn from each other and make a connection between our heads, our hearts and our kishkes (that means "guts" more or less) So the Digital Story Bee(tm) is a free, three-hour workshop where people come together with a couple of family photographs and tell each other stories, face to face, in a nice circle, a bit like an old quilting bee. Each Digital Story Bee(tm) has a theme to keep everybody on the same page. Then, you shmooze a little, see a little demonstration of how all this technology works, and follow this four step process:

1. Scan a picture

Each Woman is a Dreamer in Her Time
by Joan Roth

My mother, Clara, like her mother and mother-in-law before her was a dreamer. But few of her dreams, if any, ever came true. She's an inventor. She invented the first hair curler, eye lash curler and portable dish dri, she really did! Even though no one believes her and no one cares, because the one time her hair curler got to the market place, World War II broke out and she couldn't get the material she needed quick enough to produce fast enough.... so the story goes. But I've seen her patents and I believe her. I know she is a genius. A beautiful, gentle woman who gave much too much of herself to others; who never gave up hope; stopped loving those who abused her generousity and never lost her faith in God.

Clara.

Dora on the other hand was more domineering. Dora was Clara's mother. She was born in New York City, March 24, 1890. The third daughter of ten children, only seven of whom lived. The boys were all educated, of course. Abe, the oldest became a professor. He was the Dean of the night school at Hunter College and is written up in *Who's Who in America*. Louis became a doctor and was noted in the family as the doctor to Irving Berlin's father-in-law. Joseph became a dentist. Both men built their practices in their father's big old house on 189 Mineola Avenue, in Mineola, Long Island. Dora, too, wanted to be a doctor. Realizing she had no chance because," only the boys were being sent to college," she spent the rest of her life wishing she had become a nurse. She did hospital volunteer work and when she turned 70 years old , she was awarded a nurses certificate and a Red Cross pin.

Dora

Bertha has always been a mystery to me. She died before I was born, so I never knew her. I don't know if she and my mother liked each other, though I imagine even though they were from different worlds, they share a genuine innocence of being. Bertha was born in the Ukraine, in a village called Tarasha, somewhere around 1860. Her husband came to America first and she had to care for and escape with the children on her own. There was a color photograph of her on everyone's living room table, but no one ever mentioned her. Not my father, nor my aunts and uncle on my father's side. Neither did my zede. Whenever I asked about her, everyone always went shhhh.I never understood the reason for their silence. I don't think there was one.

Bertha.

My Working Grandmother
by Radhi

In my years as a working woman, living far from home, my grandmother's letters have been a constant inspiration. "I love my work. My work is my life," they have always said.

My grandmother's work has been amongst destitute women. Women without a home; without a place in society. Over the years she has rescued and rehabilitated women who are homeless in one way or another. She has raised money to build shelters for them- short-stay homes, rehabilitation centers and working women's hostels. These shelters for women have provided timely care and counseling for those fleeing dowry-deaths, escaping child-marriages or prostitution. In recent years her organization has come to the rescue of women and children affected by AIDS. This voluntary work has taken my grandmother to places where few other women would have dared to venture. She has gathered courage along the way.

Satyavati Shah at the age of eighteen

Widowed at twenty eight, my grandmother was left with two little girls and a bleak future. Young widows in Hindu families were seen as a dark omen, and faced lives as outcasts. Their hair was shorn. Their red wedding bangles were broken and their ornaments taken off. They wore white saris. They were housebound and survived on family left-overs. My grandmother was proud of her long, dark hair that fell to the ground. She protested having to cut it off. She was young and unprepared to be isolated from the world.

In her grief, a neighbor visited her and suggested participating in some social work at a Gandhian women's group. It would be socially acceptable, and it would be her chance to go out and meet people again. From that day on she embraced the cause of women who, like herself, wanted to live with dignity above all else. She slowly built a new life. In years to come she built her own home and lived independently. She has always said that helping others has given her strength and courage in her own life. She has listened to their stories and learnt to help in every way she could. Her work has taken her to remote parts of the country, very far from where she started.

A few years ago the government recognized and awarded Satyavati Shah for a lifetime of dedicated work. It was a proud moment for her, and an inspiring one for us.

Today, at eighty-four, my grandmother still has a full day at work, attends conferences, and believe it or not- is still raising money to build new homes! Her recent letter contains her usual refrain. " I am very busy, but I love my work." It keeps her going... Going strong!

My grandmother as a young widow

Grandma Aeschliman
Phyllis Aeschliman Shedroff

Grandma Aeschliman's wedding picture

Grandma Aeschliman was born Lucy Novak in a small town in north central Czechoslovakia. She immigrated as a young child and moved to the midwest (Missouri and Kansas). She married Daniel and had 5 sons by him.

Lucy had taught school in a one room school house before she married. I guess I got my interest in education from her. One of my greatest possessions is a set of the Kansas State Reading Series: Primer to 6th Grade which I was able to purchase some years ago. She had kept a few copies in her attic, along with lots of other books, and I spent a lot of time up there when I visited her on the farm as a young child.

The joke about grandma was that she was very stubborn. She refused to take Social Security because

---

photographs: Laurie Blavin

Who haunts **you?**

the Fray

The past haunts me.

The Fray was one of the first websites to allow readers to share their own stories—and it is still one of the best. What sets *The Fray* apart is its approach to using prepared original stories (written, edited, designed, and produced) as a catalyst to touch people and entice them to share their thoughts and reactions—that is, their own stories—as they relate to the prepared stories.

The first danger of any audience participation is that an audience won't, in fact, participate. Using well-written and well-designed stories as catalysts reduces this danger drastically. Reviewing any of the stories on the site reveals a dizzying number of responses, proving the effectiveness of this technique.

Another danger of audience participation is always the appropriateness of the responses. Often, the audience isn't sufficiently engaged or their motives aren't aligned with the purposes and expectations of the site creators. What works here, is that the topics are personal and emotional enough to be engaging and just long enough to be enveloping. By the time readers get to the end of the story (where their opportunity to participate begins), they're more likely to share their own stories in line with the spirit of the site, rather than change the tone of the experience. There is a kind of subtle peer pressure at work here that helps guide people to be thoughtful and respectful of each other, as well as open with their own feelings.

The Fray has been successful in terms of the amount as well as depth of the participation throughout the site. It is one of the best examples of how successful—and how special—personal storytelling can be.

ghosts

hope

drugs

www.fray.com
designer and creator: Derek Powazek

experience design nathan shedroff

Papa's ghost finds me in the garage. It's where we both keep our tools.

Papa was a carpenter, a cabinetmaker. One of the garages in back is still filled with his power tools: drill press, lathe, table saw, band saw, jigsaw, router, joiner, all made by Rockwell. He lost a finger on one of the saws, made the dining room table at my parents' house with those tools, made a lot of the furniture in my house. The dresser in my room, the dining room table and chairs, and the mightiest speaker cabinet you can imagine. He's in all of that wood, but he only speaks to me in the garage.

I call it my shop. My bike tools live there: chain whip, chain tool, truing stand, housing cutters, spoke wrench, allen wrenches, headset wrench, the Big Ass Crescent wRench (or BACR, as my friends call it), Pedro's ATB lube, Tri-Flow cannisters, repair stand, and bike stickers all over the place. The garage is a two door, one half is my shop, the other Papa's. The tools all seem to get along; I just hope I don't see all my tools picking on Papa's for being too old. Those Rockwell beasts would stomp all over my Parks without even breaking a sweat.

I tune up my bike late at night, when I'm home from work, and Papa is with me in the garage. It's cold, and I'm covered with oil and mung and cursing at my brakes for not aligning properly, and Papa is watching what I do. Just like Grandma, he's not too sure why I'm fussing so much over a bike, but he can see I'm using my hands and making them calloused and being a prideful bastard and not taking my bike to a shop. I'm doing this myself, because there is no excuse for not taking care of yourself. Papa's ghost visits both of our shops, and he doesn't mind, since I'm his grandson.

The ghosts only seem to come out at those times, but I make sure to visit them often. The house is mine now, my home to make memories in, but I'd damn well better remember the ones that lived there before.

Who haunts you?

star wars memories
The lights go down and I'm
laughing at the pure joy of
seeing giant yellow words
scroll up the screen.

resolutions
It always seemed so far away,
but here we are in 1999.

the nicest person in san francisco
I cranked the stereo up and the
windows down. I was ready for an

"Don't you have some lipstick or something?" she asks, as she examines my lip, now *blue from the blow* it received the night before.

"Yeah, I do," I answer quietly, then start rummaging.

He joins us, looks at me in the mirror. He reaches out and lays his hand on my hair for a few moments, stroking it. "Have a good day at school!" he adds, then walks off.

She grabs one of my lipsticks and checks the color.

"Here you go, that'll go well with the sweater. You have to look pretty, or else what will the boys think, right?"

She smiles.

I am seventeen years old.

Smiling hurts.

nathan shedroff **experience design**

The structure of a story often affects its experience—especially how it is understood. While the vast majority of narratives (stories, reports, speeches, etc.) follow a simple linear progression (beginning, middle, and end), many of the most engaging stories play with this structure in novel ways. Whether using traditional, improvisational, or "street" theater techniques, structures are a part of the interaction among actors, and between the actors and audience. These interactions stabilize or provide departures for dynamic parts of the action (the characters, the environment, the script, the performance, etc.). Improvisational theater techniques, in particular, play with making these elements dynamic or static in order to explore possibilities, while keeping an interesting narrative building for an audience. Any exploration of theater techniques and narrative structures should explore improvisational techniques, as well as more traditional theater and storytelling techniques.

David Siegel has identified two-goal story structures in many successful books and movies. This narrative device allows the story to change substantially, as the hero—who had been focused on one goal—switches when a larger, more important goal comes to light during the story. This switch provides tension and an opportunity for emotional and dramatic development. Sometimes the goal switches again (to a third goal; though too many switches can become confusing). In other stories, the goal may switch back to the original one (a reversal). Brenda Laurel reminds us that "in theater, perception is more important than reality." That is, whatever the structural changes, the narrative still needs to have a cognitive clarity that people can follow, even if it isn't realistic or accurate.

Brenda also informs us that all narratives require **action** even when there are no characters. Action is what holds our attention and creates meaning. All experiences that strive to be interesting, engaging, entertaining, or informing must be designed to act—even react and interact—on some level. The action is also the best place to start development and design (as opposed to the environment, the characters, or props).

Computers as Theater, Brenda Laurel, Addison-Wesley, 1991
isbn: 081011313

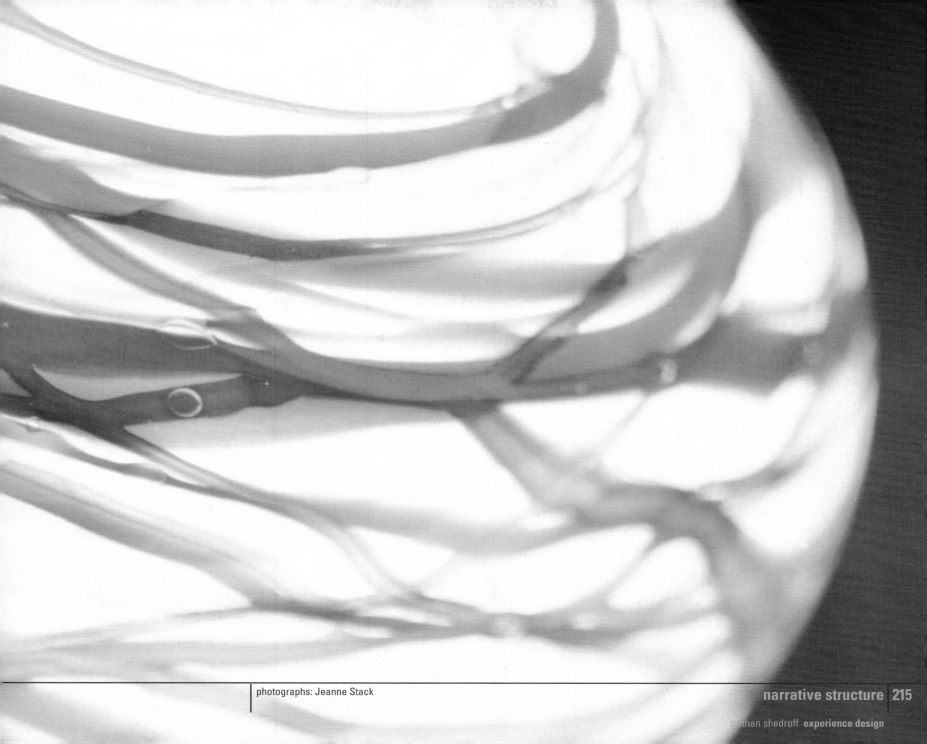

The presentation and organization of this Holocaust Museum at the Simon Wiesenthal Center in Los Angeles, California is innovative, sensitive, and powerful. The experience uses different points of views (represented by three characters who represent the design perspectives of the museum) to present the information and build the story, which is brilliantly implemented. The three perspectives represent a historian, an exhibit designer, and a photo editor. The three discuss key issues of the Holocaust experience and explain how the elements of the museum's design help the visitors understand this experience. At one point in the museum, visitors can obtain an identity card that describes a real person who experienced the Holocaust. Throughout the museum, in different rooms, there are small machines that read the cards and describe the history of the represented person at that point. It's important to note than many of the people described don't live through the entire holocaust, which makes a personal connection between visitors and victims.

The interactive exhibits in the Museum of Tolerance could be more powerful and engaging, but this museum deserves credit for targeting the subject of tolerance (of many different cultures), instead of merely building a shrill memorial.

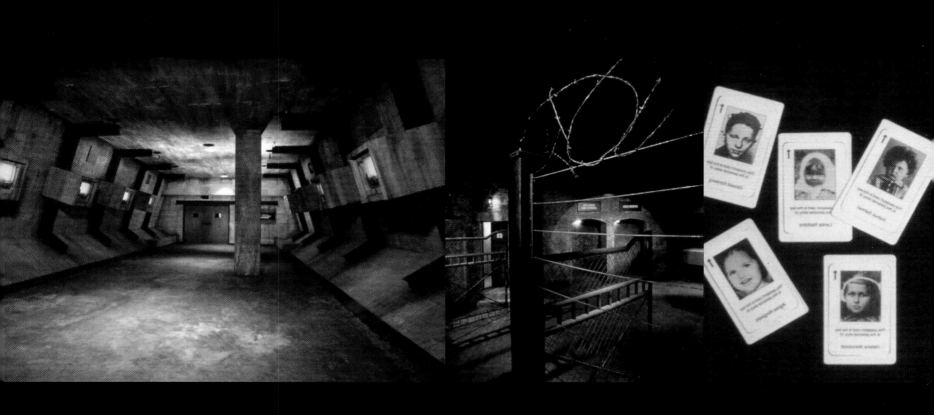

research.microsoft.com/vwg/projectsheets/comicchat.htm
principal designers: David Kurlander, Tim Skelly, and David H. Salesin
date: 1996

We are mostly familiar with non-linear navigation through our use of hypermedia like the Web, but this is not the first example of such navigation in this medium. There are many common experiences in which we move about non-linearly— that is, where we have choices of how and where to proceed along the way. Driving or walking in a city, for example, are non-linear experiences, as are almost all real-space, physical experiences. There is nothing inherently better about non-linear experiences, though the choice offered, if appropriate, often creates a sense of participation and can be more satisfying.

For many decades—if not longer—non-linear navigation has been a dream of storytellers. These non-linear narratives are experiments that allow the audience to help create the story or, at least, help shape its enfolding. Mostly, these stories have been unsuccessful since the majority of audiences are mostly interested in hearing a compelling story well told than in helping to create what usually becomes a marginal one. Most people don't feel they have the ability to tell stories themselves and, therefore, are reluctant to do so. Also, most storytellers aren't prepared for the explosion of choice and exponential work required with each point that represents a choice in a story, and the elements

necessary to weave a consistent, meaningful story with somewhat random choices on the part of the audience.

In her book *Computers as Theater*, Brenda Laurel outlines five basic structures that relate to narrative flow...

• single thread, no choices (traditional linear stories)
• single thread, minor detours
• multiple threads, preset choices
• multiple threads, unprompted choices
• exploratory

It is this last structure, exploratory, that most computer-based storytellers are after—as it is the ideal (or goal) of non-linear navigation; it is also the most difficult to produce because of the infinite choices and combinations. Even multiple threads with preset choices create exponentially more work than single threaded stories.

Computers as Theater, by Brenda Laurel, Addison-Wesley, 1991
ISBN 081011313

My favorite book as a child was a non-linear narrative that included a spinner that directed the story from page to page. I would spin and read for hours; rereading the same pages but in different sequences. Twenty years later, after learning about non-linear, computer-based narratives, I would still marvel at how simple and successful my experience was using what is generally accepted as a non-interactive medium.

experience design nathan shedroff

author: Dr. Lee Mountain
illustrator: Dane Love
copyright 1970 Pictorial Publishers

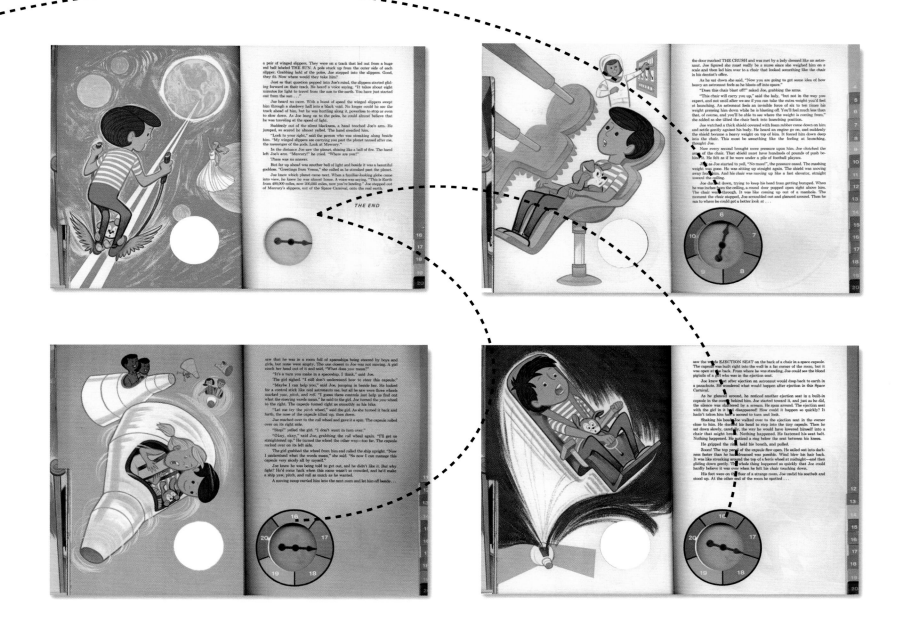

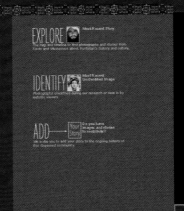

When documentary photographer Susan Meiselas traveled to Iran and Kurdistan, she had no idea she would be so moved by the experience and the people. This site and the accompanying book document her experiences and the stories of the people she met there, as well as stories from others who have a connection with Kurdistan.

While most websites are (by their nature) non-linear, this site excels in its ability to portray a coherent and moving impression of this region no matter which path the visitor takes. One of the most unusual and important features of the site is the ability for people to post unidentified pictures and have the

community members, whether ethnic Kurds, scholars, or travelers, contribute whatever they know about the image. More than oral storytelling, this becomes oral history; in some cases is the first time it's been recorded in text to be shared.

The Story Map in the site presents a geographical navigation to stories while the timeline presents a chronological one. Each story is personal and powerful and deserves to be read at some point. The navigation of this site allows users to read along an interest path, or browse serendipitously.

224 | **akakurdistan**

www.akakurdistan.com

creators: Susan Meiselas
and Picture Perfect: www.picture-perfect.com
date: 2000

experience design nathan shedroff

UNKNOWN IMAGE ARCHIVE

The act of memory unlocks the life within each photograph and it reclaims its place in history.

Every picture tells a story and has another story behind it. Who is in the photograph? Who made it?
Who found it? How did it survive?

Finding a photograph is often like picking up a piece from a jigsaw-puzzle box with the cover missing.
We have the image, but the history of how it came to be is lost.

Can you tell us anything about these images?

SEND us a picture you want
to know more about

Recent Submission

Do you know anything about this image?

Pис. VIII. Наахв.

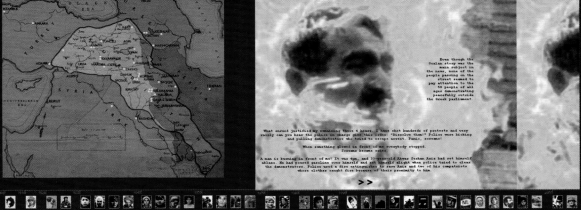

Even though the
Ocalan story was the
main subject in
the news, none of the
people passing on the
street seemed to
pay attention to the
50 people of all
ages demonstrating
peacefully outside
the Greek parliament.

What ensued justified my remaining there 4 hours. I have shot hundreds of protests and very
easily can you hear the police in charge give this order: "Dissolve them!" Police were kicking
and pulling demonstrators who tried to escape arrest. Panic, screams!

When something glowed in front of me everybody stopped.
Screams became cries.

A man is burning in front of me! It was 6pm, and 33-year-old Akvar Serhan Axis had set himself
ablaze. He had poured gasoline over himself and set himself alight when police tried to clear
the demonstrators. Police used a fire extinguisher to save Axis and two of his compatriots
whose clothes caught fire because of their proximity to him.

> >

One of the most creative experiences you can ever know—or witness—is improvisational theater.

These experiences require actors or participants to develop consistent, cogent, and interesting stories without rehearsing. They must do so immediately and, often, using random (and usually incongruous or ridiculous) elements from the audience. Improv comedians additionally must shape the result into something funny.

Improvisational actors (or **interactors** as Keith Johnstone, one of the leading improvisational theater teachers, defines) must deal with numerous random variables and still create something that audiences find satisfying. While interactors require specific training to perform under these circumstances,

most online experiences must perform similarly—often dealing with random inputs from audiences, and creating a meaningful experience in real time.

Improv, by Keith Johnstone
isbn: 0878301178

experience design nathan shedroff

Even designers of real-space experiences can learn from the constraints and practices of improvisers to make more interesting experiences for their audiences and participants.

Improvisers tend to view every action or statement as an opportunity (called an **offer**), and it's critical that they use these opportunities to create more opportunities (rather than blocking them) for each other. While this may sound simple, our normal actions (e.g., conversations) often serve to conclude statements and other actions (and therefore end opportunities). Every action, position, movement, or utterance, not only serve to create characters but also serve to continue the possibility of more action. Good improvisers accept offers made by others and learn that the best offers are not forced but assumed. When you design an experience, rather than concentrate on creating offers for your audience, assume that the things they are already doing (see *User Behavior*, page 116) are offers to you to pick up and use.

Experienced interactors reveal characteristics that are critical to all action and storytelling—not just improvisational acting—which they use to make the experience interesting and meaningful. For example, every movement, inflection, question, phrase, and action implies some kind of status or changing of **status** in one of the characteristics of action and interest. Therefore, experiences that allow changes of status—or even force them—among participants, or the experience and the audience, often create interest and tension. The status level of the system or experience in relation to the user or audience is often critical to how the experience is both understood and considered. Finding appropriate ways of resetting these levels can make the difference between a successful experience and a disastrous one.

Theater Sports is a form of improv practiced all over the world like a sporting event—complete with local, regional, nationals, and even international competitions. Competition is a bit of a strong word for the bout, as the judging is mostly arbitrary and the actors are interested only in the play. If you can imagine tag-team improv, you're pretty close.

Theater Sports has its own set of rules and a collection of formats that mix players into different types of interactions, includes the audience in suggestions (and sometimes action), and varies the experience for all involved. Many troupes around the world teach these forms in classes so that others can join the fun.

If you've never seen improvisational play this fast and frenetic, you might not be able to imagine the experience. Suffice it to say that it is probably the most creative experience you'll ever watch as players try to be quick, funny, and creative, but have only themselves, the audience's reactions, and real-time interactions to rely upon.

Bay Area Theater Sports, director: Kirk Livingston
www.improv.org
www.infotainment.com.au/theatresports

experience design nathan shedroff

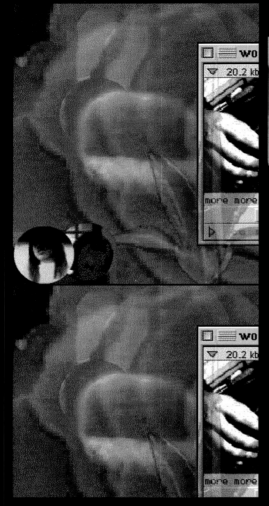
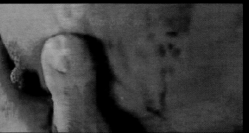

LIVE
Online performances
every Thursday at Midnight in Belgium

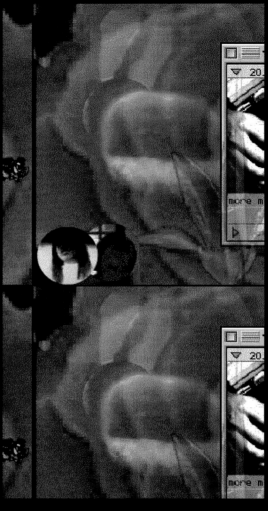

See Wirefire:ReMixed on
the GMI Screen, Leicester Square, London, England
September 18 - October 31, 2000

Please try the
beta random Wirefire generator
Just sit back and let the machines do the work.

Wirefire is a live performance that occurs every Thursday night at midnight from Belgium. Artists Auriea Harvey and Michaël Samin create an improvisational experience using several technologies to present ever-changing and unexpected performances that defy description. There aren't a lot of ways for viewers to participate, but this is a direction that the performances will surely move in the future as technologies continue to develop.

artists: Auriea Harvey and Michaël Samin
date: 2000

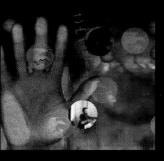

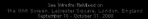

Wirefire

LIVE
Online performances
every Thursday at Midnight in Belgium

(*i*)

(*r*)

See Wirefire:ReMixed on
the GMI Screen, Leicester Square, London, England
September 18 - October 31, 2000

Please try the
beta random Wirefire generator
Just sit back and let the machines do the work.

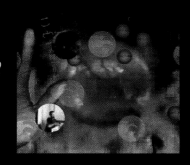
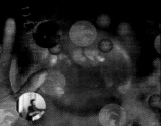
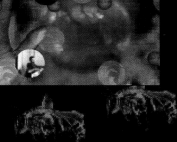

in
Wirefire

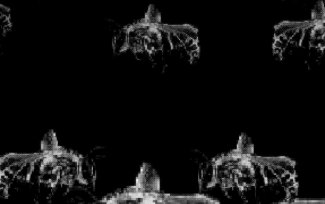

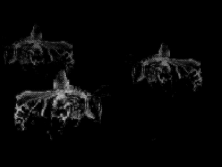

The perspective of the activity or content in an experience can affect how it is understood. Certainly, the point of view of the experience itself can have an affect on how people interact and relate to it. Consider how immersive computer and video games can be with their (mostly) first-person and second-person perspectives. Stories, movies, and theater also draw us in at different levels based on the perspective from which we view them.

Point of view is also relevant to the content and environment of an experience, in terms of the opinion and context that may be embodied in it. For example, an encyclopedia that offers only one opinion or perspective on a subject might not be seen as balanced and authoritative as one that offers several. Experiences that allow the audience to share their experiences can be more satisfying than those that don't, and these viewpoints can deepen understanding.

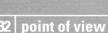
experience design nathan shedroff

At the time of its publication in 1991, the book *Griffin & Sabine* was touted as one of the best book experiences because of its innovative interface, which was tied to a narrative that supported such an unusual construction. The book was written as a correspondence between two people on opposite sides of the world. They communicate in postcards and letters, and the book's story is this conversation made physical. The postcards were printed directly onto the pages (back and front), and the letters were printed and stuffed into envelopes attached to the pages. Readers actually open the envelopes and pull out the letters to read them (and to continue the story), as if they were actually intercepting the communiqués from the two writers.

It would have been easy for this idea to turn into a hollow gimmick. What saved the book and contributed to its success were the points of view of each writer, used as devices of both orientation and mysterious draw.

Griffin & Sabine: An Extraordinary Correspondence
www.chroniclebooks.com

written and illustrated by Nick Bantock, 1991
isbn: 0877017883

experience design nathan shedroff

GRYPHON CARDS
41 YEATS AVENUE
LONDON NW3

JUNE 8

Sabine

I am an honourable man (most of the time),and although I could spend this whole
letter asking you more questions.I will hold back,do the right thing and spill
my life story. But it's going to seem awfully dull compared to your colorful
existence. I see what you mean about getting shy...I feel like climbing under
the carpet.
My mother was Italian-Irish,my father Hungarian-Scottish,Iwas born in Dublin,
and when I was one,we moved to England. As you might guess,I wouldn't know my
nationality if it came up and bit me.
We lived off the Holloway Rd.in darkest London. Our s
house was as dismally predictable as the others in th
outside. The inside was slightly different. Our hous
We owned thousands,nay millions of books. They line
and turned the floor into a maze far more comlex tha
ruled our lives. They were our demi-gods. Occasiona
enactment of The Battle of Britain in the front roo
flying round like a pair of demented fighter planes
at one another. My father would be wearing his trac
and moth-eaten dressing gown and my mother her lem
My entrance would make no difference to their dogf
accidentally(and inevitably)knocked over a pile o
and unite to examine the extent of the damage.
Life continued in this pleasant vein until the da
newspaper van that thoughtlessly mounted the pave
It sounds heartless,but looking back,I would say
because at 15 I was whisked off to live with my
Devon. Vereker was a potter,and the kindest person I've ever met. The firs
thing she asked me was whether I wanted to carry on with school or learn to pot.
No one had ever asked me what I wanted to do before. I would have made her my
idol if she'd let me. Instead,I became her apprentice.
Some people find it hard to move from the big city to the country,but for me it
was a piece of cake. Not only did I fall for Vereker,but also for the town of Totnes.
In that green and pleasant land the cider is so strong you have to hold on to
the bar as you drink it. I spent 3 blissful years in Vereker's house quietly
being instructed on how to use my hands and my eyes. Eventually she convinced

P.T.O.

PAR AVION
航空郵便

SABINE STROHEM
PO BOX ONE F
KATIE
SICMON ISLANDS
SOUTH PACIFIC

Timbuktu - sunrise   Timbuktu - afternoon

Jerusalem - sunrise   Angkor - sunset

BeNowHere is one of the earliest experiments in immersive virtual reality using cinematic techniques instead of computer graphics. The experience allows one person at a time to explore four different sacred sites (Angkor, Jerusalem, Dubrovnik, and Timbuktu) from a central point. These real places are overlapped virtually, and are switched gradually. As well as a geographic change, each place has a temporal change that offers a different view of the site. What makes this project successful is its field-of-vision-filling perspective as much as its cinema-quality resolution.

www.naimark.net

principal designer: Micahel Naimark
first installation: 1995

usalem - sunrise
7 Jerusalem - early evening

rovnik - early evening
Dubrovnik - afternoon +

Extending existing narratives in new ways (taking an existing book and making a movie or theme park ride around it, for example) is an increasingly common design problem fraught with many challenges. One of the most difficult is trying to keep some form of consistency in style and tone, even though the medium may change drastically. Of course, each medium has its own strengths and weaknesses, which result in an evolution of the narrative as it takes new forms. The more complex the new experience, and the more challenges involved in creating it, the greater the risk of the new experience reflecting poorly on the original one.

For these reasons, narrative extensions are frequently unsatisfying as they rarely achieve the expectations of the audience. Too often the narrative themes are used merely as patinas over stereotypical experiences. For example, a roller coaster ride tied to a movie narrative is rarely more than an existing ride painted a new color with new signage. While very small children may be swayed with such pale translations, almost everyone else is sophisticated enough to see through such transformations and regard them as cheap and disappointing.

More complex is the translation of a theme or story into a restaurant (an increasingly common endeavor). Themed restaurants, like the Rain Forest Café, have some good ideas but usually implement them so poorly as to make them caricatures.

The idea of creating new environments and experiences around existing narratives and themes isn't new nor is it inherently wrong. The problem is that most audiences have grown quite sophisticated in their experiences and expectations and will only accept the experience if it feels authentic, inspired, and consistent with the original theme. Experiences that do not make this transition successfully actually run the risk of destroying, or at least hurting, the brand value of the original experience.

experience design nathan shedroff

nathan shedroff **experience design**

Las Vegas Hilton, Las Vegas, NV
www.ds9promenade.com

experience design nathan shedroff

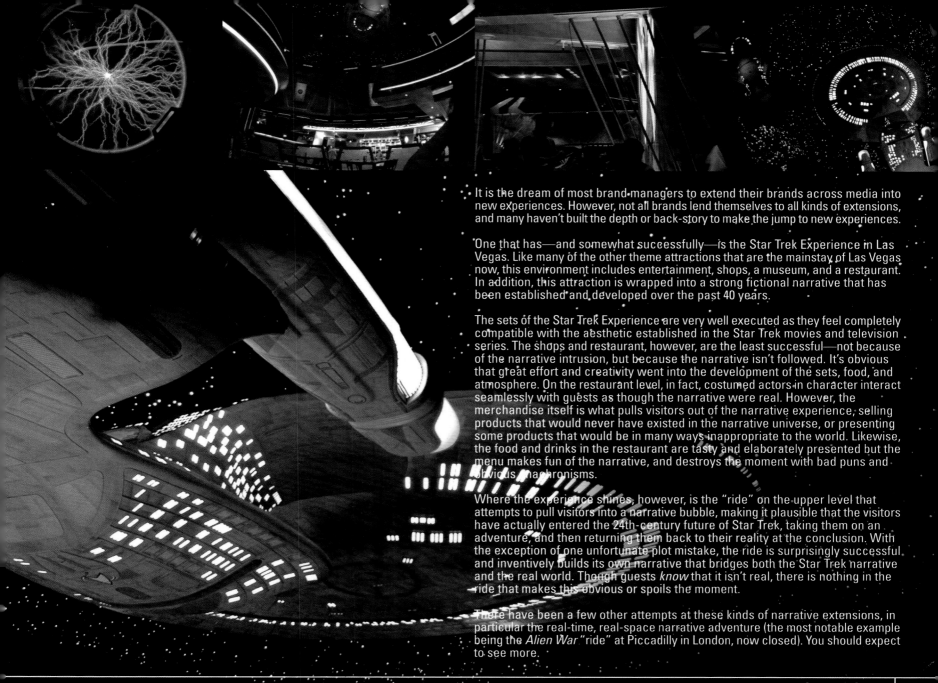

It is the dream of most brand managers to extend their brands across media into new experiences. However, not all brands lend themselves to all kinds of extensions, and many haven't built the depth or back-story to make the jump to new experiences.

One that has—and somewhat successfully—is the Star Trek Experience in Las Vegas. Like many of the other theme attractions that are the mainstay of Las Vegas now, this environment includes entertainment, shops, a museum, and a restaurant. In addition, this attraction is wrapped into a strong fictional narrative that has been established and developed over the past 40 years.

The sets of the Star Trek Experience are very well executed as they feel completely compatible with the aesthetic established in the Star Trek movies and television series. The shops and restaurant, however, are the least successful—not because of the narrative intrusion, but because the narrative isn't followed. It's obvious that great effort and creativity went into the development of the sets, food, and atmosphere. On the restaurant level, in fact, costumed actors in character interact seamlessly with guests as though the narrative were real. However, the merchandise itself is what pulls visitors out of the narrative experience, selling products that would never have existed in the narrative universe, or presenting some products that would be in many ways inappropriate to the world. Likewise, the food and drinks in the restaurant are tasty and elaborately presented but the menu makes fun of the narrative, and destroys the moment with bad puns and obvious anachronisms.

Where the experience shines, however, is the "ride" on the upper level that attempts to pull visitors into a narrative bubble, making it plausible that the visitors have actually entered the 24th-century future of Star Trek, taking them on an adventure, and then returning them back to their reality at the conclusion. With the exception of one unfortunate plot mistake, the ride is surprisingly successful and inventively builds its own narrative that bridges both the Star Trek narrative and the real world. Though guests *know* that it isn't real, there is nothing in the ride that makes this obvious or spoils the moment.

There have been a few other attempts at these kinds of narrative extensions, in particular the real-time, real-space narrative adventure (the most notable example being the *Alien War* "ride" at Piccadilly in London, now closed). You should expect to see more.

Slash fiction is a well-known, and active form of a larger category of audience participation known as fan fiction. While not new (people have been writing their own versions of their favorite television shows, comics, and movies for as long as these media have been successful), the Internet has given rise to a diaspora of fiction as writers share, critique, and compare their stories online.

Most any popular television show, comic routine, or movie has active audiences writing extended narratives; the science fiction genre is definitely one of the most prolific. Fan fiction is a way for audiences to extend the narratives they enjoy into parts of their lives that the media owners either haven't gotten to or dared to approach. Most fan fiction stories are explorations of the storylines, consequences, and characters in the official stories, but some of it takes relationships among the characters to a new level—often explicitly sexual. Slash fiction (the name is derived from the pairing of two or more characters separated by a slash in the title of the story) has been around for decades, starting surreptitiously in published homemade newsletters, and now residing primarily online. It is believed that the first slash fiction originated with the Star Trek characters Captain Kirk and Mr. Spock, who were carrying on a torrid, secret love affair over most of the life of the show—and even today now that the show is in reruns.

Publishers, studios, and other media owners strive for a precarious balance with fan fiction. On the one hand, each story is unofficial and creates alternate, often incompatible realities with ongoing storylines of existing series. On the other, to crack down and try to eliminate these stories would most likely alienate and enrage the very fans who are the most loyal viewers (and therefore customers) of these stories. So far, most studios have simply ignored fan fiction as a harmless addition to the worlds they have created; and, since these stories don't tend to break into the mainstream, it is unlikely that they would somehow compete or ruin the value of the official stories.

for an index of fan fiction, try: members.aol.com/ksnicholas/fanfic/

excerpts from Valery's *Buffy the Vampire Slayer* fiction at www.geocities.com/SoHo/Coffeehouse/1275/fanfiction.html

er German shepherd, Charlie. No tra

le girl has

d in the Sunny Dale area."

you kidding?" Spike aske

ed up to flip the T.V. off. She sighe

her bag and heading out the door on

hool. It's all my fault.

led out of his office when he heard t

nis library open and something hit on

d wooden tables with a bang. He flinc

scraped against

Smell
The olfactory system gre...
as lumps from our limb...
system (before we
developed cerebra...
hemispheres)

Evolution

Very
Yes
10,000
Yes
N...

Memorable
Explosive?
Distinguishable
Precise/Richness
Describable
Always sensing
Distance

Organ

We don't always take time to evaluate our own senses and their roles in our lives. Everything we perceive must enter our minds through one of our senses. This becomes so automatic through our growing years that we easily take our senses for granted. However, a deeper understanding (or at least a re-addressing) of our senses can lead us to innovative experiences that allow us and our audiences to experience new reactions to even the most common experiences.

There's some debate about how many senses we have. Many people regard kinesthetic, electromagnetic, and even psychic senses as viable, important senses; others stick to the traditional five senses: vision, hearing, taste, smell, and touch.

One way to understand how senses can be used in experiences is to build a taxonomy and populate it with your own opinions. Since our senses are such an intimate and immediate part of us, they tend to be difficult to translate to others. This means conducting a more thorough exploration of not only our own reactions to senses, but the reactions of others as well.

One of the best introductions to the power of the different senses is the excellent book, *A Natural History of the Senses*, by Diane Ackerman. It would be a great place to start before exploring and creating your own taxonomy.

A Natural History of the Senses, Diane Ackerman
isbn 0679735666

Vision
Abstract thinking may have evolved from the amount of visual patterns).

Hearing

Taste

Evolved membranes.

Moderate to Far

Moderate to Very Far

3 Small bones

70% of our brain's sense receptors are clustered in the eyes. Rods (contrast) are thin, straight. 125 Million. Cones (color) ~7 Million (three kinds: green, blue, red). Blind spot (no rods or cones). Fovea (only cones in the center of the pack of the eye). This makes it difficult to see at night. Each cones has a direct connect to the brain. 1/10 second transmission time for nerve signal.

Not much
Not as rich
Not easily?
Effective immediately after birth

Yes, affects other senses

Moderate Intimate
Yes, most

the senses

Color: Hue, Lightness, Saturation

Completely synthetically reproduceable

Tone, Timber, Octave, etc.

4: Sweet, Sour, Salt, Bitter

Hot, Cold, Pain, Pressure

Synthetically reproduceable

"25,000 more molecules needed than for smell"

Completely synthetically reproduceable

19-20,000 Hz (cycles/second) at best (almost ten octaves). This decreases with age. Middle C is 256 Hz.

Direct signal/connect to limbic system (intensely emotional section)

Affects levels of hunger, hormones, growth process.

Glutamate, salt, and sun can be detected.

Sense of gravity
Awareness?
Communicat

Ultrasonic and Infrasonic, Infrared and Ultraviolet
Sight
hearing

Categories
Natural/Synth.
Amount needed

Synthetically reproduceable

Musky smells can create a bit hormone changes in

Affects levels of hunger,

Body react

Sun can bleach smell out of things. Weightlessness makes astronauts lose smell.

Absense

Other Phenomena

Smell is one of those poorly understood and often ignored senses—yet it can be one of the most memorable and powerful. Many people speak of memories elicited by a smell long forgotten. Experiences which carefully incorporate smells can add an extra dimension that is both robust and surprising. Shopping mall planners and store owners have long known that different scents can enhance not only the shopping experience (by enticing customers to come inside, or make them feel more comfortable once they are), but can increase sales as well.

Smells act upon a primal part of our brain over which we have little control. Our reactions to smells are more instinctive than any other sense. Pheromones, for example, are said to trigger reactions in our body as well as our mind, often with such subtlety that we're hardly even aware of either the stimulus or the reaction—at least at first. Odors can be subtle as well as overt, and they can trigger a variety of reactions that can elicit complex combinations of feelings.

Most computer manufacturers are still trying to perfect the use of sound and vision and have not shown much interest in creating devices that enable computers to communicate via any other senses. Some have created smell display devices that use cartridges of scent essences to recreate any odor artificially. With only seven component scents, scientists (and now these devices) can recreate any scent humans can smell. Unfortunately (or fortunately), it's not likely that these devices will become standard in consumer computers anytime soon, but they still can be used in specialized experiences quite effectively.

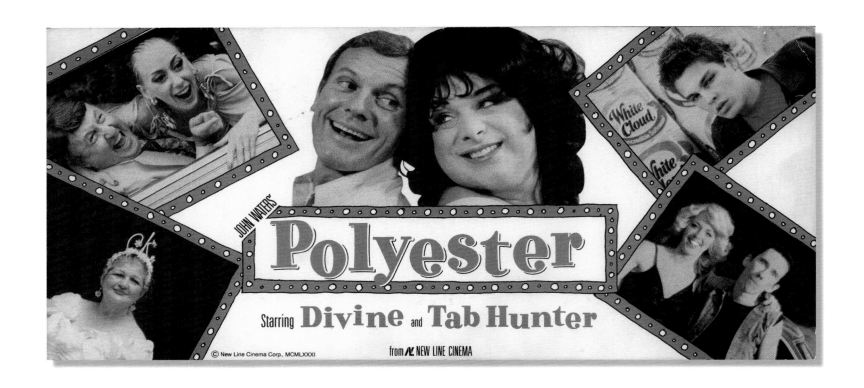

souvenir poster giveaway
movie: *Polyester*

release date: 1981

In 1981, when director John Waters wanted to push the boundaries for his latest movie, he created a way to bring the smells from the story directly to his audience. Since many of his camp movies were reminiscent of the low-tech 1950s, he used Scratch-n-Sniff technology to encase nine different odors onto a card handed to members of the audience with their movie tickets. At specific times in the movie, a number would flash in the corner indicating the odor to be activated and the smell would be associated with the action in the movie—often to humorous and tasteless effect.

Today, researchers experiment with elaborate theaters with sophisticated hidden technology to create a "realistic" experience that includes the sense of smell, but John Waters accomplished all of this much more easily—and for far less money—exposing the audience to the mechanism, and requiring that they play along.

One of the few attempts to create online olfactory experiences, the iSmell is a device that emits scents constructed from seven elemental odors. These scents, in the correct combinations, can simulate any naturally-occurring aroma, allowing a Web page to trigger the device that will create an olfactory experience for any suitably equipped user. Perfume manufacturers are some of the biggest proponents of these devices (which could have a great impact on their ability to sell perfumes and colognes online). Aromatherapists are also interested in the technology for treating people over the Web.

However, there are several potential problems with these devices, aside from the fact that they will be an extra expense that most users will deem unnecessary. Poorly refreshed devices will produce incorrect odors when one or more of their elemental scents are not replenished (much like a color printer). Also, users may find that they aren't happy with many of the smells that are triggered from some websites, and would respond by turning down the volume or even muting it as they would with the speakers in their computers.

It will be a long time, if ever, before these devices are common; until then, there's no way to provide this kind of sensory experience for people.

Smelly Games Aromatherapy **digiSCENTS.** A Revolution of the Senses

Product Testing Scented Websites

Search | Contact | Translations

Inside DigiScents | Products | Developers | Business Scents | Scent City

DigiScents brings the sense of smell to your computer with iSmell digital scent technology.

The SCOOP

FAQ:How Does it work?
The DigiScents Story
Media Coverage
Awards
Events
Scent Science

Business Scents
Research: DigiScents has a strategic research alliance with Procter & Gamble. Distribution: Through our relationship with Real Networks, hundreds of millions of Internet users will be able to experience scents through the RealPlayer.

Products
Learn about our revolutionary iSmell Technology and check out our iSmell Designs.

Developers
Join the 3900 ScentWare developers who are adding smell to games, Web sites and applications. Sign up now!

CARDS & WALLPAPER

FIRST WHIFF

Join the revolution of the senses! Sign up now for the program that keeps you downwind of the latest in Digital Scent Technology and get a chance to demo the iSmell.

Quote of the Week

"It's easy to joke about smelly email, but the customers will be there and so will the money."
- Ed Stear
Gartner Group Analyst

digiSCENTS. POLL

Which scent most strongly reminds you of your childhood?
- Play-Doh
- mimeograph paper
- crayons
- fresh baked cookies
- wet grass
- model glue
- cotton candy
- paste

What's Cookin'

Fragrance industry endorses DigiScents in unprecedented joint strategic investment. Givaudan and Quest invest in iSmell technology.

Translations of our corporate overview are now available (currently in five flavors). Click a flag to download a PDF in your own language.

DigiScents wins the EMMA Award for Technical Innovation! See the Press Release and the flash presentation.

iSmell a winner! Check out our Awards page, featuring awards from Saatchi and Saatchi, RetailVision and CNET! Ahh, the sweet smell of success.

Is your Web site stinky? Read the White Paper for our ScentWare Web Development Kit (WDK).

DigiScents in the news... Forbes.com gets a whiff while Beyond 2000 sniffs digital scent technology all over the gaming space and beyond. Check out our Media Coverage for more!

DigiScents is launching the ScentWare Web Development Kit (WDK)! Go to our Developer's area and apply now to get yours.

 FirstWhiff campaign announced!

Answer a few fun questions and sign up to join the revolution. Be the first to find out

digiSCENTS™ On Location at Burning Man

Stopping to "smell the roses" at the Ol'Fac-Tree

Like smell, taste is often overlooked as an element of designed experiences. There are currently no artificial devices that can recreate taste, but taste is well understood by professional food laboratories. In real-world experiences, food has long been an important consideration, whether for parties, restaurants, theme parks, movies or even theater. However, aside from nicer restaurants and some parties, food is rarely integrated into the experience—even as an enhancement. Rather, food is viewed as nourishment or an accompaniment. Finding ways to integrate tastes into an experience requires more originality than any other sense, but the result can be a stronger, more memorable experience for the participants.

experience design nathan shedroff

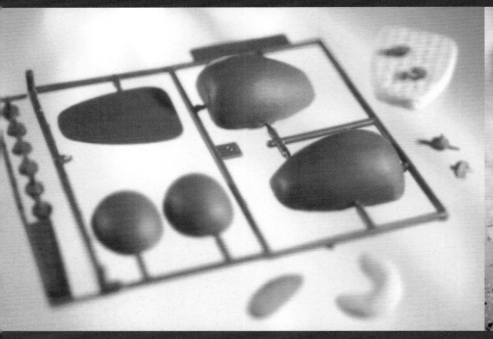

Any meal or food can qualify as an exceptional taste experience but few take the opportunity to be both delicious and conceptually challenging—or even fun. It was exactly this spirit that led IDEO, a global design firm, to sponsor its own internal design competition using chocolate to see where the creativity of its designers could lead them.

The results are as unexpected as they are wonderful. One design was for a set of model-like chocolate parts to be assembled in different forms to create different tastes. Another was chocolate stirrers for coffee and tea. A different design used chocolate bolts and nuts for building dessert assemblies of different flavors and materials. There were flowers and cases for exquisite jells, and lots of new ways of presenting and packaging chocolate.

IDEO chocolate prototypes
www.ideo.com/studies/choco.htm

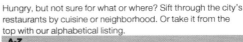

zagat.com℠

CHICAGO AREA   Change locations

Find the right restaurant fast

HOME | SEARCH | BROWSE | LISTS | SHOP | VOTE | JOIN   LOG IN

Welcome
zagat.com delivers the dish on more than 20,000 restaurants, bistros, cafes, coffee-houses, diners, hotels and takeout joints in the city of your choice

SPONSORS

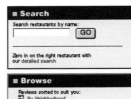

Smart   AMERICAN EXPRESS

On Sale Now!

ZAGAT IN YOUR PALM
The Zagat Restaurant Guide for Connected Organizers
Buy yours today

■ **Search**

Search restaurants by name:

[_____] GO

Zero in on the right restaurant with our detailed search

■ **Browse**

Reviews sorted to suit you:
→ By Neighborhood
→ By Cuisine
→ Alphabetically

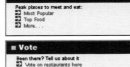

■ **Lists**

Peak places to meet and eat:
→ Most Popular
→ Top Food
→ More...

■ **Vote**

Been there? Tell us about it
→ Vote on restaurants here

BUY ZAGAT BOOKS AT A DISCOUNT
Save up to 25% on our guides, maps and gifts.
Find out how

ON OUR TABLE

Baby, it's cold outside: Top-rated restaurants where the fireplace is as warming as the fare.

Unfit for print: Our reviewers let loose

WEEKLY QUICK VOTE

Which retro dessert deserves a reprise?
○ Chocolate fondue
○ Cookies and milk
○ Floating islands
○ Ice cream sundaes

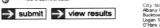

→ submit   → view results

HOME | SEARCH | BROWSE | [ ] | SHOP | VOTE | JOIN

---

zagat.com℠

CHICAGO AREA   Change locations

BY POPULAR VOTE

HOME | SEARCH | BROWSE | LISTS | SHOP | VOTE | JOIN   LOG IN

■ Browse

Hungry, but not sure for what or where? Sift through the city's restaurants by cuisine or neighborhood. Or take it from the top with our alphabetical listing.

A-Z

A B C D E F G H I J K L M N O P Q R S T U V W X Y Z

NEIGHBORHOODS	CUISINE
City North	American (New)
Andersonville/Edgewater	American (Regional)
Lakeview/Wrigleyville	American (Traditional)
Lincoln Park/DePaul	Argentinean
Rogers Park/West Rogers Park	Armenian
Uptown/Lincoln Square	Asian
	Austrian
City Northwest	Bakeries
Albany Park	Bar-B-Q
Bucktown	Brasserie
Logan Square	Cafeterias
O'Hare Area/Edison Park	Cajun/Creole
Wicker Park	Californian
	Caribbean
City South	Chinese
Chinatown	Coffee Shops/Diners
Hyde Park/Kenwood	Continental
Pilsen	Cuban
South Shore	Czech
Southwest Side	Delis/Sandwich Shops
	Dim Sum

■ **Search**

Search restaurants by name:

[_____] GO

Zero in on the right restaurant with our detailed search

■ **Lists**

Peak places to meet and eat:
→ Most Popular
→ Top Food
→ More...

■ **Vote**

Been there? Tell us about it
→ Vote on restaurants here

There are currently no sites that use taste as a part of the Web surfing experience. Of course, there are plenty that use taste as a theme, for example sites about food, cooking, or restaurants. One of the most famous restaurant review websites actually started as a very respected printed guide. What makes Zagat different from other guides is that it focuses solely on restaurants, includes a detailed, multi-part rating system, and uses reviews from restaurant-goers, not just professional reviewers.

Anyone can contribute to the ratings by reviewing restaurants on the Zagat site. Likewise, a vast array of restaurants are reviewed on the site and they can be easily searched and found. The Zagat guide has always been know for finding great restaurants before they become known. Restaurants like *Picholine* in New York's Upper West Side and *Arun* in Chicago (see page 186) aren't where most people look for great local restaurants, but they appeared on the Zagat radar before most others.

---

zagat.com℠ BY POPULAR VOTE
HOME | SEARCH | BROWSE | LISTS | SHOP | VOTE | JOIN   LOG IN
CHICAGO AREA   Change locations

zagat.com℠ BY POPULAR VOTE
HOME | SEARCH | BROWSE | LISTS | SHOP | VOTE | JOIN   LOG IN
CHICAGO AREA   Change locations

▪ Review

F	D	S	C	
26	23	25	VE	VOTE

ARUN'S
Albany Park
4156 N. Kedzie Ave. (bet. Belle Plaine & Berteau Aves.) Chicago, IL, 60618-2440 (773) 539-1909

✉ E-MAIL THIS REVIEW

☑ "Master chef" Arun Sampanthavivat "is an artist" whose "exquisite" presentations of "unique", "top-notch" Thai entice the faithful to this "out-of-the-way" North Side "class act"; ordering is easy because a "breathtaking" $75 tasting menu is the only option, and if some are "alienated" by the "excessive" cost, aficionados agree there's "no better Thai" anywhere -- "and that includes Thailand."

VOTE ON THIS RESTAURANT

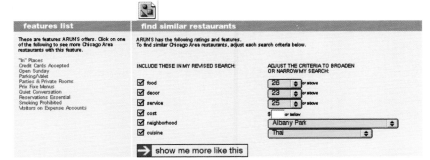

features list	find similar restaurants

These are features ARUN'S offers. Click on one of the following to see more Chicago Area restaurants with this feature.

"In" Places
Credit Cards Accepted
Open Sunday
Parking/Valet
Parties & Private Rooms
Prix Fixe Menus
Quiet Conversation
Reservations Essential
Smoking Prohibited
Visitors on Expense Accounts

ARUN'S has the following ratings and features. To find similar Chicago Area restaurants, adjust each search criteria below.

INCLUDE THESE IN MY REVISED SEARCH: ADJUST THE CRITERIA TO BROADEN OR NARROW MY SEARCH:

☑ food   [26] or above
☑ decor   [23] or above
☑ service   [25] or above
☑ cost   [$] or below
☑ neighborhood [Albany Park]
☑ cuisine   [Thai]

➡ **show me more like this**

▪ Top by Cuisine

Top American (New)	Food Rating
TRU	28
SEASONS	27
CHARLIE TROTTER'S	27
302 WEST	26
COURTRIGHT'S	26

Top American (Regional)	Food Rating
Crofton on Wells	24
Prairie	23
Meritage Cafe & Wine Bar	23
Zinfandel	22
Blackhawk Lodge	20

Top American (Traditional)	Food Rating
SEASONS CAFE	25
Ritz-Carlton Cafe	23
Lawry's The Prime Rib	23
Genesee Depot	21
Plaza Tavern	20

Top Asian	Food Rating
Yoshi's Cafe	23
Le Colonial	23
Chinoiserie	21
Red Light	20
LuLu's Dim Sum & Then Sum	20

Top Bar-B-Q	Food Rating

The sense of touch is much more prevalent in experiences because it is easier to address, as every experience requires us to touch something. Even personal computers use a mouse to control the cursor on the screen. While most computer programs make little or no use of this fact, the contact is still there. There are plenty of alternative mice and other input devices that create touch displays for users, transferring information via our hands. This haptic research has been in development for a few decades, yet there are few commercial examples that have been even remotely successful.

More common are physical experiences that make touch a part of the encounter. Petting zoos and touch pools in aquariums, for example, rely mainly on introducing touch to a learning experience that conventionally would use only sight.

Touch is an awkward sense for most people because we are not accustomed to dealing with only touch, and our other senses, particularly sight, are so much more dominant in our perceptions. Experiences in which we cannot see or hear and only have our hands to guide us are interesting, but frustrating for all but those people who have already lost their sight and have spent time learning to do without. Touch is also inherently intimate, although not as intimate as taste; therefore touch experiences are often uncomfortable for us when inappropriate. Comfort and familiarity have a lot to do with creating this sense of appropriate touch, and these feelings can change quickly and dynamically based on the topic, purpose, and parts of the body involved.

experience design nathan shedroff

nathan shedroff **experience design**

The ability to convey touch—especially to transmit it—has been ignored for most of the computer age. Because touch is one of our most important intimate sensations, it can create some controversy or feelings of discomfort when used as part of an electronic experience. Surely the ridiculous claims of cyberdildonics (artificial sensation devices for networked sex) make enough people queasy at just the thought of a device-mediated touch.

However, IDEO, a global design firm, has built a prototype that shows how wonderful human touch can be by using advanced technologies such as wireless networks.

The Kiss Communicator comes as a pair of devices that are linked only to each other via a wireless network (pick one: cellular, spread-spectrum, it doesn't matter). When one device is activated, perhaps by a gentle blowing across its top or a caress of the surface, the message is sent to the other device where it is received and "played" as a warming of the device and a gentle glow. Though the device doesn't exactly replicate a genuine touch, the symbolic meaning is clearly communicated.

prototype from IDEO

experience design nathan shedroff

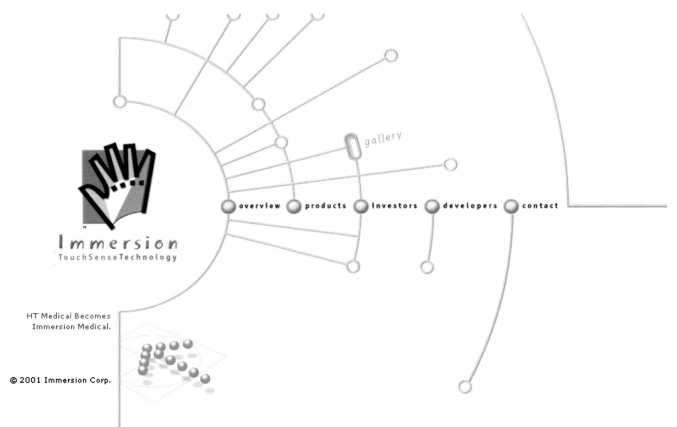

Immersion
TouchSenseTechnology

HT Medical Becomes
Immersion Medical.

© 2001 Immersion Corp.

gallery

overview   products   investors   developers   contact

Immersion is a company that produces software patches to existing applications so that touch can be an added sense when using the applications. TouchSense is Immersion's software that allows a force-feedback mouse or joystick to push back against the user's hand to create the sensation of tactility where previously there was none. Imagine your cursor slipping into the groove of a scroll bar for the first time. Instead of merely a flat, smooth slide, the mouse actually bounces on the edges as if the 3D shading was physical. While this is hardly a necessity for most people, it does add a new dimension and a more physical experience to what is usually an abstract and virtual experience. Also, visually impaired users can now get more of a sense of what is happening on a computer screen by adding sound cues.

TouchSense requires a special mouse or joystick but these are only slightly more expensive now than the best non-tactile mice. Avid gaming fans can enhance their game play with these devices as they respond to the textures and situations encountered in the games. Other entertainment opportunities are also being explored but it may be professional uses such as medical simulations, product development, 3D modeling, and manufacturing where advances will appear first.

Immersion Corporation
www.immersion.com

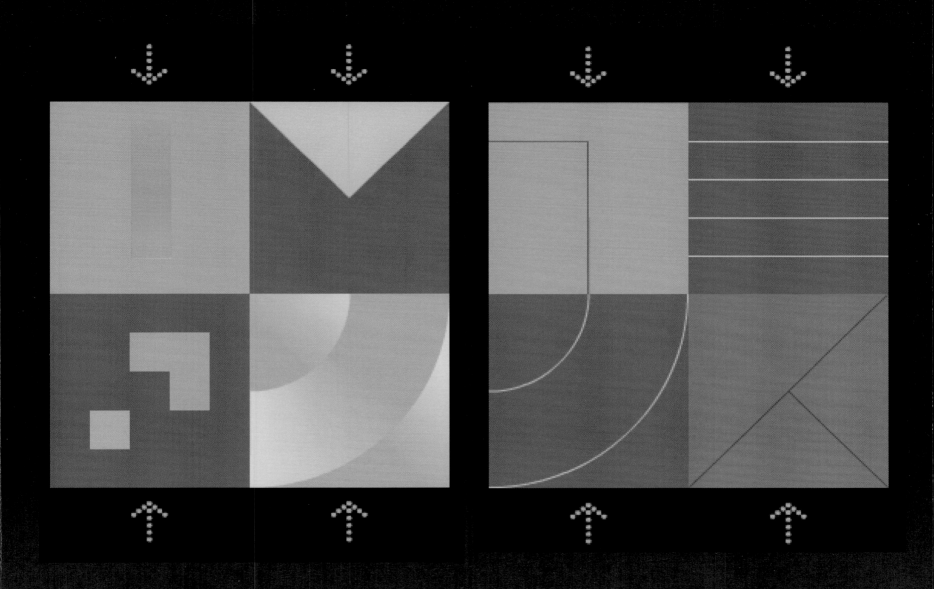

Sound is one of the most sophisticated senses we have since we regularly experiment and create innovative displays specifically for our ears. From the time we are very small, our entire world is filled with sounds targeted at stimulating or affecting our behavior. We grow to expect pleasure or annoyance at surprising new sounds as well as established ones.

Like vision, sight is a reaction to certain frequencies of electromagnetic energy, which includes light, x-rays, and microwaves, our ears are able to interpret. There are certainly sounds (**ultrasonic**) most human ears cannot pick up that other animals (like dogs) can hear routinely.

Sound comes in a variety of forms—whether voice, music, sound effects, or other forms of communication—and they can be incredibly complex, rich, and often subtle. It is the primary way most of us receive data, information, and knowledge. While we encounter much of these through reading, still, and increasingly, the majority of our understanding comes from hearing. Even visual media, such as television and movies, deliver the majority of information through speech and other sounds, and the majority of emotions through music. This isn't to say that there aren't compelling visuals that stimulate our emotions or convey information. However, try turning off the sound on the television and interpret what is happening. You'll most likely find it's more difficult than simply turning off the picture and keeping the sound (essentially, radio).

nathan shedroff experience design

Creating experimental audio events often requires sophisticated environments configured to surround an audience with speakers. The Audium is exactly this kind of experience. For over 20 years, Stan Shaff and Doug McEachern have created and maintained this audio sculpture space in San Francisco.

The performance takes place in total darkness and the 50-person audience is surrounded by 169 speakers, which are controlled using only analog technology. Ultimately, what the Audium proves is that the environment itself isn't nearly as important as the content itself. Some of the Audium's score is more reminiscent of 70s rock opera and a tired computer synthesizer, while other parts are adept transformations of audio space by juxtaposing different sonic environments, and then morphing the two. Audium's performance succeeds best when using natural sounds and recordings.

| **audium**

1616 Bush Street, San Francisco, CA 94109
TEL 415 771 1616
www.audium.org

creators: Stan Shaff and Doug McEachern
date opened: 1975

experience design nathan shedroff

enter

YOU WILL NEED THE FLASH4 PLUG-IN TO VIEW THIS SITE
IF YOU DON'T HAVE IT, PLEASE DOWNLOAD IT BY CLICKING HERE

g to see at this site, only sounds to hear. In fact, it's a blank
ith an interactive soundtrack that leads you through a sequence
sounds themselves aren't the focus, the process is. In fact, it's
eat experiment in audio cues. It's so interesting, in fact, that
here's nothing to see and you quickly realize that the soundtrack,
ng a narrative, has completely engrossed you without a single

nathan shedroff **experience design**

Sight is one of our most precious senses. We use it to guide ourselves and interact with others, to orient ourselves in our world, and to interact with nature. Sight allows nature to convey a great deal of data about itself (weather, time of day, and so on) and we use this data in subtle and often unconscious ways.

Of course, as we experience it, vision is only a small slice of the electromagnetic spectrum and it doesn't even encompass all of the spectrum that is visible. The slice of light that our eyes can see includes a seemingly endless spectrum of **colors** moving from red to violet. Outside of this range, however, light still exists and some animals and many machines can see in these ranges. Bees and other insects can see in the **ultraviolet** and this helps them distinguish among flowers. **Infrared** light is used in most small wireless devices like remote controls. It is also used in night-vision equipment because it allows us to distinguish heat sources (like bodies) and, thus, "see" in the dark.

Machines use a variety of vision types to perform their tasks. Some use the visible (to us) spectrum, others make use of infrared—either exclusively or to augment the visible spectrum. It is one of the dreams of robot creators to construct a machine that appears to see and understand the things we do so that it can act on these the way we do.

Because of how our eyesight works, when we design, it is often more important to make our designs work first in grayscale before color as they then will be clearer and easier for an audience to read (whether human or machine). Black-and -white copiers, for example, see color based on their light values and have a hard time distinguishing light blue from white or dark red from black. Other grayscale sensors will, most likely, have the same problems even though the difference in colors are clear to us.

experience design nathan shedroff

Human vision is composed of small rods and cones in our eyes which are sensitive to the spectrum of visible light. In fact, the rods are sensitive to the amount of light (allowing us to distinguish light from dark), and the cones are sensitive to frequency of light (allowing us to distinguish colors). We have many more rods than cones, which means that we actually see the amount of light (white, black, and grays) before we see color. While rods give us more and stronger light information, cones enable us to see detail more sharply. Because cones are more prevalent than rods in the fovea (an area at the center of our field of vision), we don't perceive any difference in our environment even though we aren't seeing in the same way from our center of focus to our peripheral vision.

Our eyes are also attuned to seeing movement, as are most predatory animals (for example cats and birds). This means that experiences that require us to discern small subtle differences or movements are easier for us than distinguishing detail in large, broad movements.

Knowing how the eye sees (and how machines perceive light) can lead us to new experiences that exploit or play with these phenomena in novel ways.

nathan shedroff **experience design**

One of the media controversies in 2000 was a mini-tempest over infrared vision features in SONY video cameras. The fury was over the fact that infrared video (and photos, for that matter) can often make it appear as if you are seeing through clothing. While this isn't really the x-ray vision 1950s advertisers promised (the camera can't actually see visual spectrum light through clothing or any other materials), infrared vision used in the daytime (as opposed to night viewing, which is common in the military) does have the *appearance* of looking at someone's naked silhouette.

The truth is that all CCDs (Charged Coupled Devices are the light-sensing part of an electronic camera) are sensitive to infrared light, however, only SONY products have bothered to enable this part of the spectrum to be recorded. After the controversy arose, SONY disabled the feature for daytime use (a light sensor turns off the feature if it senses daylight), but it's easily defeated by simply covering the sensor.

Rather than concentrating on the *faux* nefarious use, instead we should be experimenting with a new way of seeing and recording images. Many insects and animals can be viewed in the infrared spectrum, and for the first time humans can inexpensively record them in their environments. The experience of seeing in a new way should be an opportunity to see what is new to us.

NightShot™ Infrared vision system available on some SONY video cameras

nathan shedroff **experience design**

While not strictly an online experience (it can be used if it is not connected to a network), EarthBrowser is at its best when it is able to download real-time pictures from weather satellites, as well as other geographical and weather data of the Earth. With these photos, you are able to construct a near real-time representation of the Earth, spinning on your computer.

It is quite a feat to bring such an important and special image to people directly. Imagine having a live view of the Earth rotating on your screen, available at any time. This is the beginning of a dream many have had—not only of being able to see something never before possible but as a way of organizing their personal world and orienting it to the larger world in which we live.

Lunar Software
www.earthbrowser.com

creator: Matthew Giger

experience design nathan shedroff

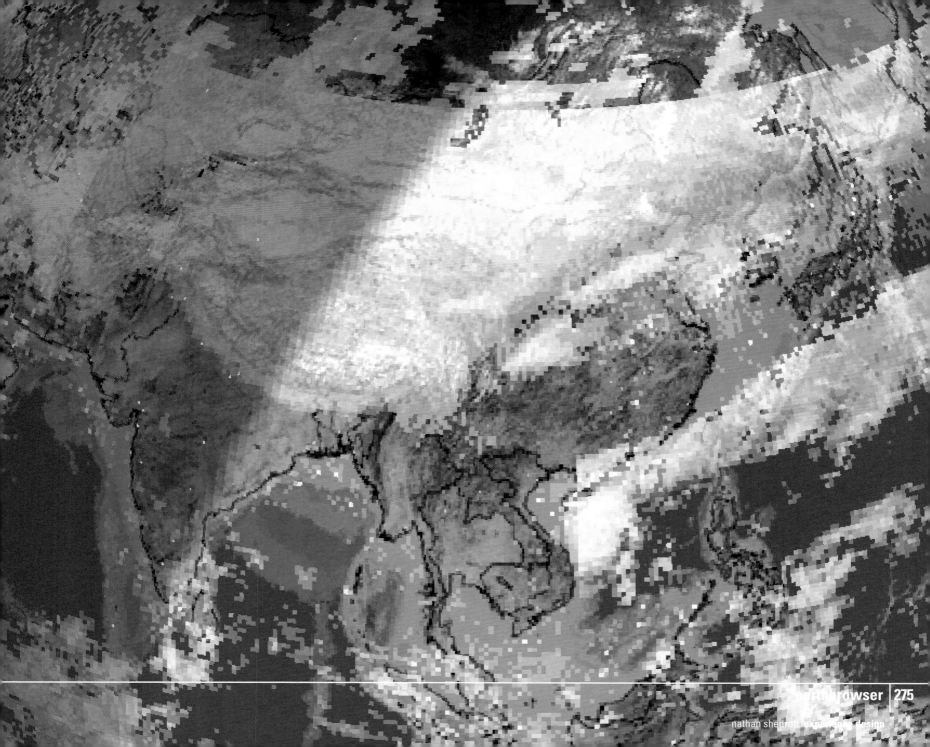

nathan shedroff experience design

Sensorial design is merely a catch-all phrase for the design disciplines which create experiences that interact directly with our senses. These include traditional design disciplines (for example, graphic design), writing, and media design disciplines (such as videography and animation). Each of these has a complex history and numerous principles. Each also has a myriad of books, courses, degrees, seminars, and other materials that cover them in more depth than we can here. However, it's important to, at least, get a sense of the diversity and the relationships among these disciplines, and to recognize their relative strengths and weaknesses in communicating and in experience creation.

experience design nathan shedroff

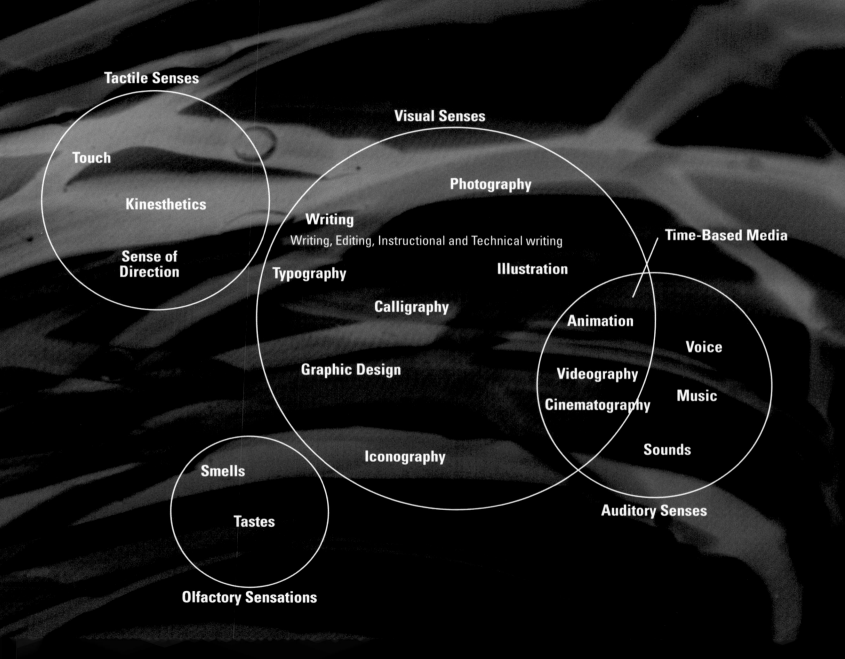

While visual design traditionally has been concerned with appearance, it can communicate more than mere beauty; it can convey meaning in any decision that builds on visual appearance. In particular, graphic and illustrative **styles** convey cultural cues that help people indentify designs with different values. Though most designers make choices based on what they prefer or what "looks nice" (and, unfortunately, are taught to), the best designers choose each element of visual design, including typography, color, layout, and photography based on how they want to communicate the goals and the message to the intended audience. The overall design must still feel consistent and clear, and it should certainly be handsome, but great designs communicate first and are beautiful second. Likewise, these designs tend to transcend trends more readily since they are built upon a more meaningful and less stylish foundation.

Style is difficult to categorize or characterize because different elements will communicate different meanings to different people. Few people have a well-educated understanding of design or a high visual literacy. However, this isn't their fault as much as it's merely a missed opportunity in our society. This makes it more challenging for designers to construct experience. As long as designers focus on their audiences and not themselves, they will communicate more successfully.

Cirque du Soleil® is more theater than even circus, and where it does overlap with the stereotype of a circus, it is so advanced and elaborate that it seems wholly new and magical. *Mystère*,® one of its latest productions, makes a standard circus seem more like a series of athletic events than the feats of strength and agility, beauty, and mystery that the Cirque du Soleil performers create. One of the important ways they do this is by creating narratives around the acts, and then weaving them throughout the evening with recurring characters. They include the audience on occasion, first making them the butt of the joke, then including them as fellow performers.

Mystère, and most of the Cirque du Soleil productions, are not light-hearted, happy, silly shows. More often than not, they are dark, brooding, emotional, and intense productions.

All interaction aside, the Cirque du Soleil productions are also known for their incredible beauty. Their particular mix of lighting, set design, costumes, and music create a seamless experience that transforms the story and actors into something other-worldly and fantastic. Afterward, the performance seems more like a dream than a memory, and the translucent, multi-dimensional nature of the design, imagery, and activity can take much of the credit.

Cirque du Soleil
http://www.cirquedusoleil.com/en/piste/mystere.html

Aerial High Bar act from *Mystère*
costumes: Dominique Lemieux

nathan shedroff **experience design**

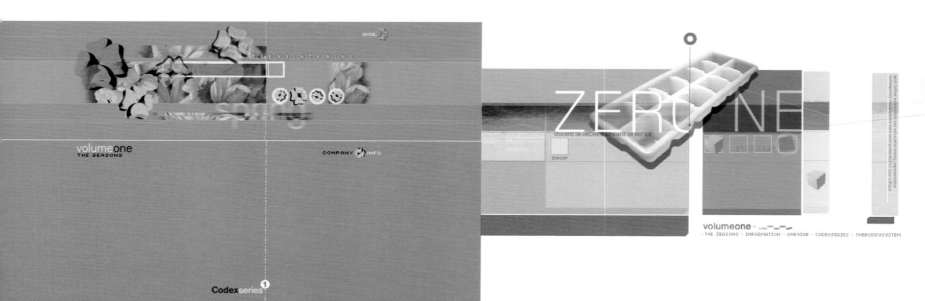

For several years, Matt Owens has been leading the online industry in sophisticated and original visual design. His site, Volume One, changes its appearance every three months but the level of quality never wavers. Throughout the past four years the designs have changed on regular intervals, exploring styles ranging from simple to complex, from stark to colorful, and often incorporating animation and transparency.

When Volume One first launched, it heralded a level of design that seemed more reminiscent of print than of websites. Since then, online design has almost unilaterally improved but Matt Owens and associate Warren Corbitt still manage to delight their audiences by differentiating themselves through visual design.

www.volumeone.com

creators: Matt Owens and Warren Corbitt
site launched Spring 1997

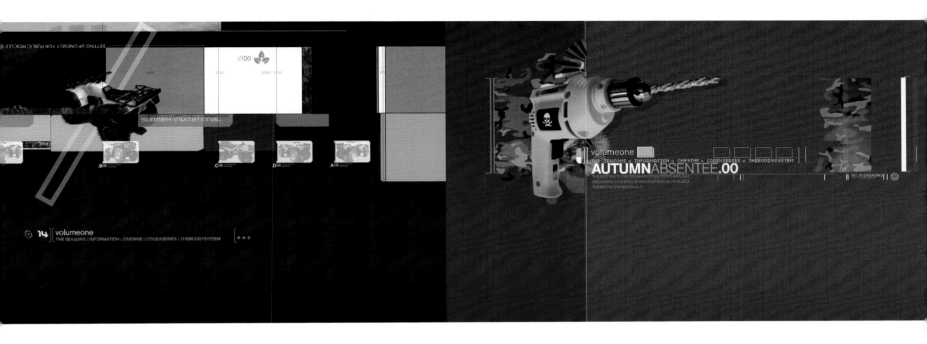

volumeone

AUTUMNABSENTEE.00

nathan shedroff **experience design**

Most designers of digital experiences dream of building an experience so immersive that the participants regard it as all-encompassing and forget that the experience may be artificial. This is usually accomplished through virtual reality technologies like goggles displaying computer-generated imagery, and headphones often supplying 3D sound. What most designers of these systems fail to understand is that immersive experiences surround us in the real world, and we have well-developed expectations for such experiences. Indeed, our sense of reality is so sensorially stimulating that it's nearly impossible to design an experience that could even approach the immersiveness of reality.

This being the case, it's often a better strategy to build experiences that cannot exist in reality and, therefore, sidetrack our senses with novelty and originality rather than simulating reality as we have become accustomed to experiencing it. These are the approaches that often make us forget that we are not in our normal reality.

Immersion does, however, require more than mere novelty. To be an immersive experience (as opposed to just an engrossing one), it needs to stimulate—if not redirect our attention on—our major senses (usually being vision and hearing). Films do this regularly without using any unfamiliar technology. When the story is interesting and the sound and visions capturing, we fall into the experience with rapt attention for that time. Most people can remember instances where they fall out of such experiences (suddenly remembering they're in a theater, or noticing the people or environment around them). This

might be due to the noises of those around us or a disruption in the environment. However, it could result just as easily from a disruption in the narrative, such as anachronistic development or a lapse in consistency or believability.

Thus, immersion is as much a result of the narrative's ability to capture and hold our attention as it is the visuals, audio, or other sensory displays that divert our attention toward the experience. In fact, a good story (whether told aloud or read in a book) can more often immerse us in another world than the most advanced technological systems.

Immersive experiments tend to favor the technological—that is, more often than not, more attention is paid to the technological tricks of diverting our attention—than in building a cognitively interesting and consistent experience. These technological tricks usually aim at stimulating our senses in novel ways or building elaborate environments that enclose us.

Theater has always experimented with ways to immerse the audience. The theater tends to create more cognitively cohesive experiences and to experiment with non-digital ways to immerse people. Theater often mixes elements like live actors, sets, recorded and live music, lighting, interaction, sets, and rehearsal more than its digital counterparts. It tends to focus less on interactivity and meaning and more on elaborate, expensive, and digitally-prejudiced solutions to problems—often solving problems much easier and more elegantly—and less disruptively—than with computers.

experience design nathan shedroff

nathan shedroff **experience design**

One of the most exciting additions to the Star Trek universe was the Holodeck from *Star Trek: The Next Generation.* It's a multi-purpose, immersive, and interactive technology that allows people, places, climate, and sensations to be created from "thin air." This is probably the most recognizable innovation of Star Trek, and it has become an archetypal experience, as well as the pinnacle of immersive spaces. Naturally, this is a fantasy and the technology to create such an experience is not likely to be developed—certainly not for a very long time.

However, Debra Solomon, an artist who lives and works in Amsterdam has taken this concept and insinuated it into her online and offline installations. More than merely a simulation space, the-living has staged events, demonstrations, and four-day improvisations in the various spaces she has constructed. Past installations switched between the Holodeck's recognizable grid lines (made almost psychedelic with new surfaces) and sets of her creation. Visitors were presented an environment that was both familiar and fantastic, recognizable and disorienting, determined and still open to interpretation.

Her latest installation, the artist-astronaut project, not only creates a virtual environment from a physical one, but there is a narrative thread on which participants can create a future scenario concerning artists becoming astronauts. The mission of these astronauts was to interpret the experience and opportunities of space for the rest of us. The participants were hypnotized with a constructed, shared history outlining major events, and then were awakened in the year 2035 when they received awards for their achievements as artist-astronauts. The participants then created the rest of the story within this state and described their roles and achievements, outlining what they had accomplished and what they learned from their experiences. The installation was a simulation in both space and story as well as in time.

One outcome of this project has been the creation of an independent agency to integrate artists into the European space program, making the artist-astronaut installation a test simulation in yet another form.

www.the-living.org/artist-astronaut

artist: Debra Solomon
date: 1999 and continuing

experience design nathan shedroff

nathan shedroff **experience design**

Placeholder is one of the most human, innovative, and successful experiments in virtual reality. Its innovation is in participant movement and control within a system. In particular, people have not one but two hand controls (with corresponding representations, since we have two hands) that enable them to grasp things. Another innovation is that rather than pointing one's fingers into a gun-like shape and pulling the imaginary trigger as a way of flying through the virtual space, one does something much more natural and representational, they flap their arms like a bird.

Placeholder has several specialized environments, each offering different objects to play with, and several characters that participants can "capture" and become. When merged with one of the characters, participants temporarily take on their perceptions (for example, a change in visual perception), and their mode of movement (such as a slithering snake). Placeholder is one of the only VR environments that allow participants to change basic perceptions and explore life—or, at least, activity—through these other perspectives.

www.tauzero.com/Brenda_Laurel/Severed_Heads/CGQ_Placeholder.html
principal creator: Brenda Laurel
date launched: 1998

experience design nathan shedroff

Time and motion are the underpinnings of animation and video. Though we're familiar with time and movement, we are usually unfamiliar with the design details used to craft an experience using animation and video. As with all other computer-enabled disciplines, novices quickly begin to appreciate that creating a satisfying design requires a wealth of time, experience, and knowledge—more than just access to a low-cost, powerful system for developing animation or editing video.

As with immersion, creating satisfying animation or video has as much to do with the cognitive or narrative solution as it does with the actual imagery. Experienced animators, for example, understand that the illusion of motion must be carefully created not just from slight changes from scene to scene but with characters and objects specifically drawn to imply motion and action. Likewise, cinematographers know that planned editing from scene to scene and view to view is almost as critical as the action caught by the camera.

What differentiates successful video and animation is the care and appropriateness in illustrating motion and using the edits as a player in the story, which is just as important as lighting, acting, and costumes.

Another factor of time is in pacing; and this, like motion, is an element as critical as the subject matter itself. Alfred Hitchcock, for example, used timing and pacing in a film to create suspense in ways previously not conceived. Music videos use time and motion to create moods and influence emotions.

There is a visual literacy to timing, editing, and motion that we learn through experience. By the time we're young adults, we often take for granted the visual cues employed to tell a story—often used to tell it more efficiently. Just as we take for granted the act of talking to another person through a plastic, impersonal device like the telephone (something that babies must learn); so, too, do we take for granted the visual devices we've become accustomed to in the telling of stories on screen, such as close-ups, jump-cuts, establishing shots, and speed lines.

Theater directors are always looking for innovative ways of involving their audiences, and new ways of creating an experience. Most have never thought to use or move through the space above their audience. At De La Guarda, there is no stage, only the space hanging above the audience, the walls, and the same floor where the audience stands. The performance begins with the audience standing shoulder-to-shoulder in a small room with a low ceiling. As the performance starts, the silhouettes of the performers move across the ceiling as the audience realizes that it is translucent. The ceiling then becomes a canvas of light, paint, objects, and people until it is finally punctured by the performers and, ultimately, destroyed—revealing a large, cavernous space above the audience.

This space is then a new kind of canvas that the performers hang, spin, and dance within (as well as on the walls) while creating narratives with movement and light. The performance is so captivating that the audience barely notices—if at all—crew and other performers moving into the crowd to begin new phases of the show. Soon, and for the duration of the production, the audience is dancing furiously along with the performers, interacting with them on the floor—and in the air.

Daryl Roth Theater, New York City, NY
Rio Casino Hotel, Las Vegas, NV
www.delaguarda.com

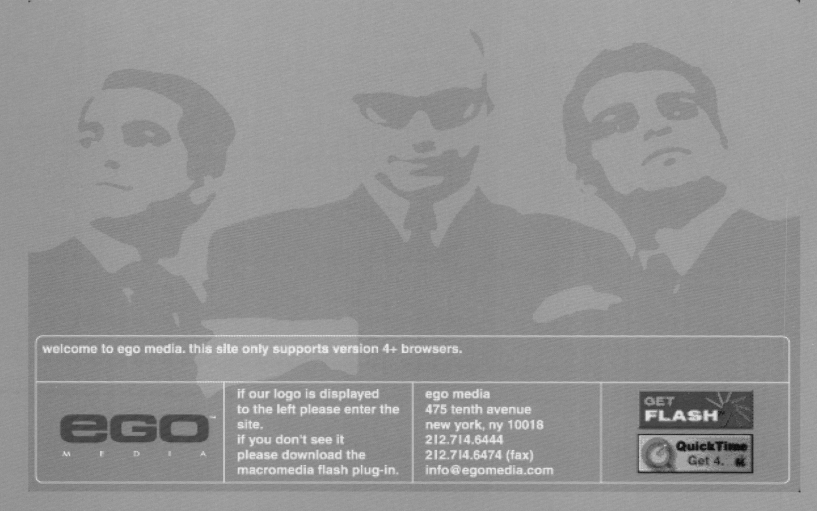

welcome to ego media. this site only supports version 4+ browsers.

| | if our logo is displayed to the left please enter the site. if you don't see it please download the macromedia flash plug-in. | ego media 475 tenth avenue new york, ny 10018 212.714.6444 212.714.6474 (fax) info@egomedia.com | GET FLASH™ QuickTime Get 4. |

Animation is difficult to do well in a medium with severe bandwidth problems. Egomedia has carefully crafted an experience that successfully keeps an audience's attention, yet it spools seamlessly on the slowest common connections. One way they accomplish this is through minimal use of elements, and choosing a particular visual style that allows for fast performance. This minimal, simplified style uses a posterized-like effect to render people and movement with little detail or color variation. Any visual depth is accomplished merely through scale of figure over the ground. The "retro" style is reminiscent of the 1960s and helps add interest since it creates a special, and now seldom-seen appearance.

music on

ego   work   lab

:: menu

:: main

mission

process

services

careers

partners

contact

ego agents

EGO AGENTS

raymond roubeni
chief ego

proceed

headlines

10/13/00 Astoria Federal Savings Selects Ego Media for Online Branding
07/30/00 ORB Inc. Selects Ego Media for New Website
07/27/00 Ego Media Wins Pixie Award for Best Web Design
07/20/00 Ego Media Joins Ogilvy Interactive Consortium
07/19/00 Ego Media to Design DetterbeckWider Website
07/17/00 Ego Media Redesigns KPNQwest Site in Flash and HTML
04/07/00 Ego Media Launches Flash and HTML Sites for Intellispace
03/03/00 HMG Worldwide Chooses Ego Media for Re-branding
09/28/99 HMG Worldwide Acquires Ego Media

the ego drink of the month

every month we'll feature an exotic drink

exit site

Symbols can be used as a way of collapsing information into a smaller form. They also can be used as a mnemonic for the original information. Symbols can demonstrate or illustrate a process or identify something. What makes symbols powerful is their ability to transmit meaning under difficult circumstances—especially across linguistic and language barriers. However, just because something is a symbol, doesn't mean it automatically possesses the ability to communicate to everyone. Cultural differences make symbol, icon, and logo design even more risky and dangerous since they rely on much more shared context than other forms of communication. Not understanding the full range of meaning within a culture often causes designers to design symbols that not only fail to communicate what is intended, but often communicate false or defamatory information.

Where symbolism excels is when it is paired with other forms of communication (like a diagram or text label). This allows symbols to be more easily recognized and remembered (and used as a true mnemonic device). This is especially important for complex or critical information. Expecting a symbol or icon to function clearly on its own when representing new information or communicating to novices is probably asking too much of a symbol.

Abstraction is also a difficult concept to communicate because abstract concepts, inherently, are more open to judgment, experience, and interpretation. Conceptual information relies heavily on personal contexts. However, when done well, this is precisely why abstraction can be so powerful; it can pull into an experience otherwise difficult or unconnected meanings that lend to a richer, more complex experience. This is what great art does. These wider connections can lead to more emotional, personal, and surprising experiences that leave us more satisfied than representational experiences that simply "stick to the facts."

Disney's *The Lion King* is one of the most elaborate and beautiful spectacles of theater. The musical production uses many untraditional theatrical techniques to tell the story of the lion cub, Simba. Director Julie Taymor uses the techniques of the Thai shadow puppets, Bunraku puppetry, and stark symbolism, which are more reminiscent of experimental theater, to create moods and convey an animal's characteristics, as well as to advance the story.

One of the first decisions Taymor made was not to conceal the actors in animal costumes. In fact, in most cases, the actors who portray animal characters (and those who act more as puppeteers) are revealed, making the costume design all the more radical and wonderful. When the full cast assembles on the stage at both the beginning and end of the production, the magnificence of the costumes and the way the actors and puppets move is astounding.

| **the lion king**

experience design nathan shedroff

New Amsterdam Theater, New York City, NY
Pantages Theater, Los Angeles, CA
Lyceum Theater, London, England

director and chief designer: Julie Taymor
date opened: 1993 (NYC)
www.disney.co.uk/MusicalTheatre/TheLionKing/

Elsewhere in the musical, shadow puppets are used to connect the scenes in a natural bridge while the stage is reset (behind curtains) for the next scene. Not only is this form of storytelling economical, it also serves to add variety and a change in perspective for an audience that is more familiar with the changes of perspective and scale in television and movies than in theater (where, for example, close-ups are impossible).

Perhaps the most effective and symbolic storytelling comes at the moment in the story when the passing of time brings a severe drought. Rather than a voice-over explaining the amount of time passing and how bad the drought has become (a common technique), the curtains open on a large light blue circle of cloth covering the stage that is slowly pulled through a hole in the center of the stage. The metaphor is clear and powerful—and beautiful—without being overstated or obvious.

photographs: Joan Marcus

the lion king |

nathan shedroff **experience design**

Interface Design...

Books

The Art of Human-Computer Interface Design, Brenda Laurel, editor, Addison-Wesley, 1990, ISBN 0201517973.

Apple Human Interface Guidelines: The Apple Desktop Interface, Apple Computer, Inc., Addison-Wesley, 1988, ISBN 0201177536.

The Design of Everyday Things, D.A. Norman, Basic Books, 1988, ISBN 0465067093.

A Natural History of the Senses, Diane Ackerman, Vintage Books, 1991, ISBN 0679735666.

The Meaning of Things: Domestic Symbols and the Self, Mihaly Csikszentmihalyi and Eugene Rochberg-Halton, Cambridge University Press, 1981, ISBN 052128774X.

Bringing Design to Software, Terry Winograd, editor, et al., Addison-Wesley, 1996, ISBN 0201854910.

Interface Culture, Steven A. Johnson, Harper San Francisco, 1997, ISBN 0465036805.

Online Articles

IBM Ease of Use Guidelines: www.ibm.com/ibm/easy/design/lower/f020200.html

IBM RealPlaces Guidelines: Elements for Creating 3D User Environments: www.ibm.com/ibm/hci/guidelines/design/3d

Organizations

ACM Multimedia, www.acm.org/sigmm

SHORE: University of Maryland Student HCI Online Research Experiments, www.otal.umd.edu/SHORE

SIGCHI (the Special Interest Group in Computer Human Interface issues of the Association of Computing Machinery) www.acm.org/sigchi

SIGGRAPH (the Special Interest Group in Computer Graphics of the Association of Computing Machinery), www.acm.org/siggraph

Conferences

CHI, www.acm.org/sigchi
SIGGRAPH, www.acm.org/siggraph

News

ACM **interactions** *Magazine,* www.acm.org/interactions
The SIGCHI Bulletin, www.acm.org/sigchi/bulletin

Other Resources

ACM Online Digital Library www.acm.org/dl
HCI Index is.twi.tudelft.nl/hci
HCI Resources usableweb.com

Information Design...

Books

Information Design, Robert Jacobson, Ph.D., Editor, MIT Press, 1999, ISBN 026210069X.

Information Architects, Richard Saul Wurman, Watson-Guptill Publishers, 1997, ISBN 1888001380.

Information Anxiety, Richard Saul Wurman, Doubleday, 1989, ISBN 0553348566.

Information Anxiety 2, Richard Saul Wurman, Que, 2000, ISBN 0789724103.

Envisioning Information, Edward Tufte, Graphics Press, 1990, ISBN 0961392118.

The Visual Display of Quantitative Information, Edward Tufte, Graphics Press, 1983, ISBN 096139210X.

Hats, Richard Saul Wurman, *Design Quarterly* No.145, MIT Press, 1989.

The Age of Missing Information, Bill McKibben, Plume/Penguin, 1992, ISBN 0452269806.

Conferences

TED Conferences www.ted.com

Vision Plus Conferences www.vision-plus.net

Information Design 2000 www.infodesign2000.com

Organizations

American Center for Design www.ac4d.org

International Institute for Information Design (IIID), Vienna, Austria (contact Peter Simlinger) www.iiid.net

Information Design PIC of the Society for Technical Communication stc.org/pics/idsig

Information Design Network www.csad.coventry.ac.uk/IDN

Resources
www.informationdesign.org

Information Design Resources www.xs4all.nl/~plato/InfoDesign.html

Information Architecture Resources www.jjg.net/ia

Rochester Institute of Technology Information Design Archive, design.rit.edu/DAO/main.html

Interaction Design...

Books

New Games, Andrew Fluegelman, Editor, Headlands Press Book, Dolphin/Doubleday, ISBN 038512516X.

Generation X, Douglas Coupland, St. Martin's Press (discussion of "Takeaways" on pages 91–104), 1992, ISBN 031205436X.

Life on the Screen: Identity in the Age of the Internet, Sherry Turkle, Simon & Shuster, 1997, ISBN 0684803534.

The Media Equation: How People Treat Computers, Television, and New Media Like Real People and Places, Byron Reeves and Clifford Nass, Cambridge University Press, 1998, ISBN 1575860538.

Tell Me a Story: Narrative and Intelligence, Roger C. Schank, Northwestern University Press, 1995, ISBN 0810113139.

Influence: The Psychology of Persuasion, Robert B. Cialdini, Ph.D., Quill/William Morris, 1984, ISBN 0688128165.

Computers as Theater, Brenda Laurel, editor, Addison-Wesley, 1991, ISBN 0810113139.

Interactive Acting, Jeff Wirth, 1994, ISBN 0963237497.

Hosting Web Communities: Building Relationships, Increasing Customer Loyalty, and Maintaining A Competitive Edge, Cliff Figallo, John Wiley & Sons, 1998, ISBN 0471282936.

The Great Good Place: Cafes, Coffee Shops, Community Centers, Beauty Palors, General Stores, Bars, Hangouts and How They Get You Through the Day, Ray Oldenburg, Marlow & Co., 1989, ISBN 1569246815.

Communities in Cyberspace, Marc Smith and Peter Kollock, Routledge, Editors, 1998, ISBN 0415191408.

Online Articles

Film Structure, by David Seigel, www.dsiegel.com/film/Film_home.html

Two-Goal Film Structure, by David Seigel, www.dsiegel.com/film/two_goal.html

The Center for Digital Storytelling, www.storycenter.org

Online Community Articles

Online Community Report, www.onlinecommunityreport.com

more resources available at:
www.nathan.com/resources

Return on Community: Proving the Value of Online Communities in Business, www.participate.com/research/wp-return_on_community.asp

Building Profitable Community on the Web One Page at a Time, www.msnbc.com/news/151714.asp

There Goes the Neighborhood, Janelle Brown, www.salonmagazine.com/21st/feature/1999/01/cov_19feature.html

The Community is the Brand, Margaret Wertheim, www.laweekly.com/ink/00/28/cyber-wertheim.shtml

Conferences
Digital Storytelling Festival in Crested Butte, CO, www.dstory.com

Doors of Perception, www.mediamatic.com/doors

Organizations
Stanford University Project and People, Computers and Design, www-pcd.stanford.edu/pcd

Stanford CAPTology Lab, www.captology.org

MIT Media Lab, www.media.mit.edu

Institute for the Learning Sciences, www.ils.nwu.edu

The Center for Digital Storytelling, www.storycenter.org

The Improv Comedy Page, www.improvcomedy.org

ComedySportz Improv Comedy, www.teleport.com/~comedy

Good Experience, www.goodexperience.com

Hyper Island School of New Media, www.hyperisland.se

Multimedia...

Books
Multimedia Demystified, Apple Computer and **vivid** studios, Random House, New York, 1993, ISBN 0679756035.

Careers in Multimedia, **vivid** studios, Ziff Davis Press, 1995, ISBN 1562763113.

Online Articles
***vivid** studios' Process Outline,* **vivid** studios, 1995, www.vivid.com/practices/meth.phtml

Visual Design...

Books
A Primer of Visual Literacy, Donis A. Dondis, MIT Press, 1973, ISBN 0262540290.

Design Yourself, Kurt Hanks, Larry Belliston, and Dave Edwards, Willam Kaufmann, Inc., 1978, ISBN 0913232386.

Experiences in Visual Thinking, Robert H. McKim, PWS Engineering, 1980, ISBN 0818504110.

Understanding Comics, Scott McCloud, Kitchen Sink Press, 1993, ISBN 0878162453.

Symbols Sourcebook, Henry Dreyfuss, McGraw-Hill, 1972, ISBN 0471288721.

The Icon Book: Visual Symbols for Computer Systems and Documentation, W. Horton, Wiley & Sons, 1994, ISBN 047159900X.

Handbook of Pictorial Symbols, Rudolf Modley, Dover Publications, Inc., 1977, ISBN 048623357X.

Signs + Emblems, Erhardt D. Stiebner and Dieter Urban, Van Nosrand Reinhold Company, ISBN 0442280599.

Dimensional Typography, J. Abbott Miller, Princeton Architectural Press, 1996, ISBN 1568980892.

The Photographer's Handbook, Third Edition, John Hedgecoe, Dorling/Kindersley, Knopf, 1992, ISBN 0679742042.

The Book of Video Photography, David Cheshire, Dorling/Kendersley, Knopf, ISBN 0394587448.

No Logo, by Naomi Klein, Picador, 2000, ISBN 0312271921.

Brand.New, Jane Pavitt, Editor, Princeton University Press, 2000, ISBN 069107061X.

Selling the Invisible, Harry Beckwith, Warner Books, 1997, ISBN 0446520942.

Hey, Whipple, Squeeze This, Luke Sullivan, John Wiley & Sons, 1998, ISBN 0471293393.

Relationship Marketing, Regis McKenna, Addison-Wesley Publishing Company, Inc., 1993, ISBN 0201567695.

The 22 Immutable Laws of Marketing, Al Ries & Jack Trout, HarperBusiness, 1994, ISBN 0887306667.

Organizations
American Center for Design, www.ac4d.org

Design Management Institute, www.designmgt.org

Conferences
Living Surfaces, www.ac4d.org

Strategic Design Conference, www.ac4d.org

Online Resources
Visual Literacy Site, www.pomona.edu/visual-lit/intro/intro.html

Art and Culture, www.artandculture.com

Design Online, www.designonline.com

experience design nathan shedroff